CHURCH AND STATE IN WESTERN SOCIETY

To Jane
Always my Love

To my Mother, Elfriede Eberle

And in memory of my Father, Edward C. Eberle

Church and State in Western Society

Established Church, Cooperation and Separation

EDWARD J. EBERLE
Roger Williams University School of Law, USA

Routledge
Taylor & Francis Group
LONDON AND NEW YORK

courts of judicial review—the focus of this volume—reflect each country's distinctive history and culture. Reflectively engaging these differences, however, has the merit of taking Americans, and others as well, out of their legal comfort zones, prompting them to rethink aspects of their own constitutional jurisprudence on free exercise and church-state relations.

When assessing law and religion, it is always helpful to consider the perspectives of other constitutional democracies. Professor Eberle's decision to compare the United States with the United Kingdom and Germany is particularly astute. The church-state relations in these three countries fairly represent models found elsewhere in the democratic world. The United Kingdom is an established church model that is currently moving toward a more open approach to religious groups. By contrast, the United States is a separationist model, while Germany's model of accommodation involves various forms of cooperation between church and state. For Americans in particular, study of British and German judicial decisions can be a fertile source of ideas and insights that enrich the study of the equivalent jurisprudence of their own Supreme Court, revealing both flaws and strengths in the interpretation of the US Constitution.

Singled out for comparison in this book are leading cases Americans usually organize under the headings of the free exercise and non-establishment of religion. The free exercise cases focus mainly on controversial rituals, practices, or observances that have come under attack in all three jurisdictions. These include the display of religious symbols or the wearing of religious garb in public school settings or places of work, compelled oath-taking in courts of law, the ritual slaughter of animals in defiance of anti-cruelty laws, Sabbath Day observances that require religious persons to refrain from work, and the refusal to undergo blood transfusions for religious reasons even to save the life of a patient. On religious establishment, Professor Eberle's main comparison is between Germany and the United States. Germany's Constitution, known as the Basic Law, authorizes a church tax to support the main religious denominations, provides for religious instruction in state schools, grants certain religious groups the elevated status of "corporations under public law," and sets aside religious holidays "as days of spiritual improvement." But the Basic Law is equally emphatic in declaring that "[t]here shall be no state church" and that any participation in state-sanctioned religious activities shall be voluntary, a prerogative that extends to the collection of the church tax. Despite radical differences in the written texts of the two constitutions, the author finds as many similarities as differences in the jurisprudence of the German and American high courts of judicial review.

A major premise of this book is that Germans, Americans, and the British have a great deal to learn from one another's jurisprudence. Professor Eberle does more than simply compare constitutional doctrine. He holds each country's constitutional case law up to the light of the other in a self-critical quest to explore what is the most philosophically persuasive in the three bodies of law. He finds too that the comparative perspective helps to crystallize and clarify the empirical and normative assumptions behind the religious liberty and church-state jurisprudence of the three countries. The author's project prompts the reader to do nothing less than to wonder whether a synthesis of the cooperation and separationist models of religious liberty would produce "better" outcomes. The presumption is, as noted, that we can learn from the wisdom of other high courts of judicial review, for their opinions contain rays of light drawn from alternative traditions of freedom. What then are the possibilities of convergence in the constitutional policies of the three democracies? (Professor Eberle already sees a degree of convergence taking place in the financial support of religious schools.) Would some measure of convergence between the positive and negative models of religious liberty help to maximize freedom of religion in American society? Or enhance the equal treatment and protection of both religious and non-religious persons? Professor Eberle's book will prompt readers to reflect seriously on these and related questions affecting the relationship between religion and government.

Donald P. Kommers
University of Notre Dame

Preface

This is a book about the role of church and state in Western society. Religion plays a major role in Western society and in most other societies in the world. But it is critical that government figures out ways to evaluate religion. Can religion play an important role in determining basic values and norms in society? Is this good for people and does this lead to the establishment of a cohesive and coherent society? Or can religion play an important role in wreaking havoc in society? How is the havoc caused? Is it a rise of religious fanaticism or dominant majorities controlling based on religious doctrines?

The book addresses the different perspectives on religion in the three countries, the United Kingdom (UK), Germany and the United States (USA). The UK system is one of an established church. That model has been in place a long time, but now the UK is moving toward a much more accommodating idea of establishment. The German model is one of cooperation between church and state, but the German model is also now moving toward a more liberal and accommodating model of cooperation. The USA model is one of separationism, but the USA is also now moving toward a more accommodating model, providing more support for religion. We will look at each of the models and assess them and determine what new perspectives they offer and how this will work in their own countries and countries outside their border.

Crucial to the idea of religion is the constitutional order within the countries. Western countries are rooted in constitutionalism. Constitutionalism is necessary to constrain freedoms and protect people's rights. The UK has the longest running constitutional system in the world. While there is not a fully written constitution, constitutional principles have been in place a long time. The German Basic Law has been in place since 1949 and is widely considered to be one of the most influential constitutions in the world and poses a challenge to the US Constitution. The American Constitution is the oldest continuous written constitution in the world. Each of the German and American constitutions is important and shows the key strategy to achieving the proper balance between human freedom and social order.

What is critical in the book is the assessment of the force of modern constitutionalism in each of the countries and how it plays a major role in supporting or curtailing religious and other freedoms. Today, constitutionalism is a dominant force in Western and other countries. After all, the role of the constitution is to provide security within a democracy.

Acknowledgments

I conceived this book over the past several years and owe its existence to work done in earlier articles that explored and developed these themes. The book relies, in some respects, on these articles of mine: "Religion in the classroom in Germany and the United States," 81 *Tulane Law Review* 67 (2006); "German religious freedoms: the movement toward protection of minorities 1," in *II/III Annual of German & European Law* (2004/2005); "Free exercise of religion in Germany and the United States," 78 *Tulane Law Review* 1023 (2004); "Roger Williams's gift: religious freedom in America," 4 *Roger Williams University Law Review* 1 (1999).

I owe a debt of gratitude to many people who read and commented on my book. Another round of thanks is due them: Larry Cata Backer, Mark Kende, Donald Kommers, Ron Krotosynski, Peter Quint, Mel Topf, and James Whitman.

Thanks are also in order to a number of persons and institutions that encouraged and supported this project. Versions of portions of this book were presented at the Universities of Heidelberg and Muenster in Germany and the University of Southern Denmark in Denmark. I owe a debt of gratitude to Dean David Logan of Roger Williams Law School, who helped support my travel and scholarship. A number of my research assistants researched topics and collected materials. These include: Kathyrn Blythe, Kristin Hermitz, and Christopher Rogers, all of whom I owe a round of thanks. I owe a great debt of gratitude to my librarian, Nan Balliot, who was crucial in gathering the materials that were critical to this book, and thanks also to Stephanie Edwards.

Finally, I wish to thank my wife, Jane, to whom this book is dedicated, and my children, Sarah and Edward Benjamin, for their love and support. And I want to thank and dedicate this book to my mother, Elfriede Eberle, and in memory of my father, Edward C. Eberle.

Table of Cases

Germany

Auschwitz Lie, 90 BVerfGE 241 (1994)
Baden Christian Community School Case, 41 BVerfGE 29 (1975)
Baha'i, 83 BVerfGE 341 (1991)
Bavarian Christian Community School Case, 41 BVerfGE 65 (1975)
Bavarian Official Oath Case, 79 BVerfGE 69 (1988)
Berlin Sunday Opening Law, BVerfG, 1 BvR2857/07 (December 1, 2009)
Blood Transfusion Case, 32 BVerfGE 98 (1971)
Brandenburg I, 104 BVerfGE 305 (2001)
Brandenburg II, 105 BVerfGE 235 (2002)
Brandenburg III, BverfG, 1 BvQ 25/02 (July 28, 2002)
Brandenburg IV, 106 BVerfGE 210 (2002)
Bremen Pastor Case, 42 BVerfGE 312 (1976)
Catholic Hospital Case, 70 BVerfGE 130 (1985)
Classroom Crucifix I, 85 BVerfGE 94 (1991)
Classroom Crucifix II, 93 BVerfGE 1 (1995)
Conscientious Objector Case, 69 BVerfGE 1 (1985)
Cross in Courthouse, 35 BVerfGE 366 (1973)
Denial of Witness Oath, 33 BVerfGE 23 (1972)
Eppler, 54 BVerfGE 148 (1980)
Islamic Teacher's Head Scarf, BVerfG, 2 BvR 1436/02 (September 24, 2003)
Jehovah's Witness, 102 BVerfGE 370 (2000)
Jewish Organization, BVerfG, BvR 890/06 (May 5, 2009)
Kalifstaat, BVerfG, 1 BvR 536/03 (October 2, 2003)
North-Rhein Westfalis Christian Community School Case, 41 BVerfGE 88 (1975)
OSHO, 105 BVerfGE 279 (2002)
Prayer in Kindergarten, BVerfG, BvR 1522/03 (October 2, 2003)
Ritual Slaughter, 104 BVerfGE 337 (2002)
Rumpelkammer, 24 BVerfGE 236 (1968)
School Prayer Case, 52 BVerfGE 223 (1979)
Scientology Artist, 99 BVerfGE 185 (1998)
Soldiers are Murderers I, 45 NJW 2943 (1994)
Soldiers are Murderers II, 22 EuGRZ 443 (1995)

United Kingdom

Ahmad *v*. UK, [1982] 4 E.H.R.R.126
Aston Cantlow et al. *v*. Wallbank and another, [2003] UKHL 37, 1 AC 546
Azmi *v.* Kirklees Metropolitan Borough Council, UKEAT/0009/07/MAA (transcript)
Birmingham City Council, Ex p Equal Opportunities Commission, [1989] AC 1155
Board of Governors of St. Matthias Church of England School *v.* Crizzle, [1993] ICR 401, IRLR 472
Campbell *v.* UK, [1982] 4 EHRR 293
Chondel *v.* Liverpool City Council, Employment Appeal Tribunal, UKEAT/0298/08/JOJ (transcript) (February 11, 2009)
Church of Jesus Christ of Latter Day Saints *v.* Henning, [1963] 2 All ER 733, [1964] AC 420
Copsey *v.* WWB Devon Clays Ltd., [2005] EWCA Civ.932, ICR1789, IRLR 811
Costello-Roberts *v.* UK, [1994] 1 FCR 65
Dawkins *v.* Dept. of the Environment, [1993] ICR 517, IRLE 284
Denbigh High School Case, [2007] EWHC 298 (Admin); 1 All ER 249, ELR 278
Esson *v.* London Transport Executive, [1975] IRLR 48
Eweida *v.* British Airways, UKEAT/012/08/LA (transcript)
Gallagher *v.* Church of Jesus Christ of Latter-Day Saints, [2008] UKHL; 4 All ER 640
Glasgow City Council *v.* McNab, [2007] IRLR 476 (January 17, 2007)
Harris *v.* NKL Automotive Ltd., UKEAT/0134/07/DM (transcript)
Hussain *v.* London Country Bus Services Ltd., [1982] 4 E.H.R.R. 126
Hussain et al. *v.* Secretary of State for the Environment, 23 P & CR 330, 221 EG 627 (Queen's Bench 1971)
In re A (Children), [2001] Fam. Law 147 (2000)
In re L, [1998] 2 FLR 810, [1999] 2 FCR 524, [1998] Fam. Law 591 (1998)
Jane *v.* Jane, 4 FLR 712, 13 Fam. Law 209 (Court of Appeal, Civil Division 1983)
James *v.* Eastleigh Borough Council, [1990] 2 AC 751
James *v.* MSC Cruises, Case No.2203173/05, reported in 157 Equal Opportunities Act
Kingston & Richmond Area Health Authority *v.* Kaur, [1981] ICR 631, IRLR 337
Mandla et al. *v.* Dowell Lee et al., [1983] 2 AC 548, 1 All ER 1062
Mohmed *v.* West Coast Trains Ltd, UKEAT/0682/05/DA (transcript)
Panesar *v.* Nestle Co., [1980] IRLR 64, ICR 144
Regina *v.* Bishop Challoner Roman Catholic Comprehensive, [1992] 2 AC 182 (House of Lords)
Regina *v.* Bishop of Stafford, Court of Appeal (Civil Division) (2000) (transcript)
Regina *v.* Chief Rabbi of the United Hebrew Congregation, [1992] 2 ALL ER 249, 1 W.L.R. 1036
Regina *v.* Governing Board Body of JFS et al., [2009] UKSC 15
Regina *v.* Lancaschire County Council, [1995] ELR 33

Regina *v.* Lancaschire County Council Ex Parte , [1994] ELR 478
Regina (on the application of Begum) *v.* Denbigh High School, [2006] UKHL 15
Regina (on the application of X) *v.* Head Teachers and Governors of Y School, [2007] EWHC 298 (Admin); 1 All ER 249, ELR 278
Regina (on the application of Watkins-Singh) *v.* Aberdare Girls' High School, [2008] EWHC 1865 (Admin) 3 FCR 203
Regina *v.* Rabbincal Commission for the Licensing of Shochetim, *The Times* (December 22, 1987); *The Independent* (December 28, 1987) (transcripts) Court of Appeal 1987)
Regina *v.* Registrar General, [1970] 2 QB 697, 3 All ER 886, 3 WLR 479
Regina *v.* Secretary of State for Education, [1994] ELR 495
Saini *v.* All Saint's Haque Centre, Employment Appeal Tribunal, UKEAT/0227/08/ET (transcript) (October 24, 2008)
Singh *v.* Lyon Maiden Ltd., [1975] IRLR 328
Singh *v.* Rowntree Mackintosh Ltd., [1979] IRLR 199, ICR 554
Stedman *v.* UK [1997] 23 EHHR 168
Surayanda *v.* Welsh Ministers, [2007] EWCA Civ 893 (transcript) (2007)
Williamson *v.* Secretary of State for Education and Employment, [2005] UKHL 15, [2005] ALL ER 1

United States

Abington School District *v.* Schempp, 374 U.S. 203 (1963)
Adarand Constructors, Inc. *v.* Pena, 515 U.S. 200 (1995)
Aguilar *v.* Felton, 473 U.S. 402 (1985)
Agostini *v.* Felton, 521 U.S. 203 (1997)
Berghuis *v.* Thompkins, 78 U.S.L.W. 4479 (2010)
Board of Education *v.* Allen, 392 U.S. 236 (1968)
Braunfeld *v.* Brown 366 U.S. 599 (1961)
Cantwell *v.* Connecticut, 310 U.S. 296 (1940)
Chaplinsky *v.* New Hampshire, 315 U.S. 568 (1942)
Church of the Lukumi Babalu Aye *v.* City of Hialeah, 508 U.S. 520 (1993)
Comm. for Public Educa. *v.* Regan, 444 U.S. 646 (1980)
Cutter *v.* Wilkinson, 544 U.S. 709 (2005)
Davis *v.* Beason, 133 U.S. 333 (1890)
Edward *v.* Aguillard,482 U.S. 578 (1987)
Employment Division, Dept. of Human Services *v.* Smith I, 485 U.S 660 (1988)
Employment Division, Dept. of Human Services *v.* Smith II, 494 U.S 872 (1990)
Engel *v.* Vitale, 370 U.S.421 (1962)
Epperson *v.* Arkansas, 393 U.S. 97 (1968)
Everson *v.* Board of Education, 330 U.S. 1 (1947)
Frazee *v.* Illinois Dept of Employment Security, 489 U.S. 829 (1989)
Goldman *v.* Weinberger, 475 U.S. 503 (1986)

Good News Club *v.* Milford Central School, 533 U.S. 98 (2001)
Gooding *v.* Wilson, 405 U.S. 518 (1972)
Hernandez *v.* IRS, 490 U.S. 680 (1989)
Hobbie *v.* Unemployment Appeals Comm'n, 480 U.S. 136 (1987)
Hunt *v.* Washington State Apple Advertising Commission, 432 U.S. 333 (1977)
Illinois *v.* Caballes, 125 S. Ct. 834 (2005)
Lamb's Chapel *v.* Center Moriches Union Free School District, 508 U.S. 384 (1993)
Lawrence *v.* Texas, 539 U.S. 558 (2003)
Lee *v.* Weisman, 505 U.S. 577 (1992)
Lemon *v.* Kurtzman, 403 U.S. 602 (1971)
Lopez *v.* United States, 514 U.S. 549 (1995)
Lynch *v.* Donnelly, 465 U.S. 668 (1984)
Lyng *v.* Northwest Indian Cemetery Protective Association, 485 U.S. 439 (1988)
Marsh *v.* Chambers, 463 U.S. 783 (1983)
McCollum *v.* Board of Education, 333 U.S. 203 (1948)
McDaniel *v.* Paty, 435 U.S. 618 (1978)
Meek *v.* Pilterger, 421 U.S. 402 (1985)
Meyers *v.* Nebraska, 262 U.S. 390 (1923)
Minersville *v.* Gobitis 310 U.S. 586 (1940)
Miranda *v.* Arizona, 384 U.S. 436 (1966)
Mitchell *v.* Helms, 530 U.S. 793 (2000)
Mueller *v.* Allen, 463 U.S. 388 (1983)
O'Lone *v.* Estate of Shabazz, 482 U.S. 342 (1987)
Palko *v.* Connecticut, 302 U.S. 319 (1937)
Pierce *v.* Society of Sisters, 268 U.S. 510 (1925)
Planned Parenthood *v.* Casey, 505 U.S. 833 (1992)
Police Dep't of Chicago *v.* Mosley, 408 U.S. 92 (1972)
R.A.V. *v.* St. Paul, 505 U.S. 377 (1992)
Reynolds *v.* United States, 98 U.S. 145 (1879)
Roe *v.* Wade, 410 U.S. 113 (1973)
Rosenberger *v.* Rectors and Visitors of the Univ. of Virginia, 515 U.S. 819 (1995)
Saenz *v.* Roe, 526 U.S. 489 (1999)
Santa Fe School District *v.* Jane Doe, 505 U.S. 290 (2000)
School District of Grand Rapids *v.* Ball, 473 U.S. 373 (1985)
Shapiro *v.* Thompson, 394 U.S. 618 (1969)
Sherbert *v.* Verner, 374 U.S. 398 (1963)
Sloan *v.* Lemon, 413 U.S. 825 (1973)
Thomas *v.* Review Board, 450 U.S. 707
Torcaso *v.* Watkins, 367 U.S. 488 (1961)
United States *v.* Ballard, 322 U.S. 78 (1944)
United States *v.* Carolene Products, 304 U.S. 144 (1938)
United States *v.* Seeger, 380 U.S. 163 (1965)
Wallace *v.* Jaffree, 472 U.S. 38 (1985)
Walz *v.* Tax Comm'n of New York City, 397 U.S. 664 (1970)

Washington *v.* Davis, 426 U.S. 229 (1976)
West Virginia *v.* Barnette, 319 U.S. 624 (1943)
Wisconsin *v.* Yoder, 406 U.S. 205 (1972)
Witters *v.* Washington Dept. of Service for the Blind 474 U.S. 481 (1986)
Wolman *v.* Walter, 433 U.S. 229 (1977)
Yick Wo *v.* Hopkins, 118 U.S. 351 (1886)
Zelman *v.* Simmons-Harris, 536 U.S. 639 (2002)
Zobrest *v.* Catalina Foothills School District, 509 U.S. 1 (1993)
Zorach *v.* Clauson, 343 U.S. 306 (1952)

Introduction

Religion is and always has been a major inspiration for people. People's belief in a God, non-God, divine being or other transcendental tenet helps drive people to the types of missions they want to pursue in their daily life. Religion is both a motivating force—inspiring people to live up to their convictions and do good for others—and a contentious force—motivating people to insult or demean others who do not agree with their religious views. These religious influences play out in society, helping constitute some of the elements that comprise a community, such as ideas, values, customs, or practices. Religion is a major influence in the morals and structure of a society and the ethos and character of its people.

Religious freedom is one of the original fundamental rights that helped start the Western movement toward constitutionalism. Freedom of conscience formed the basis for a person's inner citadel of freedom. The beliefs, ideas, and attitudes grounded in conscience help direct a person to the path he or she wants to pursue. But to protect religious freedom, there must be boundaries between a person and the state.

Protection of the boundaries between a person and the state consists of two frameworks. First is the religious realm of a person. Religion is a personal matter which is determined through the inner workings of the soul. An individual's conscience helps determine faith, belief, and behavior. We can think of this as the inner citadel of freedom. Second is the role of government in relationship to religion. Government and the policies that it creates can be influenced by religion. For example, consider some events inspired by religion in the United States. Rules limiting obscenity and other forms of sexual depiction were motivated primarily by religion, a movement led by Andrew Comstock following the end of the American Civil War.[1] Prohibition of alcohol was led by the religious-influenced temperance movement, resulting in the adoption of the Eighteenth Amendment to the United States Constitution in 1919, which was later repealed by the Twenty-first Amendment in 1933.

Religion can also have a negative effect on government. For example, the English Civil War of 1642–48 was initiated in part by the religious friction between Protestants and Catholics, although another major influence was the Crown versus Parliament. With the Protestants winning the war, non-Protestants,

1 The movement resulted in the passage of the 1873 Comstock Act, which Comstock oversaw from 1873 until his death in 1915. Bret Boyce, Obscenity and Community Standards, 33 *Yale J. of Int'l L.* 299, 313 (2008).

such as Catholics and Jews, were often discriminated against and banned from government offices.

Thus, the need for demarcation between religion and the state is important. If religion and the state are conjoined more closely, then majoritarian forces will often control over minorities. If the line between religion and the state is drawn more clearly, there is often a greater likelihood that the integrity of both religion and the state will be better preserved. It is important to focus on the value of religion to a person, the society, and the state.

Western society is traditionally Judeo-Christian, as Judaism formed the basis for certain elements of Christianity. The Catholic (universal) Church maintained dominance over Europe until two pivotal events. The Catholic Church's refusal to grant permission to King Henry VIII of England to divorce his wife and marry Anne Boleyn led to England's break with the Catholic Church and the founding of the Church of England in 1534. The Church of England later became the official state church, with the monarch supervising church functions. While the Church of England is Protestant, it shares many common bonds with the Catholic Church. Today, with the contention among conservatives and liberals within the Church of England, there is an ongoing dialogue between the Church of England and the Catholic Church over whether Church of England congregants should join the Catholic Church.

Under the idea of an established church, the state officially recognizes one religion as the state religion. Under the established church approach, the state can have significant influence over religion. In the United Kingdom (UK), this meant historically that religions other than the officially recognized Anglicanism, a form of Protestantism, were often discriminated against, especially Catholics, Jews, and dissenting Protestants. The UK still has in place the state Church of England and the Church of Scotland, with the Church of Ireland and Church of Wales yet retaining the characteristics of an established church, but are not formally an established church. Under this approach, religion is considered to be a positive matter which should be supported by the state.[2] Today, the UK has become much more tolerant of other religions. Today there are far fewer established churches in western Europe than in the past.

An even more pivotal event was the Protestant Reformation, led by Martin Luther, begun in 1517 with Luther's posting of 95 theses on the door of a Catholic Church in Wittenberg, Germany. Luther's act triggered widespread revolt against the Catholic Church in most of northern Europe. The protracted struggle led to widespread friction among Catholics and those who rebelled as Protestants. Each considered the other a heretic and therefore wanted to kill the rebel. The brutal struggle ended with the Peace of Augsburg (1555), the central principle of which was *cuius regio, eius religio* (whose rule, his religion). The Peace of Augsburg

---

2 Judith D. Fischer and Chloe J. Wallace, God and Caesar in the Twenty-First Century: What Recent Cases Say About the Church-State Relations in England and the United States, 18 *Florida J. of Int'l L.* 485, 487, 489 (2006).

led to the division of Europe between Catholic and Protestant areas. The Peace of Augsburg also led to state control of religion, providing England with supremacy over the Church of England and some state control over churches in northern Europe.

Given Germany's locus as the center of the religious battle ground, there is a mutual relationship between church and state. The German approach, historically, and today can be characterized as one of cooperation. The government helps support religion, and religion has some influence on government. However, today, there is much less religious influence on government. The key focus of government support of religion is by allowing religious instruction in public schools and by the government providing a system of tax collection for religious bodies.

A third approach to church-state relations is separation of church and state. The separationist model originated in the United States (USA) with the country's founding, and was made concrete in the First Amendment, part of the 1791 Bill of Rights, added to the 1787 Constitution, which was formally ratified in 1788 after nine states approved it. The idea behind separation of church and state is that each has independent and important tasks and it is, therefore, critical that the influence of church on state or state on church be prevented as much as possible in order to preserve the integrity of each domain.

We can now see that we have three approaches to church-state relations in Western society: established church (established), cooperation between church and state (cooperationist), and separation of church and state (separationist). Under the established church model, one religion is made the official religion of the state. Under this approach, church and state can each influence another. Under the established church model, however, the state will often have a great impact on the church.

In Germany, the model is one of cooperation between church and state. Under the German model of cooperation, church and state can have a significant mutual effect on one another. The state supports church through state machinery that provides for the raising of tax revenues to support financially the church and allows religious instruction in public schools. The state also provides the structure to help religion, mainly Protestant and Catholic, but now also some support for Muslims, other Christians, other religions, non-Christian denominations and sometimes, maybe, for philosophical-based sects. And religion can have a role in helping form the value structure of society. Thus, the German approach of cooperationism can be mainly characterized as the government providing a framework for religious liberty, with religion playing an important role in the formation of values. The cooperationist model is the most prominent in Western society.

Both the UK and Germany are subject to two constitutional orders: their native constitutional order and the constitutional framework of the European Union (EU). EU law is a supranational system and sets out the core norms that member states must abide by. There is a difference in approach to EU law between the UK and Germany. As the UK does not have a formal written constitution that sets out clear constitutional norms, the UK is much more compliant with EU constitutional norms. By contrast, the German Basic Law sets out core constitutional values, such as human dignity and a democratic and social welfare state that cannot be threatened. So, if European Court of Justice or European Court of Human Rights decisions are not compatible with the core norms of German constitutionalism, the German Constitutional Court may not adhere to them. The justification for this is that the EU does not yet have a written constitution setting out the core constitutional norms that would set out a vibrant set of fundamental rights.

Under separationism, the idea is to separate church and state as much as possible to avoid one entangling into the affairs of the other. Church and state must each maintain its own independence and integrity in order to avoid church forces affecting state and state forces affecting church. The wall of separation is designed to prevent breaches of church into state or state into church. The United States is the world's first experiment in separation. France followed the USA model in 1789, and Turkey, since the 1920s, also has a model of separation of church and state.

In comparing the models of establishment, cooperation, and separation, I plan to describe the components of each of the models, illustrate how they operate, examine their strengths and weaknesses, and then reach a conclusion as to which is best, for what reasons, and what each model can learn from the others. A comparative treatment of important legal issues, such as constitutionalism and religion, is important to shed light on the role religion plays in Western society. In particular, Germany is worth considering, as in the post Second World War era following the debacle of the Holocaust, Germany has been a model for a secure and important constitutional order based on human dignity and the value of a person. The German constitution (known as the Basic Law) is one of the most influential constitutions in the modern world, acting as a rival to the US Constitution. Looking outside the borders of our native land can shed insight into other perspectives and free native citizens from their natural cognitive biases.

I start the book by providing a brief overview in Chapter 1 of the religious history in the UK, Germany, and the USA. Past religious events can have a major impact on a society, such as Henry VIII's break-off from the Catholic Church or Martin Luther's initiation of the reformation. I also want to lay out a brief description of the religious complexion of each of the three countries. The UK and Germany are very similar in religious orientation today, with about 49 per cent of the UK population believing in God and the German population about 53 per cent believing in God. By contrast, the USA is significantly more religious in orientation, generally a population of about 95 per cent believing in God.[3]

In Chapter 2 I describe the constitutional text and structure of the three countries. The UK, without a written constitution, instead relies on a series of charter documents and written laws which is often characterized as an unwritten constitution, but could as well be described as a series of written foundational documents and customs, such as the Magna Carta and the English Bill of Rights.

3 http://www.thearda.com/internationalData/MultiCompare5.asp?c=41, 90, 234.

The German Basic Law sets out the core norms of the constitutional order. The Basic Law is extremely detailed in keeping with the emergence of post Second World War constitutionalism. The Constitution of the Commonwealth of Massachusetts, drafted by John Adams, is the oldest written constitution in the world. As a country, the United States Constitution is the oldest written constitution in the world but relatively short, about five to six pages; it may be the shortest constitution in the world. The United States Constitution is notable for its creation of separate and independent branches of government: the legislative, executive, and judicial. The USA was the first country to establish hard independent judicial review, with the notable 1803 decision of *Marbury v. Madison*,[4] although earlier Supreme Court decisions also laid the foundation for judicial review.[5]

In Chapters 3–5 I focus on personal religious freedom. Free exercise of religion is the constitutionally protected right to act on your religious convictions. The core elements of personal religious freedom consist of freedoms of conscience, belief, practice of religious rites (such as communion, worship or kosher diet), and religiously motivated behavior, such as refusing to work on the Sabbath. Free exercise of religion is like free speech: both are individual freedoms to act on thoughts. In the case of religion, it is individual action based on religion. In the case of speech, it is expression based on a person's viewpoint. Because the UK has no written constitution, the common practice is that citizens are free to do what they like unless constrained by laws or rules derived from the common law. Generally, the UK has taken a conservative approach to enforcing personal religious freedoms, but more recent legal developments demonstrate a more accommodating approach. Chapter 3 covers UK free exercise of religion.

Chapter 4 covers the German approach to free exercise of religion. The German constitutional order accords broad scope to the freedom to believe or not believe in God or a philosophical tenet, and the freedom to act on such belief through free exercise of religion. Insofar as a person can prove religious conviction, the German Court will accord broad protection to religious freedoms.

In Chapter 5 I address the American approach to free exercise of religion. In the United States, free exercise of religion has been upheld as a constitutional right only rarely. It started with *Sherbert v. Verner* (1963), where the Supreme Court upheld the free exercise rights of a devout Christian who refused to work on Saturdays because of her faith and was then denied unemployment benefits in South Carolina.[6] At present, personal religious freedoms are protected, but receive less protection today than in the past with the pivotal *Employment Division, Department of Human Resources, Oregon v. Smith* case of 1990, which has tended to favor majoritarian control through general laws that results in constraining minorities' religious practices.[7]

4 5 U.S. (1 Cranch) 137 (1803).

5 See, e.g., *Calder v. Bull*, 3 U.S. (3 Dall.) 386 (1798).

6 374 U.S. 398 (1963).

7 494 U.S. 872 (1990).

In Chapters 6–8 I discuss the relationship between church and state, such as the teaching of religion in schools, public or private; display in public places of religious symbols; and use of prayer in public settings. I describe the elements of each of the systems of religion present in the UK, Germany, and the USA. In Chapter 6 I describe the UK model of an established church, meaning that the state officially recognizes one church as the state church. In the UK, the state church is the Church of England, a Protestant church. Under the established church approach, the government will assist the state church and likewise the church will assist the government. Religious education is mandated by law to be taught in all schools, public or private. Today, the Church of England has a much more limited role as an established church, with the relationship between church and state less tight and much more accommodation being given to other churches. The established church approach has increasingly lost favor in Europe.

Chapter 7 covers the German approach to church-state relations, which is one of cooperation between the two institutions. For example, the government provides the administrative apparatus to collect and disperse tax money to financially support churches. Religious education can be taught in public schools. And religious symbols can sometimes be displayed. Crosses are now generally not allowed to be displayed, in either a classroom or a courtroom. However, prayer in the school is allowed so long as it is voluntary, not a duty. And I look at a range of cases that deal with minority religious groups, such as the Jehovah's Witnesses, the Baha'i and some fringe groups, such as OSHO, a Bhagwanian movement.

In Chapter 8 I cover the American approach to church-state relations. In the USA, the approach historically is separation of church and state, designed to protect the integrity of government and church so that one does not unduly influence the other. Today, there is a contest in the USA over church-state relations in the school system. Where public schools are involved, the approach is still primarily one of separationism. However, in certain school districts where private schools are located, primarily religious schools, there is an approach of accomodationism, where the government will provide funds to aid private schools, many of which are religious. As with the German chapter on church-state relations, also at issue in the USA are prayer and Bible reading in school, which the US Supreme Court has rendered unconstitutional.

In Chapter 9 I evaluate the ideas of personal religious freedoms and church-state relations in the three countries. I will gather the ideas developed and expressed and then compare the religious approaches of the three countries and assess which approach is better, for what reasons, and what kind of insights might be gained. Comparative law has a valuable role to play in shedding light on a native legal system. A central purpose of comparative law is to learn: we learn by looking at others, important truths about our own native legal system, truths that can be reevaluated and reaffirmed. There is much one legal system can learn from another legal system.

Chapter 1
History

United Kingdom

As with most European countries, in the pre-Christian era there were indigenous religions that practiced their own religious rites, such as celebrations at monuments like Stonehenge. Christianity was a religious mission that influenced and took root in the UK starting in the second or third century. During Anglo-Saxon times, the line between church and state was not so clearly drawn. With the Norman invasion of 1066, the English church was given new life and brought more in line with the form of church in continental Europe. Christianity was known as Catholic (meaning universal). A squabble between Henry II and Thomas Becket, appointed by Henry II as Archbishop of Canterbury, over who would have supreme authority—the state or the church—led to great dissension and, ultimately, the murder of Thomas Becket in Canterbury Cathedral in 1170.[1] Henry II was appalled by the murder. In 1167 the first English university was founded, Oxford, based on the influence of the first Western university founded in Bologna, Italy.[2] Oxford and later Cambridge University would ultimately also play a large role in influencing religion in the UK. Vernacular translation of the Bible began in the Middle Ages, notably with Wycliffe.

The Catholic Church remained in effect in the UK until Henry VIII broke off from the Roman Catholic Church because of the refusal of the Church to grant him permission to divorce and remarry. With his divorce, Henry VIII formed the Church of England, in 1534, breaking off from Rome and Catholicism. The monarch would now be in charge of religion. In 1535, Henry VIII shut down the monasteries. Church money had to go to the state. The first English Bible was published in the 1530s, a consequence of the Martin Luther-led Reformation. In 1554–55, there was an attempt to reconcile with Rome during the Counter-Reformation. This movement was successful for a very short period, restoring much of the medieval church. But the Counter-Reformation was short lived. Roman Catholicism was restored only for a short time under the rule of Mary (1553–58). At this time, the country was divided into three religious groups: Catholics, Protestants, and a middle group, the Church of England, which strove for no servility to Rome or Geneva, the main influence of Protestantism in the UK, and a cleansing of the abuses gathered from the Middle Ages.

---

1 John R.H. Moorman, *A History of the Church of England* 80 (1959).

2 Ibid. at 87.

In 1559, the Act of Supremacy restored the monarch as the supreme leader of the church, allowing the monarch to control the church and appoint officials to religious offices.[3] In 1570 a Papal Bull was issued finalizing the separation of the Church of England from Rome. A Papal Bull is a type of letter, patent or charter, with a metal seal, issued by the Pope for the granting of a decree or document. Ultimately, the separation of the Church of England from Rome led to the Spanish invasion of England; the English easily defeated the Spanish fleet, preserving the independence of the Church of England.

With the formation of the Church of England, the UK generally favored Protestants and treated less favorably Catholics, Jews and other denominations. Catholics' and other denominations' civil rights were severely curtailed, including rights to own property or inherit land, burdened with special taxes, could not generally vote and Catholics could not send their children abroad for Catholic education. Roman Catholic priests were sometimes liable for imprisonment. Many Catholics retreated to isolation from the Protestant mainstream.[4]

The tensions came to a boil in the seventeenth century, when the Stuart dynasty succeeded the Tudor dynasty, as Queen Elizabeth I had no children. Much of the grounding of the Church of England goes back to Queen Elizabeth I, who wanted a unity of church and monarch.[5] The Stuarts were from Scotland and wanted to reestablish the divine right of kings, a concept that had origins in English history. James, the first Stuart king, was Protestant, and suspicious of Catholics and Puritans. Still, he did not want to persecute Catholics and tried to restore some form of reconciliation with Catholics. In 1605, this led to the Gunpowder Plot, when a group of fanatics tried to blow up the Parliament building with the king, lords and members of the House of Commons present. The plot, which failed, led to the requirement of an oath for repudiation of Papal claims.

There was also great contention among Protestants, as separatists believed that the Church of England was corrupt. Many separatists were purged and forced to emigrate to other countries, such as Holland, and ultimately migrated to the United States, with Puritans forming the Massachusetts Bay Colony. This led to great controversy and the outbreak of civil war, pitting the Parliament, whose members were mainly Protestant, against Charles I, the successor to King James, the first of the Stuart kings. The war started when Charles I was desperate for cash and reconvened Parliament, which he had suspended a number of times, and had not been in session for 11 years. His attempt to arrest five members of parliament sparked the civil war. Charles I wanted to purge the country of all Calvinists and Puritans and restore it more along his religious ways. The parliamentary forces

---

3 Peter Cumper and Peter Edge, First Amongst Equals: The English State and the Anglican Church in the 21st Century, 83 *U. Det. Mercy L. Rev.* 601, 603 (2006).

4 http://en.wikipedia.org/wiki/Roman_Catholic_Church_in_England.

5 Judith D. Fischer and Chloe J. Wallace, God and Caesar in the Twenty-first Century: What Recent Cases Say About the Church-State Relations in England and the United States, 18 *Florida J. of Int'l L.* 485, 491 (2006).

won the war, leading to the continuity of Protestantism and the end of the Church of England as the official state church and the end of the Book of Common Prayers. Charles I was beheaded in 1649.

In 1658, the monarchy was restored as was the Church of England as the official state church. The Book of Common Prayer was reintroduced and later revised. The Clarendon Code included the 1661 Corporation Act, which required those holding civic office to renounce the Solemn League and Covenant and to swear not to take up arms against the monarch and also to be communicants of the Church of England. The Act of Uniformity (1662) and Conventicle Act (1664) prohibited anyone over the age of 16 from attending any religious assembly other than the Church of England. The Five Mile Act (1666) mandated that non-conformist ministers are forbidden to live or visit within five miles of any place they had previously worked. In 1673, England passed the Tests Act, requiring any holder of a civil or military office to take an oath of allegiance to the Crown and the sacrament according to the rites of the Church of England, and to denounce the doctrine of transubstantiation. The goal of the Tests Act was to prevent and force from office Catholics, who were viewed as a danger to the country. In 1681, the Exclusion Act took effect, prohibiting Catholics from assuming the crown. Many prominent English philosophers, such as Thomas Hobbes and David Hume, believed religion to be a divisive force and wanted the government to control it.

Movement toward more equality with Catholics started in the 1680s, with King James II, a Catholic. In 1687, James II issued his Declaration of Indulgence, suspending penal laws against Catholics. The English Act of Toleration (1689) guaranteed certain religious freedoms to believers who were not members of the Church of England. The Act was modeled on John Locke's 1688 Letter of Toleration. The Act was not that protective of non-Anglicans; it mainly allowed them to exist in society as dissenters, but they were yet treated as second-class citizens. Catholics were not covered by the Act. Ultimately, James II fled in 1688 and was succeeded by William and Mary, who were Calvinists and restored Protestantism as the key religion. Under English law, the possessor of the crown must still be Protestant and cannot be married to a Roman Catholic, established under the Act of Settlement of 1700.[6]

In the 1740s there was an evangelical revival, similar to what occurred in the United States. In 1778 a Catholic Relief Act allowed Catholics to own property, inherit land and join the army. Other reforms allowed the Catholic clergy to operate more openly.[7] In the 1790s Methodists numbered about 70,000 and led the fight to abolish the slave trade. Toleration expanded in the nineteenth century, including the removal of civil restraints on Unitarians in 1813; Catholics in 1829;

---

6 Judith D. Fischer and Chloe J. Wallace, God and Caesar in the Twenty-first Century: What Recent Cases Say About the Church-State Relations in England and the United States, 18 *Florida J. of Int'l L.* 485, 489 (2006).

7 http://en.wikipedia.org/wiki/Roman_Catholic_Church_in_England.

and Jews in 1846. In 1828 the Corporation and Tests Act were repealed.[8] Catholics were now allowed to have voting rights and to hold government offices. Jews were allowed to be members of parliament in 1858, and atheists in 1888. These Acts allowed these religious groups to serve in other government offices as well.[9] In 1833–54, the Oxford movement, Anglican inspired, helped reform politics (especially the House of Commons) and religion (mainly the Church of England) and also elements of Catholic theology.[10]

In the post Second World War era, especially the era of the 1990s and now the twenty-first century, the UK is much more tolerant of other religions, including other Christian denominations, Muslims, Sikhs and others. The Race Relations Act of 1976 forbids discrimination in the workplace over color, race, nationality, or ethnic origin. Ethnic origin is widely considered to include religious affiliation, such as Sikhs, Jews, and gypsies, but not Rastafarians or national groups.[11]

Blasphemy had a long tradition in the UK. It applied only to blasphemy against Christianity. These were mainly common law offenses and originally part of canon law.[12] The last attempted prosecution under blasphemy laws was in 2007 when the fundamentalist group, Christian Voice, sought a prosecution against the BBC over the broadcasting of the show *Jerry Springer: The Opera*, which included a scene depicting Jesus, dressed as a baby and thought to be a bit gay. The courts rejected all the challenges. The last successful blasphemy prosecution was *Whitehouse v. Lemon* in 1977, when the editor of *Gay News* was found guilty. The last person to be imprisoned for blasphemy was John William Gott, on 9 December 1921. He was punished for publishing two pamphlets which caricatured the biblical story of Jesus, Matthew 21:2–7, comparing Jesus to a clown. In 2008, an amendment was passed to the Criminal Justice and Immigration Act of 2008, which abolished the common law offenses of blasphemy in England and Wales.[13]

Today, acts of the Church of England must be approved by parliament, although this is a formality. Bishops and the Archbishop of Canterbury, who is also the Primate of all of England, and the Archbishop of York, who governs the northern area of England, are chosen by the monarch, but on the advice of the prime minister. Thus, the idea of establishment no longer carries much influence of the church in state affairs. Many now see the Church of England as a moderate, non-dogmatic and pragmatic body. Church and state are no longer unified; the

8 Mark Hill, The Permissible Scope of Legal Limitations on the Freedom of Religion or Belief in the United Kingdom, 19 *Emory Int'l L. Rev.* 1129, 1132 (2005).

9 Peter Cumper and Peter Edge, First Amongst Equals: The English State and the Anglican Church in the 21st Century, 83 *U. Det. Mercy L. Rev.* 601, 605–606 (2006).

10 http://en.wikipedia.org/wiki/Roman_Catholic_Church_in_England.

11 For the history of religion in England, see John R.H. Moorman, *A History of the Church of England* (1959); Ernest Gordon Rupp, *Religion in England 1688–1791* (1986); Jim Smyth, *The Making of the United Kingdom 1660–1800* (2001).

12 http://en.wikipedia.org/wiki/Blasphemy_law_in_the_United Kingdom.

13 http://en.wikipedia.org/wiki/Blasphemy_law_in_the_United Kingdom.

Church controls religion, the state controls governmental policies.[14] The UK system is moving away from an established church model and much more toward an accommodationist model.

Germany

Like the United Kingdom, religious rights in Germany were originally indigenous in the pre-Christian era. While Christianity began in Germany in the fourth century, the chief influence on its rise in German territory was Charlemagne, the king of the Franks, who assumed the crown in 768 and had as his goal the spread of Christianity. He welcomed all scholars, encouraged education, helped the monasteries and improved the legal system. Alter and throne became united.[15]

The pivotal event in German history was the Reformation, started by Martin Luther in 1517 with his posting of 95 theses on the church door in Wittenberg. This led to a religious revolution. The Catholic Church went after Luther, attempting to excommunicate him. But he was able to gain protection from princes favorable to his cause. Luther relied on the protection of tolerant German princes from Catholic authorities to safeguard his life and teachings. He ultimately found refuge in the castle in Wartburg, where in his room he translated the Bible into German, making it accessible to the common population. Luther's translation of the Bible into the vernacular had a major influence on the rise of Protestantism. Reliance on state power to protect religion is another factor leading toward a cooperative church-state relationship. Protestantism also was the crucial force in the literacy campaign of this time. Protestants founded schools so every child could read the Bible, the defining focus of Luther's Reformation. Reading allowed a person to understand scripture by his or her own lights, facilitating direct communication with God.

The religious struggle ultimately led to war, pitting Catholics against Protestants, in line with the Civil War in England a century later. Catholics and Protestants each thought the other was a heretic. Eventually the mutual slaughter ended with the 1555 Peace of Augsburg, which lasted to 1618. The core principle of the Peace of Augsburg was *cuius regio, eius religio* (whose rule, his religion). Under the principle, the ruler would choose the religion, and then the population would have to choose the ruler's religion or emigrate to another region in keeping with their religious faith. Ultimately, the Peace of Augsburg collapsed with the Battle of Pilsen on All Saint's Day, 1 November 1618.

Religious strife led to the 30 Years War, which decimated 15 per cent of the European population, much in German areas. The war was not just based on religion, but also the political interests of rulers. For example, Catholic France

14 Judith D. Fischer and Chloe J. Wallace, God and Caesar in the Twenty-first Century: What Recent Cases Say About the Church-State Relations in England and the United States, 18 *Florida J. of Int'l L.* 485, 490–91, 497 (2006).

15 *History of the World* 111 (Dorling Kindersley Book, Gillian Denton, Sr. Ed. 1994).

allied with Protestant Sweden, the last war Sweden participated in. The last battle was fought at Lens, on 2 August 1648. The war ended with the Treaty of Westphalia, on 24 October 1648, which was concluded in Münster and Osnabrück, and embodied the core principles of the Peace of Augsburg (*cuius regio, eius religio*), maintained the division of Europe between Catholic and Protestant regions, and also led to the founding of the Netherlands and Switzerland and core principles of international law.

Protestantism, mainly Lutheranism, has effectively functioned as a de facto established church in several of the German states before unification. Germany achieved unity as a country relatively late, only in 1871, under Bismarck. By this time, Lutheran, Catholic, and Jewish religions were well established in Germany. In the later nineteenth century, the *Kulturkampf* (culture war) broke out, pitting Protestants against Catholics and Jews. Catholics and Jews were often barred from office.

Religious tolerance came late to Germany. Until the Weimar Constitution of 1919, church-state relations were close and religious discrimination was widespread. With Protestantism effectively operating as the official church in much of the Prussian-dominated German Reich in the nineteenth century, Roman Catholics (who were one-third of the population) were often barred from high positions in the Reich government, and Jews were routinely excluded from public service and the army. Historically, German constitutions distinguished between dominant churches (Lutheran, other Protestant and Roman Catholic) and minor sects. During the Hitler era, Nazi Germany exerted substantial control over religion, including the dominant Protestantism and Catholicism. Minority religions were discriminated against and Jews were persecuted, leading to the Holocaust.

The modern Basic Law is framed specifically against the horrors of the Hitler era. Most notable is the securing of the social order on the premise of the inviolability of human dignity. This centers the society around the human person and their flourishing. Religious freedoms, in particular, are indispensable to this vision because the spirituality of religion or belief in some other ideal is a core element of the development of human personality. Only with the lessons learned from the Hitler era did Germany secure freedom from coercion of conscience, the essence of religious freedom discovered and elaborated on centuries earlier by Roger Williams,[16] John Locke,[17] and James Madison.[18] Development of religious freedom along these Enlightenment lines in Germany was thus a late affair.

16 Roger Williams, *The Bloody Tenet, of Persecution, for Cause of Conscience* (Samuel L. Caldwell ed., 1867) (1644).

17 John Locke, *A Letter Concerning Toleration* (1689).

18 James Madison, *Memorial and Remonstrance Against Religious Assessments* (1785). (Liberty of conscience is "precedent, both in order of time and in degree of obligation, to the claims of Civil Society."). Reprinted as appendix, *Everson v. Board of Education*, 330 U.S. 1, 28 app. at 63 (1947) (Rutledge, J., dissenting) (hereinafter "Memorial and Remonstrance").

In Germany, blasphemy is covered by Article 166 of the *Strafgesetzbuch*, the German criminal law. If a deed disturbs the public peace, blasphemy is actionable. Germany might now be the only country, covered in this book, that allows blasphemy.

In the post Second World War era, the framers of the Basic Law continued the tradition of church-state cooperation. While the churches also had an association with the Nazis, as did other institutions, the churches were poised to help in the reconstruction of Germany. This was an additional factor in facilitating the major role of church and religion in German society.

United States

American religious history is more complicated than commonly thought and consists, at least, of a struggle between separationism and accomodationism, itself a long-running contest that percolates quite strongly today. The crucial developments in Virginia, led first by Thomas Jefferson and then, during the Assessment controversy of 1784–86, by James Madison, Patrick Henry and George Mason, were perhaps the decisive influence in framing First Amendment religious protections. In 1779, Thomas Jefferson drafted the Virginia Act for Establishing Religious Freedom, which was finally adopted in 1786:

> Well aware that Almighty God hath created the mind free; that all attempts to influence it by temporal punishments or burdens, or by civil incapacitations, tend only to beget habits of hypocrisy and meanness, and are a departure from the plan of the Holy Author of Religion, who being Lord of both body and mind, yet chose not to propagate it by coercions on either, as was in his Almighty power to do; that the impious presumption of legislators and rulers, civil as well as ecclesiastical, who, being themselves but fallible and uninspired men, have assumed dominion over the faith of others …

James Madison wrote the Memorial and Remonstrance Against Religious Assessments in 1785, which was designed to remonstrate against the Virginia Bill that established a provision for teachers of the Christian religion. According to Madison:

> Because we hold it for a fundamental and undeniable truth, 'that religion or the duty which we owe to our Creator and the manner of discharging it, can be directed only by reason and conviction, not by force or violence.' The Religion of every man must be left to the conviction and conscience of every man; and it is the right of every man to exercise it as these may dictate. This right is in its nature an unalienable right. It is unalienable, because the opinions of men, depending only on the evidence contemplated by their own minds cannot follow

> the dictates of other men: It is unalienable also, because what is here a right towards men, is a duty towards the Creator.

The Virginia experience resonated especially strongly in the early Establishment Clause jurisprudence of the Court.[19] An originalism of jurisprudence followed an influential strand of originalist history.

For Thomas Jefferson and James Madison, Enlightenment ideals drove their version of civic republicanism. They advocated separation of church and state as the proper institutional relationship. For Jefferson, deeply influenced by French thought—in part because he served the United States as minister to France from 1785–89—separation was mainly a strategy to protect the fragility of the experiment in civic republicanism, perhaps as an argument for secularism.[20] Jefferson's famous statement of the "wall of separation" lies, of course, in his letter to Nehemiah Dodge and Others, a Committee of the Danbury Baptist Association, in Connecticut (1 January 1802): "[A] perfect separation between ecclesiastical and civil matters" is the best course for "religion & Gov. will both exist in greater purity, the less they are mixed."[21] Other civic republicans were alarmed by the excesses of the French Revolution and sought to dampen the passion for excessive liberty. One infamous measure taken was, of course, the Alien and Sedition Act of 1798, ostensibly used to restrict the French ideology, but which the administration of John Adams used to jail political opponents.

Thomas Paine, author of the leading revolutionary tract, *Common Sense* (1776), was also a confirmed Francophile. Paine aided the French in drafting the famous *Declaration of Rights of Man and the Citizen* (1789), which helped secured religious freedoms. Paine was an extreme separatist, once observing that the union

---

19 *McGowan v. Maryland*, 366 U.S. 420, 437 (1961); *Everson v. Board of Education*, 330 U.S. 1, 11–13 (1947). *See also* authorities collected in Arlin M. Adams and Charles J. Emmerich, A Heritage of Religious Liberty, 137 *U. Pa. L. Rev.* 1559, 1572 n. 54 (1989); Michael W. McConnell, Establishment and Disestablishment at the Founding, Part I: Establishment of Religion, 44 *Wm. & Mary L. Rev.* 2105, 2108–2109 (2003).

20 Adams and Emmerich, *supra* note 19, at 1584.

For other classifications of early influences on the First Amendment religious protections, see Adams and Emmerich, ibid. at 1583–95 (distinguishing between separatists, political centrists and pietistic separatists); John Witte, Jr., The Essential Rights and Liberties of Religion in the American Constitutional Experiment, 71 *Notre Dame L. Rev.* 371, 377–888 (1996) (distinguishing between Puritan, evangelical enlightenment, and civic republican views).

21 Nehemiah Dodge and Others, a Committee of the Danbury Baptist Association, in Connecticut (Jan. 1, 1802) [hereinafter Danbury Church Letter], reprinted in *Thomas Jefferson: Writings* 510 (1984). *Accord*, Letter from James Madison to Edward Livingston (July 10, 1822), in 9 *Writings of James Madison* 102 (Gaillard Hunt ed., 1910).

of church and state bred "a sort of mule-animal, capable only of destroying, and not of breeding up."[22]

For Madison, separation was designed to protect politics and religion; he believed both in the value of the civic republican experiment and the purity and preciousness of religion. Madison, however, was not always so absolute in his view of separatism. He also spoke of a wavering "line of separation between the rights of religion and the Civil authority" in certain "unessentials" of religion.[23] In later life, Madison returned to a view of complete separation of church and state. "A perfect separation between ecclesiastical and civil matters" [is best for] "religion & Gov. will both exist in greater purity, the less they are mixed together."[24] Madison's two main themes were separation of church and state and that a multiplicity of religious sects, as a multiplicity of interests, was the best guard against faction, which could thereby better preserve liberty.[25] Jefferson (in early, pre-constitutional work) and Madison, especially, were likely the main architects of the First Amendment religious guarantees.[26]

Religious evangelicals (most prominently Baptists) aligned themselves with Enlightenment separatists to support a separation of church and state. In part, their motivation was their own self-interest and the interest of the community. As minorities, Baptists were concerned that dominant political and religious power would inhibit them and other minorities. Separation of church and state was a way to get the state out of their—and other minorities'—way.

These evangelicals echoed the essential teaching of Roger Williams, America's original religious thinker, that separation of church and state served the interests of each best by protecting the purity and integrity of each against the inevitable tensions arising from one infringing on the domain of the other. Roger Williams, after all, was the original source for the "wall of separation" metaphor,[27] not

---

22 Thomas Paine, *The Rights of Man* (pts. 1 and 2) (London 1791), *cited in* Adams and Emmerich, ibid.

23 Letter from James Madison to Rev. [Jasper] Adams, in 9 *Writings of James Madison*, ibid., at 484, 487.

24 Letter from James Madison to Edward Livinston (July 10, 1822), in 9 *The Writings of James Madison* 102 (Gaillard Hunt ed., 1910).

25 Federalist No. 10 and No. 51. Adams and Emmerich, *supra* note 19, at 1587.

26 *Everson*, 330 U.S. at 11–13 (describing and observing leading role played by Jefferson and Madison in formulating the values and drafting the religious protections of First Amendment); *Reynolds*, 94 U.S. at 164. It is, of course, hard to determine who actually drafted the First Amendment, although most people credit Madison, Adams and Emmerich, *supra* note 19, at 1581, and for good reason: Madison sponsored the Bill of Rights as part of the compromise in Virginia leading to the state's ratification of the Constitution, and he then labored mightily to craft the Bill of Rights to achieve consensus. See also *Wallace v. Jaffree*, 472 U.S. 38, 97–99 (1985) (Rehnquist, J., dissenting).

27 Edward J. Eberle, Roger Williams's Gift: Religious Liberty in America, 4 *Roger Williams L. Rev.* 425, 427 (1999) (citing Roger Williams, *Mr. Cotton's Letter Examined and Answered* (1644)) [hereinafter *Cotton's Letter Examined*], reprinted in 1 *The Complete*

Thomas Jefferson. Many people view the evangelicals as advocating separation of church and state in order to protect the purity of religion as a voluntary, non-coerced exercise, but much of their thought was deeper than that, arguing also for political independence and a theory of the state.

At the heart of the separationist argument is that religion is a private, voluntary matter between only people and God. There can be no intrusion into this inviolate sphere of a person's spirit. Official support of religion only leads to its corruption as either government tries to control religion or religion tries to comport itself to curry favor with government. "Experience witnesseth that ecclesiastical establishments, instead of maintaining the purity and efficacy of Religion, have had a contrary operation ... [leading to] pride and indolence in the Clergy, ignorance and servility in the laity, in both, superstition, bigotry, and persecution."[28] Entangling government in religion, or religion in government, moreover, leads to great divisiveness in society as religion or its particular sects will inevitably be favored or disfavored in official policies, leading to overconfidence or arrogance in those favored and hostility and rejection in those disfavored, whether religious or not. Thus, evangelicals, like Enlightenment civic republicans, desired that religious bodies be free from state favors like "tax exemptions, civil immunities, property donations, and other forms of state support for the church."[29] However, some evangelicals did not object to some state support of religion. Isacc Backus, for example, was not against "Sabbath laws, teaching Calvinistic doctrine in the public schools, proscribing blasphemy, and conducting official days of fasting and prayer."[30] The Baptist minister John Leland, echoing John Locke, put the matter bluntly: "The notion of a Christian commonwealth should be exploded forever."[31] Locke also had written: "there is absolutely no such thing, under the Gospel, as a Christian commonwealth."[32]

Now, this experiment in separationism resonates with most Americans, positively or negatively. For it was the philosophy of separationism that marked the court's first entre into policing the border between church and state, following Jefferson's metaphor of a "wall of separation."[33] Much of Establishment Clause law that has followed has been a battle over whether a "wall of separation" is the

---

Writings of Roger Williams 313, 392 (Russel & Russel, Inc. 1963) [hereinafter *Complete Writings*].

28 James Madison, *Memorial and Remonstrance*, para. 7, *Everson*, 330 U.S at 64.

29 Witte, *supra* note 20, at 382.

30 Adams and Emmerich, *supra* note 19, at 1593.

31 John Leland, *The Writings of the Late Elder John Leland* 118 (1845), cited in Witte, *supra* note 20, at 382.

32 Noah Feldman, The Intellectual Origins of the Establishment Clause, 77 *N.Y.U. L. Rev.* 346, 387 (2002).

33 *Everson* 330 U.S. at 16, 18; *Reynolds v. United States*, 98 U.S. 145, 164 (1879).

proper rubric within which to view church-state relations, as demonstrated by the two recent Ten Commandment cases.[34]

The American experiment in separationism was unique, the first such experiment in the world, with Roger Williams' experiment in Providence colony, in 1638, being the very first. Even today, there are few experiments in strict separation of church and state; France[35] and Turkey[36] are probably the only two other notable experiments. The last established church in the United States was in Massachusetts, the Congregational church, whose establishment ended in 1837.

But separationism was not the only early American philosophy to demarcate church-state relations. The Puritan tradition advocated separation of church and state in institutional matters so that the internal governance of church and state could be preserved.[37] Puritans conceived church and state as "two seats of Godly authority in the community." The role of the church is to tend to matters spiritual; the role of the state was to maintain peace and order.

Church officials were prohibited from holding political office, serving on juries, interfering in government affairs, endorsing political candidates, or censuring the official conduct of a statesmen. Political officials, in turn, were prohibited from holding ministerial office, interfering in internal ecclesiastical government, performing sacerdotal functions of clergy, or censuring the official conduct of a cleric.[38]

But Puritans also advocated cooperation between church and state to aid religion and support the state. Under Puritanism, government could support religious education, pay the salaries of clergy, provide land to churches and grant tax exemptions to religious organizations, among other aids.[39] Of course, only Christian churches—primarily Congregational (the successor to the Puritans)—received such state benevolence. Church officials, in turn, aided the state by hosting town assemblies, political rallies, educational instructions, acting as libraries and "preaching obedience to the authorities" and more general encouragement of right and lawful conduct in citizens, among other aids.[40]

---

34 Compare *McCreary v. ACLU*, 545 U.S. 844 (2005) (finding display of Ten Commandments in courtroom unconstitutional) with *Van Orden v. Perry*, 545 U.S. 677 (2005) (finding it constitutional to display monument inscribed with Ten Commandments on grounds of Texas state capital, together with other monuments).

35 Constitution of the French Republic, art. 2 (8 July 1958): *La France est une République indivisible, laïque, démocratique et sociale.* (France is an indivisible, laic, democratic and social Republic.)

36 Constitution of Turkey, art. 24.

37 John Witte, Jr., The Essential Rights and Liberties of Religion in the American Constitutional Experiment, 71 *Notre Dame L. Rev.* 371, 378–79 (1996).

38 John Witte, Jr., The Essential Rights and Liberties of Religion in the American Constitutional Experiment, 71 *Notre Dame L. Rev.* 371, 378–79 (1996).

39 Ibid. at 379–80.

40 Ibid. at 380.

This Puritan tradition was carried forward by other prominent American civic republicans, such as George Washington, John Adams, Samuel Adams, Oliver Ellsworth, and James Wilson.[41] Puritan thought "provided the moral and religious background of fully 75 per cent of the people who declared their independence in 1776."[42] Of course, these accommodationist civic republicans had elements in common with their enlightenment and evangelical counterparts. They advocated liberty of conscience for all and free exercise of religion, encouraged a plurality of religions, and discouraged "political intrusions on religion that rose to the level of religious establishments."[43] These sets of values—free conscience, free exercise, pluralism, separationism, disestablishment and equality—are what we might call a core of "essential rights and liberties of religion."[44] But in contrast to their Enlightenment counterparts, they desired and encouraged a common religious ethic. The civic republican religious ethic was, of course, less stringent and intolerant as compared with the Puritan ethic. Dissenters from Puritan ideology were banished, such as Roger Williams and Anne Hutchinson from Massachusetts Bay.[45] They were banished because they did not follow the pure Puritan religious tenets. George Washington, for example, observed that "Religion and Morality are the essential pillars of Civil society."[46] As Washington stated in his Farewell Address of 17 September 1796: "Of all the dispositions and habits which lead to political prosperity, religion and morality are indispensable supports. In vain would that man claim the tribute of patriotism who should labor to subvert these great pillars of human happiness—these firmest props of the duties of men and citizens."[47] John Adams similarly observed: "We have no government armed with power capable of contending with human passions unbridled by morality and religion."[48] Religion promoted morality, and morality was important to the teaching of right conduct in citizens of a democracy, who,

---

41 Ibid. at 385–86.

42 S. Ahlstrom, *A Religious History of the American People* 124 (1972).

43 Ibid. at 386.

44 Witte, *supra* note 20, at 388, citing Elisha Williams, *The Essential Rights and Liberties of Protestants: A Seasonable Plea for The Liberty of Conscience, and the Right of Private Judgment in Matters of Religion, Without any Control from Human Authority* (1744). James Madison spoke similarly. 1 *Annals of Congress* 784 (Joseph Gales, Sr. Ed., 1834).

45 Eberle, *supra* note 27, at 432–33.

46 Letter from George Washington to the Clergy of Different Denominations Residing In and Near the City of Philadelphia (Mar. 3, 1797), in 36 *The Writings of George Washington, 1745–1799*, at 416 (John C. Fitzpatrick ed. 1931).

47 Adams and Emmerich, *supra* note 19, at 1605.

48 Letter from John Adams to the Officers of the First Brigade of the Third Division of the Militia of Massachusetts (1798), in 9 *Life and Works of John Adams* 229 (1854), both cited in Witte, *supra* note 20, at 386. In 1798, Adams observed: "Our Constitution was made only for a moral and religious people. It is wholly inadequate to the government of any other." Letter from John Adams to a unit of the Massachusetts militia (11 October

after all, are counted on more for civic virtue and proper governance than other forms of political organization.[49] If nothing else, religion was valued for its utility in inculcating proper conduct. This ideal seems to be the one animating these more centrist civic republicans.

Accommodationist civic republicans thus tolerated official support and accommodation of religion, unlike their separationist contemporaries. They "endorsed tax exemptions for church properties and tax support for religious schools, charities, and missionaries; donations of public lands to religious organizations; and criminal protections against blasphemy, sacrilege, and interruption of religious services."[50] In practice, these official favors were accorded only Protestants; "Quakers, Catholics, and the few Jewish groups were routinely excluded."[51] They also favored "government appointment of legislative and military chaplains, government sponsorship of general religious education and organization, and government enforcement of a religiously based morality through positive law."[52] "[T]he Continental Congress authorized legislative and military chaplains, provided for the importation of Bibles, and proclaimed days of thanksgiving, prayer, and fasting." Thomas Jefferson, as President, refused to render a Thanksgiving Proclamation, or any official acknowledgment of religion, believing those to be contrary to the First Amendment. As President, James Madison buckled under the political pressure of the War of 1812, and rendered several Thanksgiving Proclamations, which he later regretted and disavowed.[53]

Massachusetts was the prime example of this more accommodationist approach.[54] The Supreme Court has recognized some of this early history in sustaining the constitutionality of opening legislative sessions with a state-paid chaplain,[55] tax exemptions for churches,[56] and establishing Sunday as a

---

1798), in 9 *Works of John Adams* 229 (C. Adams ed., 1850–56 and reprint 1971) cited in Adams and Emmerich, *supra* note 19, at 1671.

49 As Madison observed in Federalist No. 55: "As there is a certain degree of depravity in mankind which requires a certain degree of circumspection and distrust, so there are other qualities in human nature which justify a certain portion of esteem and confidence. Republican government presupposes the existence of these qualities in a higher degree than any other form."

50 Witte, *supra* note 20, at 387. Adams and Emmerich, *supra* note 19, at 1571.

51 Witte, *supra* note 20, at 387.

52 Ibid. at 386.

53 *Lee v Weisman*, 505 U.S. 577, 623–26 (1992) (Souter, J., concurring); Adams and Emmerich, *supra* note 19, at 1571, 1585, 1587.

54 Ibid. at 387.

55 *Marsh v. Chambers*, 463 U.S. 783 (1983).

56 *Walz v. Tax Comm'n*, 397 U.S. 664, 677–80 (1970).

uniform day of rest.[57] There is, in fact, much historical work arguing that the First Amendment supports such an accommodationist approach.[58]

However, the historical record discloses an important qualification attached to state support of religion. By the end of the eighteenth century, "almost no one in America thought that government legitimately could compel taxes for religious purposes without offering some possibility of formally opting out of the tax."[59] It was difficult, however, to obtain a waiver in practice, resulting in many taxpayers being taxed against their will.[60] Freedom from compulsion, including forced taxation, was an essence of liberty of conscience. It was less clear whether taxes could be collected so that people could designate the church of their choice that they wanted to support. George Washington, for example, thought that compelled taxation to support a church of a person's choice was compatible with freedom of conscience, "so long as no one was obligated to support a religion with which he disagreed."[61]

Thus, if we were following a constitutional theory of originalism, Justice Scalia is quite right to observe that "With respect to public acknowledgment of religious belief, it is entirely clear from our Nation's historical practices that the Establishment Clause permits … disregard of polytheists and believers in unconcerned deities, just as it permits the disregard of devout atheists."[62] Justice Story captured this sentiment by famously (or infamously) observing that the Establishment Clause was designed "not to countenance, much less to advance, Mahometansism, Judaism, or infidelity, by prostrating Christianity; but to exclude all rivalry among Christian sects."[63] In fact, Story and others of the nineteenth

---

57 *McGowan v. Maryland*, 366 U.S. 420 (1961); *Braunfeld v. Brown*, 366 U.S. 599 (1961).

58 See authorities collected in Adams and Emmerich, *supra* note 19, at 1579 n. 88. See also *Wallace v. Jaffree*, 472 U.S. 38, 91–114 (1985) (Rehnquist, J., dissenting).

59 Noah Feldman, The Intellectual Origins of the Establishment Clause, 77 *N.Y.U. L. Rev.* 346, 351 (2002). See also Douglas Laycock, "Nonpreferential" Aid to Religion: A False Claim About Original Intent, 27 *Wm. & Mary* 875, 900–01 (1985).

60 Justice Jackson adopted this position—finding unconstitutional forced taxation without waiver—in his dissent in *Everson*, 330 U.S. at 21–23. (Jackson, J., dissenting).

61 Feldman *supra* note 59, at 394 n. 270, 416.

62 *McCreary County, Kentucky v. ACLU*, 545 U.S. 844, 886 (Scalia, J, dissenting) (observing further that George Washington's Thanksgiving Proclamation and Ten Commandments are monotheistic, embracing Christianity, Judaism and Islam). *Contra*, ibid. at 879 (Souter, J,) ("the dissent says that the deity the Framers had in mind was the God of monotheism, with the consequence that government may espouse a tenet of traditional monotheism. This is truly a remarkable view.").

63 R. Cord, *Separation of Church and State: Historical Fact and Current Fiction* 13 (1988). Chief Justice John Marshall "also believed that religion was essential to the survival of the republic," and noted the close relationship of Christianity to the United States. Adams and Emmerich, *supra* note 19, at 1590.

Table 1.1 Religious Complexion in Society in United Kingdom, Germany and USA

1. Belief in God		
UK	**Germany**	**USA**
44% (2004)	53.5% (1999)	95.6% (1999)[*]

2. Religious Complexion		
UK (2007)		
	Adherents	**Percentage**
	Christian 42,079,000	71.6
	No Religion 9,104,000	15.5
	Muslim 1,546,626	2.7
	Hindu 552,421	1.0
	Jedi Knight 390,000	0.7
	Sikh 329,358	0.6
	Jewish 259,927	0.5
	Buddhist 144,453	0.3[**]

Germany (2005)		
	Adherents	**Percentage**
	Christian	71.8
	No Religion	20.8
	Muslim	4.5
	Atheist	2.4
	Jewish	0.3
	Buddhist	0.1
	Hindu	0.1

USA (2005)		
	Adherents	**Percentage**
	Christian	82
	No Religion	11.3
	Jewish	1.9
	Muslim	1.6
	Buddhist	0.9
	Ethnoreligionist	0.5
	Hindu	0.4
	Atheist	0.4
	Baha'i	0.2[***]

Notes to Table 1.1

* http://www.thearda.com/internationalData/MultiCompare5.asp?c=41, 90, 234 …

** www.vexen.com.uk/religon.html.

*** *The World Factbook* (2005); http://www.worldvaluessurvey.org

century commonly thought that "Christianity is a part of the common law."[64] At the beginning of the country, there was a common belief in morals and ethics, grounded in Judaism and the main Christian religions of Catholicism and Protestantism. With the emergence of new religions in the nineteenth century, such as Mormonism, it is clear that they were singled out and not treated on equal footing with conventional religions. Yet, if we were being true to originalism, we would have to ask: would we tolerate such overt, invidious discrimination as was commonly practiced at the time? Would we be, as it were, original sinners?

Blasphemy in the United States is unconstitutional under the first amendment.[65]

---

64 Witte, *supra* note 20, at 407 (citations omitted). "Story disputed Jefferson's contention that Christianity was not part of the common law," observing that Christianity offered "the great basis, on which [the republic] must rest for its support and permanence." Adams and Emmerich, *supra* note 19, at 1590, citing J. Story, *Commentaries on the Constitution*, section 1867, at 724 (Boston 1833).

65 *Joseph Burstyn, Inc v. Wilson*, 343 U.S. 495 (1952).

Chapter 2
Basic Constitutional Text and Structure

United Kingdom

The constitutional system of the UK is not based on any single written document, but is a product of a range of core documents: the Magna Carta, important Acts of Parliament, such as the 1689 Bill of Rights, court decisions, royal prerogatives, political practice and custom, conventions, and the Human Rights Act of 1998, which came into effect in 2000 and has broken some of the linkage between the House of Lords and the judiciary. We might characterize UK constitutionalism as a constitutionalization of custom and practices which has led to a stable, enduring constitutional order.[1] Historically, the UK made no express provision for religious freedoms; also, no part of UK law limited religious freedoms. Instead, one traditionally looked to the common law and statutory law for any concrete protection for religion.[2] But this has now changed with the Equality Act of 2006, which explicitly protects people based on their religion, giving broader scope to religious rights.

One of the original influential sources of constitutionalism is the 1215 Magna Carta, which was an imposition by the barons to limit the power of the king. The crucial importance of the Magna Carta was in extending rights to common citizens, confirming liberties to be enjoyed by "freemen of the realm," including trial by jury and, most importantly, "the law of the land" clause, which was incorporated into the early state constitutions of the United States and later was transformed into the due process clause of the Fifth Amendment of the United States Constitution.

The 1628 Petition of Right reaffirmed the ancient rights of English citizens. A bloodless revolution in 1688 established continuous Protestant royal succession and constitutional government.[3] The constitutional settlement was the pivotal event in the establishment of constitutionalism. The Bill of Rights of 1689 acknowledged the balance of power between parliament and the crown as it emerged from the seventeenth-century civil war between the crown and parliament. The central concept of parliamentary supremacy finds its origins in the Bill of Rights, including the limitation of the power of the crown. The main principles include: the crown

---

1 http://www.oceanlaw.com/NXT/gateway.dll/ccw/Current/United%20Kingdom/GBR_Intro-2005.htm.

2 Mark Hill, The Permissible Scope of Legal Limitations on the Freedom of Religion or Belief in the United Kingdom, 19 *Emory Int'l L. Rev.* 1129 (2005).

3 Mary Ann Glendon, Paolo G. Carozza, Colin B. Picker, *Comparative Legal Traditions; Text, Materials and Cases on Western Law* 306–19 (3rd ed. 2007).

may not suspend or execute laws without parliamentary consent; levying money for use by the crown is illegal without parliamentary consent; armies may not be kept in peacetime without parliamentary consent; freedom of speech and debate in parliament cannot be questioned anywhere outside of parliament; liberty of the press is under the protection of juries; abolishment of the sacramental test which helped relieve Roman Catholics from unfair treatment; guarantee of trial by jury; abolishment of the slave trade; and meetings of parliament for redress of grievances.[4] Much of the origin of English constitutionalism in the seventeenth century was derived from a deep-seated reverence for the ancient constitution—"a set of principles—the common law—which had existed unchanged from the beginning of time." Lord Coke was a major influence on English constitutionalism, relying on ancient constitutionalism to establish vital constitutional principles, such as trial by jury, foundations of judicial review, no taxation without consent, and the reaffirmation of habeas corpus.[5]

The Act of Settlement of 1701 provides for the security of tenure for members of the judiciary "during good behaviour" and limits the line of succession to the throne to Protestants. The Union with Scotland Act of 1706 effectuates the Treaty of Union between England and Scotland. The Race Relations Act of 1976 protects people from direct and indirect discrimination. The 1976 Act protects people on the status of race, ethnicity and nationality. The courts have often considered religion to be part of race and ethnicity and often decide religious matters under the 1976 Act. The Human Rights Act of 1998 gives the UK a bill of fundamental rights for the first time. The Act incorporates the main provisions of the European Convention on Human Rights. Citizens can thus make their claims for rights protections under the terms of the Convention before any British court. The Act yet preserves parliamentary supremacy. However, the courts interpret laws in accordance with EU law, including the European Convention as enforced by the European Court of Human Rights. In 2002, the law of discrimination in employment was extended to cover religion, based on the EU Directive 2000/78.[6]

The Constitutional Reform Act of 2005 was motivated by a desire to bring the UK constitutional order into better harmony with modern constitutional orders, including stronger separation of powers between the executive, legislative and judicial branches. Its key focus was to establish an independent judiciary. There was also a concern that the English judiciary was not independent enough, which

4 http://www.oceanlaw.com/NXT/gateway.dll/ccw/Current/United%20Kingdom/GBR_Intro-2005.htm.

5 Jason S. Crye, Ancient Constitutionalism: Sir Edward Coke's Contribution to the Anglo-Saxon Legal Tradition, 3 *The Journal of Jurisprudence* 235, 238, 254 (2009) (citing James Hart and Richard J. Ross, "The Ancient Constitution in the Old World with the New" in Francis J. Bremer and Lynn A. Botelho (eds) *The World of John Winthrop: Essays on England and New England 1588–1649* 287.

6 Mark Freedland, Religious Expression in the Workplace in the United Kingdom, *Comp. Labor L. and Policy J.* 597, 598 (2009).

did not comply with EU law. The Act also created a Supreme Court of the UK, which consists of 12 judges appointed by the monarch and went into effect on 1 October 2009. The new Supreme Court takes over the functions performed by the Appellate Committee of the House of Lords. The judges of the Supreme Court hold their office for life and can only be removed on the addresses of both Houses of Parliament.[7] The Equality Act of 2006 explicitly protects people based on their religion, giving broader scope to religious rights. In this respect, we can see that the UK is moving toward a more overt and concrete constitutional order.

With the new Supreme Court in place, the UK is moving toward a more significant protection of constitutional norms, including especially fundamental rights. However, the Supreme Court, as of now, cannot overrule Acts of Parliament. The French constitutional system started with judicial review in the 1970s. While a weak judicial system, the French system has now moved more toward a harder, concrete and independent judicial review system and does find Acts of Parliament unconstitutional. It is likely the UK system will move in this direction too. In this respect, the nature of judicial review is somewhat weak as they do not have the power to act as an independent court and overrule parliamentary acts. By contrast, however, European constitutional acts require Parliament to comply with European constitutional norms. Still, however, the UK system is not like the US and German systems, which call for hard judicial review and the clear overruling of legislative or executive acts.

Germany

The relationship between church and state is centered on Article 140 of the Basic Law, which incorporates as an organic whole the provisions of the 1919 Weimar Constitution (Articles 136, 137, 138, 139, 141). The relationship is a cooperative one. The Weimar provisions set out a detailed and complicated scheme of church-state cooperation that is interpreted in the light of Article 4 free exercise of religion protections, which protect explicitly freedoms of faith, conscience and philosophical creed. The tendency today is to interpret Articles 4 and 140 as reciprocal religious protections. Religion and church each play a prominent role in German society, which these provisions facilitate.[8]

Article 136 of the Weimar Constitution secures civil and political rights, including eligibility for public office; freedom from dependence or restriction based on religious belief or exercise; protection against coerced disclosure of religious conviction, coerced performance of religious acts or ceremonies and

---

7 http://www.oceanlaw.com/NXT/gateway.dll/ccw/Current/United%20Kingdom/GBR_Intro-2005.htm.

8 Donald P. Kommers, *The Constitutional Jurisprudence of the Federal Republic of Germany* 443 (2nd ed. 1997).

coerced taking of religious oaths; and prohibits government from inquiring into membership in a religious body, except for statistical purposes.

Article 137 of the Weimar Constitution, in its first clause, states "[T]here shall be no state church." In comparison to the broad, albeit disputed, meaning of the American prohibition on "an establishment of religion," the German clause has a more widely accepted meaning. It forbids: (1) institutional interconnection between church and state; and (2) identification of the state with a specific religion. The clause does not mean strict separation of church and state.[9] The numerous remaining provisions of Article 137 guarantee the freedom of association to form religious bodies to "regulate and administer its affairs autonomously within the limits of the law,"[10] guaranteeing their independence from the state;[11] constitute religious bodies to "acquire legal capacity according to the general provisions of civil law;"[12] become "corporate bodies under public law;"[13] which corporate status allows them "to levy taxes in accordance with *Land* [state] law."[14] This last provision is completely without parallel in American law.

Official granting of charters to religious bodies was a major objection of James Madison, who thought that a federal incorporation of an Episcopal church in Washington, D.C., would constitute an establishment of religion.[15] Before the turn of the nineteenth century, Virginia outlawed religious corporations, a prohibition which it kept in place until 2002.[16] West Virginia yet prohibits religious corporations.[17] It is fair to point out that most religious organizations today are incorporated as non-profit corporations and receive tax-exempt status and, thus, bear some similarity to German religious corporations.

Under the more pervasive approach of German law, the state provides the legal framework for religious bodies to operate, and then offers the machinery of government to administer and collect taxes for religious purposes. In keeping with

9 David P. Currie, *The Constitution of the Federal Republic of Germany* 245 (1994).

10 Weimar Reichsverfassung (WRV) art. 137(3).

11 Compare with *Corp. of Presiding Bishop of the Church of Jesus Christ of Latter-Day Saints v. Amos*, 483 U.S. 327 (1987) (exempting church from federal antidiscrimination laws so that church may run autonomously its affairs).

12 WRV art. 137(4).

13 Ibid. art. 137(5).

14 Ibid. art. 137(6).

15 Currie, *supra* note 9, at 245, citing 22 *Annals of Congress* 982–85 (1811) (viewing federal incorporation of Episcopal church in Washington, D.C., as establishment of religion). See also Arlin M. Adams and Charles J. Emmerich, A Heritage of Religious Liberty, 137 *U. Pa. L. Rev.* 1559, 1587 (1989).

16 *Falwell v. Miller*, 203 F. Supp. 2d 624 (2002) (Va. Const.i art. 4, section 14 violates Free Exercise Clause). John Witte, Jr., The Essential Rights and Liberties of Religion in the American Constitutional Experiment, 71 *Notre Dame L. Rev.* 371, 385 (1996).

17 West Va. Consti art. 6, section 47.

the neutral, non-discriminatory nature of German law, these benefits are available to associations of a "philosophical persuasion" as well as religious ones.[18]

In practice, the main beneficiaries of governmental aid are dominant religious bodies, such as Protestant and Roman Catholic groups. Because church and state tend to consist of overlapping majoritarian configurations, church-state cooperation has been a comfortable fit.[19] In a sense, the structure of church-state cooperation operates as *de facto* establishments. The cooperative model has functioned well in a society of relative religious homogeneity.[20] Since the cooperative model was developed, in 1919, with an eye to pluralism, it is possible the model will continue to function well under new circumstances of emerging religious diversity. The model was designed for all religious groups, not just the big churches of Roman Catholicism and Protestantism.

The Seventh-Day Adventist Church, Church of Jesus Christ of Latter-Day Saints, Baptist Church, New Apostolic Church, Pentecostal communities, Christian Scientists, Mennonites and the Salvation Army, among others, have achieved recognition as public law corporations.[21] Other minority religions have had some difficulty achieving official recognition. This may, in part, be due to differences in held values. For example, Jehovah's Witnesses have historically been denied official privileges because the sect does not allow its members to vote and participate in the democratic process. Authorities thus viewed the sect as animated by values antithetical to the social order and, accordingly, a danger to society.[22] However, recently Jehovah's Witnesses acquired recognition as a public corporation in a significant Constitutional Court case,[23] signaling an important evolution in German thought toward toleration.

Under the system, employers withhold the monies and submit them to the state, which then distributes them to the religious denominations in a percentage equal to their membership. The churches pay the costs of administration. Religious groups use the money collected to build seminaries, churches, hospitals and

18 WRV art. 137(7).

19 Ingrid Brunk Wuerth, Private Religious Choice in German and American Constitutional Law: Government Funding and Government Religious Speech, 31 *Vand. J. Transnat'l L.* 1127, 1140, 1145 (1998) (in post Second World War Germany, church and state have promoted a consensus of values that includes promotion of democracy and tolerance).

20 Inke Muehlhoff, Freedom of Religion in Public Schools in Germany and in the United States, 28 *Ga. Int'l & Comp. L.* 405, 488–89 (2000) (observing that church-state cooperative model may be harder to implement as religious groups become more diverse).

21 Gerhard Robbers, Religious Freedom in Germany, 2001 *B.Y.U.L. Rev.* 643, 649–50.

22 Gerhard Besier and Renate-Maria Besier, Jehovah's Witnesses' Request for Recognition as a Corporation under Public Law in Germany; Background, current status, and empirical aspects, 43 *J. Church and State* 35 (2001).

23 Jehovah's Witness, 102 *BVerfGE* 370 (2000) (ruling that state cannot condition granting of public corporate status on basis of failure to vote; alternative ways must be pursued to assure loyalty to democratic order).

nursing homes and to train teachers. These arrangements are a mainstay by which religion secures its place as a main actor within society, if not a preferred one. Conversely, state support of religion allows government to exert some control over religion, including the set of values to be inculcated, such as promotion of morality, democracy, and tolerance.[24] The tax is between 8 per cent and 10 per cent of a person's state income tax. Any person whose name is on the church or religious body's register is automatically subject to the tax. A person must formally withdraw from the church or religious body to be relieved from the tax.[25] Non-church members are not assessed the tax.

Article 138 of the Weimar Constitution guarantees religious bodies rights, including the right to own property. Article 139 of the Weimar Constitution recognizes Sunday and other public holidays "as days of rest from work and of spiritual edification," expressly resolving an issue that has proved vexing to American law. In *McGowan v. Maryland*, the Supreme Court rejected an Establishment Clause challenge to Sunday closing laws on the ground that Sundays were now secular days of rest, even though originally were conceived as days of repose for religious reasons.[26] Article 141 of the Weimar Constitution provides for the rendering of religious services and spiritual care to the army, hospital, prisons, or other public institutions.

In addition to these express provisions that address religion, the Basic Law protects religion in a number of articles that cover other subjects as well. For our purposes, quite relevant is Article 6, which guarantees parental rights in the raising of their children, subject to state supervision.[27] Parental rights come into play most dramatically in connection with their children's education, which rights are guaranteed in Article 7. Also notable is the determination, in Article 7(3), that "[R]eligion classes shall form part of the ordinary curriculum in state schools, except in secular *(bekenntnissfrei)* schools … religious instruction shall be given in accordance with the tenets of the religious communities."[28] The state has supervisory obligations concerning education too, as set forth in Article 7(1): "The entire schooling system shall be under the supervision of the state." These ideas flow from the German theory of assigning duties to official power to secure civil peace, aid conceptions of freedom and concretize the core values of the Basic Law. Under German constitutionalism, the idea is made manifest in the conception of basic rights, which have an objective or positive dimension (constitutional values exist extrinsically to the state which the state must adhere to) that animates the

24 Wuerth, *supra* note 19, at 1140, 1145–46.

25 While state collection of church taxes is constitutional, it has nevertheless given rise to significant litigation. Currie, *supra* note 9, at 247; Kommers, *supra* note 8, at 484–89.

26 See, e.g., *McGowan v. Maryland*, 366 U.S. 420 (1961).

27 GG art. 6(2) ("the care and upbringing of children is the natural right of parents and a duty primarily incumbent upon them. The state shall watch over them in the performance of this duty.").

28 GG art. 7(3).

value structure as well as the subjective or negative dimension (values that limit state authority) that they share with American law. An important contrast between the two constitutions is that the Basic Law affects all legal relationships, public and private, under the theory of third-party effect (*Drittwirkung*), meaning that the constitution has an effect on private law as well. Teaching religion in the schools is relatively uncontroversial.[29]

However, the German constitutional system is careful to protect against coercion of conscience. Article 7 further provides "[T]he persons entitled to bring up a child shall have the right to decide whether the child shall attend religious classes."[30] And "[N]o teacher may be obliged against his will to give religious instruction."[31]

Because setting of educational policy is a matter for the German states (*Länder*) under German principles of federalism, the *Länder* determine what is appropriate educationally. Article 141 of the Basic Law preserves the historical right of *Länder* to determine if religion is to be offered at all. Under the principle of Article 141, the German states of Bremen and Berlin do not offer religious instruction in the schools.[32] Article 141 is known as the Bremen Clause, because it acknowledged the historical omission of religion in the Bremen schools. After German reunification, in 1990, Berlin in its entirety and the formerly East German state of Brandenburg became part of the Federal Republic of Germany. These states omitted mandatory teaching of religion. Likewise, Brandenburg does not offer religious instruction in the schools. Like the Article 137 provisions, the guarantees for religious instruction in public schools represent again the German idea of church-state cooperation in certain essential social services. And there are yet other provisions of the Basic Law addressing religion.[33]

Having described this complex of law, we can see that the German charter is indeed far more detailed and comprehensive in its treatment of religion than the United States charter. There are advantages to the German detail. The German charter expressly resolves many issues that called for US Supreme Court resolution in parsing out the sparse language of the First Amendment. For example, Article 4 resolves the status of conscientious objection to military service, an issue that has proved thorny for the Supreme Court.[34] Article 7

29 Kommers, *supra* note 8, at 471.

30 GG art. 7(2).

31 GG art. 7(3).

32 Article 141 provides: "The first sentence of paragraph (3) of Article 7 shall not be applied in any Land in which different provisions of Land law were in force on 1 January 1949."

33 See, e.g., GG art. 3(3) (faith and religious opinion are inappropriate subjects to target under the basic equality norm); GG art. 56 (federal President shall assume office upon taking oath, with or without reference to God); GG art. 64 (2) (same regarding federal Chancellor and federal ministers).

34 See, e.g., *Welsh v. United States*, 398 U.S. 333 (1970) (plurality); *United States v. Seeger*, 380 U.S. 163 (1965).

resolves significantly the role of religion in public schools, an issue of great contention in the United States. The greater detail of the Basic Law would seem to make a difference. Still, the Constitutional Court renders a significant number of cases on church-state relations, in the same manner as the United States Supreme Court.

Constitutional text is just one part of a country's constitution. History, framers' intent, and constitutional structure are other indispensable elements of constitutional law, at least under canons of American constitutional methodology. Not surprisingly, German history and constitutionalism differ from American. Under German constitutionalism, decisive in methodology is the text and structure of the charter and its applicability to contemporary social conditions. Framers' intent is not dispositive in achieving results, but may be consulted as an auxiliary aid to interpretation.

United States

In contrast to the detail of the German Basic Law, the United States Constitution enumerates religious liberty in only two places: the First Amendment and Article VI(3), which provides "no religious Test shall ever be required as a Qualification to any Office or public Trust under the United States." The religious test clause was designed to prevent the bitter English experience of flushing out dissenters or those not loyal enough to the English crown (mainly Roman Catholics, atheists or separatists), a practice which continued also in the colonies and early states before the Constitution.[35] The practice of requiring religious tests through mandated oaths persisted, stubbornly, in some states until 1961, when the Supreme Court declared it unconstitutional, illustrating how social reality can often lag behind constitutional ideals.[36] The Court concluded that the requirement of a religious test oath invaded the person's "freedom of belief and religion and therefore cannot be enforced against him."[37] There is little other jurisprudence under the religious test oath clause, as most issues relating to religion have involved interpretation of the First Amendment religious freedoms.

Textually, the First Amendment singles out religion in two ways. The Establishment Clause delimits governmental power over religion by prohibiting

35 Adams and Emmerich, *supra* note 15, at 1576–78 (American colonists commonly used English test oaths to support Anglican and Congregational establishments. Early state constitutions commonly required test oaths as preconditions to hold public office.) This history was a main motivation for requiring the prohibition of mandated religious oaths in Article VI of the Constitution.

36 *Torcaso v. Watkins*, 367 U.S. 488 (1961) (Maryland constitutional provision requiring state officials to declare belief in God unconstitutional).

37 Ibid. at 496.

it from establishing religion.[38] The Free Exercise Clause highlights religion for preferred treatment by singling it out, over other topics—such as politics, commerce, or property—as meriting freedom from governmental prohibition. So, we can see there is an interesting relationship, if not tension, between the Establishment Clause and the Free Exercise Clause.[39] The Establishment Clause appears to single out religion for official inaction; the Free Exercise Clause seems to single out religious activity for favored treatment.

The religious clauses are similar in ways and different in other respects. Both the Establishment Clause and the Free Exercise Clause have in common a concern for protection of the individual voluntariness of religious choice and especially a guarantee of liberty of conscience and its concomitant guard against coercion of conscience. We might say liberty of personal conscience is the common, core ideal of the two clauses. However, the two clauses differ over strategy. The Establishment Clause is primarily institutional based; delimitation of governmental power over religion safeguards the voluntariness of individual and group choice over religion. The Free Exercise Clause is mainly individually based; people, not government, are empowered to choose and act on religious tenets as one of the score of natural rights enshrined in the Constitution. There is thus a certain amount of tension between these clauses posed by an Establishment Clause that constrains government in respect of religion and a Free Exercise Clause that empowers personal religious exercise. Justice Kennedy's apt observation seems appropriate that the limits of the Free Exercise Clause lie in the Establishment Clause, in contrast to the clear structural protection of free speech, which contains no textual limitation. "The Free Exercise Clause embraces a freedom of conscience and worship that has close parallels in the speech provisions of the First Amendment, but the Establishment Clause is a specific prohibition on forms of state intervention in religious affairs with no precise counterpart in the speech provisions."[40]

Turning more directly to the Establishment Clause, it is fair to say the court works with very limited textual authority. While we might all agree that the Establishment Clause constrains official actions concerning religion, there is no general consensus over exactly what degree and nature of constraining is required. Maybe we can only come up with this commonly accepted meaning: 1) there

---

38 With the incorporation of the Establishment Clause into the Fourteenth Amendment, which extended its reach against state actions, it is more appropriate to speak of government, and not the First Amendment's chosen words of "Congress," as the object of the Clause. *Everson v. Board of Education*, 330 U.S. 1 (1947).

39 *McCreary County, Kentucky v. ACLU*, 545 U.S. 844, 882 (2005) (O'Connor, J., concurring) ("Reasonable minds can disagree about how to apply the Religion Clauses in a given case. But the goal of the Clauses is clear: to carry out the Founders' plan of preserving religious liberty to the fullest extent possible in a pluralistic society. By enforcing the Clauses, we have kept religion a matter for the individual conscience ..."); *Locke v. Davey*, 540 U.S. 712, 718 (2004) ("The Religion Clauses of the First Amendment ... are frequently in tension ... [but] 'there is room for play in the joints'") (citation omitted).

40 *Lee v. Weisman*, 505 U.S. 577, 591 (1992).

can be no established church; 2) there can be no preference of one religion over another religion; and 3) there can be no coercion of religious faith or practice. Still, given Establishment Clause constraint on governmental authority, the text would seem to signal a presumption against governmental involvement in religion.

Not surprisingly, the court has had much difficulty translating this majestic generality into a workable standard of law. At the end of the 2004–05 term, for example, the court ruled, 5-4 each time, that Texas could display a large monument of the Ten Commandments with explicit religious inscription on its state capitol grounds because it was surrounded by 21 other historical markers and 17 other monuments of various types and, therefore, it seemed more "historical" than "religious;"[41] but a Kentucky courtroom could not display a framed copy of the Ten Commandments, even when later surrounded by other historical material of religious meaning, because the display was too religious.[42] We can see that it is hard to reach agreement on what the Establishment Clause means.

Since the court started applying the Establishment Clause vigorously, in 1947,[43] it has vacillated uneasily between separationist and accommodationist stances. We can see this even in *Everson:* all nine members of the court employed separationist rhetoric, but the court split 5-4 in applying the doctrine to the facts, upholding state-supported bussing of Roman Catholic schoolchildren. The Court analogized state-provided bussing to other safety and welfare services, like police or fire protection.

41 *Van Orden v. Perry*, 545 U.S. 677 (2005).

42 *McCreary County, Kentucky v. ACLU*, 545 U.S. 844 (2005).

43 *Everson v. Board of Education*, 330 U.S. 1 (1947).

Chapter 3
Personal Religious Freedom in the United Kingdom

Personal religious freedom is the constitutionally protected right to act on your religious convictions. Free exercise of religious rights encompasses freedoms of conscience, belief, ability to perform religious rituals and act on religiously motivated behavior. Some basic definition of religion is important to lend some clarity. One way of describing religion is a sincere and meaningful belief in a God, spirit, or transcendental force which occupies in the life of its possessor a crucial place intimately related to daily life.

Personal religious freedom is like free speech: both are individual freedoms to act on one's own inspiration and thoughts. In the case of religion, it is individual action based on religion. In the case of speech, it is expression based on a person's thought process. A difference between religious and speech rights is that most personal religious freedoms are based on action, behavior and rites inspired by religious conviction. By contrast, most speech is based on the expression of an idea, thought, or emotion. The idea, thought, or emotion will be better constitutionally protected than conduct inspired by religion, which will be limited more forcefully by the general laws. General laws apply to all actors, no matter what their motive, whether personal, philosophical, or religious.

Because the UK has no written constitution, citizens are free to do as they like unless constrained by laws or rules derived from fundamental documents, parliamentary acts or the common law. Generally, the UK has taken a conservative approach to enforcing personal religious freedoms, although that is now changing with the UK's movement toward constitutionalism. Because the UK is a member of the EU and the European Convention of Human Rights, the role of protecting fundamental rights, including religion, is exercised significantly by these two European courts, the European Court of Justice and the European Court of Human Rights. UK courts will often respect and then utilize the principles of the European courts as a way to introduce a style of more independent judicial review. The Equality Act of 2006 explicitly protects people based on their religion, giving broader scope to religious rights. With the 2009 establishment of a UK Supreme Court, the UK is moving in a much stronger direction to a system of constitutionalism that protects rights, a movement that started in 1998 with the establishment of the UK Human Rights Act.

The general style of opinions by the UK courts, including the high courts, like the House of Lords, is one of a careful exposition of the facts and then a ruling for or against the claimant, with generally just a few pronouncements of principles of law. We can probably conclude that this style of reasoning relates to the origin of the common law, where it would be common practice to render the decision orally, with some secretary transcribing the notes, which might then be later published. In this respect, the UK style of judicial reasoning contrasts to an extent with that of Germany and the United States. In these two countries, the court will carefully enumerate the facts, and then employ strong judicial reasoning that leads to development of clear judicial rules of law. With the establishment of the Supreme Court, the UK is moving more in this direction of judicial articulation of clear rules of law. This change in judicial style of reasoning may diminish the long English tradition of oral rendering of decisions, focusing intently on the facts. In sum, the long rendition of facts is a long-rooted tradition of judicial decision-making that now, however, seems to be changing toward a style of independent judicial review involving clear exposition of the facts and articulation of principles of law.

With the establishment of a UK Supreme Court, the UK is providing much stronger protection of fundamental rights and operating as a court in an independent role. However, the Supreme Court, as of now, cannot yet overrule Acts of Parliament. While there is judicial review, the nature of judicial review is weaker in the British Courts as they do not have the power to overrule legislation. However, since the 1970s, the French *Constitutionnel Counseil* has been much more aggressive in assessing parliamentary acts, now leading to their invalidation or the parliament rewriting the act. By comparison, the German and US courts have the power to overrule acts of government, whether by the legislature, executive or administrative branch. We can characterize this as hard judicial review.

In the area of personal religious freedom, most of the cases before the UK courts have involved minority religions such as Islam, Sikhs, Rastafarians, fundamentalist Christians, especially Jehovah's Witnesses, and Jews. Of course that court practice covering minority religious believers is pretty common, as majority religions play a greater role in the development of the norms of society. In this Chapter I cover a range of cases that cover topics such as Islamic religious attire and facial manifestations, such as beards or dreadlocks, which might run afoul of dress or health codes, corporal punishment, refusal to work on a day of the Sabbath, and blood transfusions. But I am going to start with three seminal free exercise cases: *R. v. Governing Body of JFS and the Admissions Appeal Panel of JFS et al.*,[1] which dealt with a school admission policy and was the first important opinion on religious freedom rendered by the newly constituted Supreme Court; *Williamson v. Secretary of State for Education*,[2] which dealt with corporal punishment and in which the House of Lords sets out a relatively clear and careful definition as to what constitutes the definition of religion; and *Mandla v. Dowell Lee*,[3] which dealt with religious attire that poses safety hazards and where the House of Lords set

1 [2009] UKSC 15.

2 [2005] UKHL 15, 2 All ER 1.

3 [1983] 2 AC 548.

out a clear definition of what constitutes a group based on race and ethnicity. I will start with *R. v. Governing Body of JFS and the Admissions Appeal Panel of JFS et al.* and then go to *Williamson v. Secretary of State for Education.*

Religion in Schools

R. v. Governing Body of JFS and the Admissions Appeal Panel of JFS et al.: school admission policy

The UK Supreme Court decision of *JFS* is a path-breaking case in the development of free exercise rights. The case involved the application of a 13-year-old boy to the JFS school, considered an outstanding school. The boy's father was Jewish and his mother, originally an Italian Roman Catholic, had converted to Judaism. The parents were now divorced. Under the admissions policy of the JFS school, a prospective student must be recognized as Jewish by the office of the Chief Rabbi of the United Hebrew Congregation. The criterion for admittance to the school is that the prospective student must have been born by a mother who was Jewish at the time of his or her birth or the mother had converted to Judaism in a manner that satisfies the Orthodox faith.[4] The school concluded that the boy did not sufficiently satisfy the criterion for admission and denied his admission to the school. The case went through the lower courts and then reached the Supreme Court.

The Supreme Court upheld the Court of Appeals decision on the basis of direct discrimination, coming out 7-2: five justices voted for direct discrimination, two for indirect discrimination, and two for no discrimination.[5] The Supreme Court decided the case under the 1976 Race Relations Act, which provides:

> 1. Racial Discrimination
>
> (1) A person discriminates against another in any circumstances relevant for the purposes of this Act if-
>
> (a) On racial grounds he treats the other less favourably than he treats or would treat other persons …
>
> 3. Meaning of "racial grounds … "
>
> (1) In this Act, unless the context otherwise requires—
>
> "racial grounds" means any of the following grounds, namely colour, race, nationality or ethnic or national origins;

4 [2009] UKSC 15, 2 All ER at 10.
5 [2009] EWCA Civ 626.

> "racial group" means a group of persons defined by reference to colour, race, nationality, or ethnic or national origins;
>
> (2) The fact that a racial group comprises two or more distinct racial groups does not prevent it from constituting a particular racial group for the purposes of this Act.[6]

The Race Relations Act still appears to be the main basis for the determination of what religion means. With the new Equality Act, there is now hope for a better and more precise definition of the meaning of religion.

Critical here now would be the legal definition of what constitutes qualification under the Race Relations Act. The Supreme Court looked to two tests: the objective test, developed in the significant *Mandla v. Dowell Lee*[7] case, which will be discussed later, and the subjective test used by Orthodox Jews and requiring that the child be of a Jewish mother. Under the subjective test, consideration of being a Jew is determined by the religious law laid down by Orthodox Jews. This test focuses on religion, not ethnicity. Under the objective test, set out by Lord Fraser in *Mandla*, the test comprises seven characteristics that form an ethnic group:

> The conditions which appear to me to be essential are these: (1) a long shared history, of which the group is conscious as distinguishing it from other groups, and the memory of which it keeps alive; (2) a cultural tradition of its own, including family and social customs and manners, often but not necessarily associated with religious observance. In addition to those two essential characteristics the following characteristics are, in my opinion, relevant; (3) either a common geographical origin, or descent from a small number of common ancestors; (4) a common language, not necessarily peculiar to the group; (5) a common literature peculiar to the group; (6) a common religion different from that of neighbouring groups or from the general community surrounding it; (7) being a minority or being an oppressed or a dominant group within a larger community, for example a conquered people (say, the inhabitants of England shortly after the Norman conquest) and their conquerors might both be ethnic groups.
>
> A group defined by reference to enough of these characteristics would be capable of including converts, for example, persons who marry into the group, and of excluding apostates. Provided a person who joins the group feels himself or herself to be a member of it, and is accepted by other members, then he is, for the purposes of the Act, a member.[8]

6 Ibid. at 5.
7 [1983] 2 AC 548.
8 [2009] UKSC 15, 2 All ER at 11–12.

In reviewing the test of the Race Relations Act, the Supreme Court concludes that "racial grounds" includes "ethnic or national *origins* … Origins require one to focus on *descent*."[9] This now becomes the crucial factor: what is the basis for religion? Is it just religion? Or is it the common ethnicity that shares a religious bond? The Supreme Court concludes that:

> One of the criteria of ethnicity … is a shared religion. In the case of Jews, this is a dominant criterion. In their case, it is almost impossible to distinguish between ethnic status and religious status. The two are virtually co-extensive. A woman who converts to Judaism thereby acquires both Jewish religious status and Jewish ethnic status.[10]

The Supreme Court then goes on to review the standards set by Orthodox and Reform Jews as to conversion to being Jewish and concludes that "the test of descent is not restricted to Orthodox Jewry, but is a universal test applied by those who consider themselves to be Jews … whatever their racial, national and ethnic background, conversion unquestionably brings the convert within the *Mandla* definition of Jewish ethnicity."[11] With this, the Supreme Court concludes that "the relevant characteristics of the relative to whom the maternal line leads are not simply religious. The origin to which the line leads can be racial and is, in any event, ethnic."[12] This leads the court to the conclusion that the mother is Jewish. Under the Race Relations Act, religion plays a key role in the determination of ethnicity.

So determining that the mother is Jewish, the court looks again to the subjective test of an Orthodox Jew and the objective *Mandla* test. The court states "But one thing is clear about the matrilineal test; it is a test of ethnic origin. By definition, discrimination that is based upon that test is discrimination on racial grounds under the Act."[13] This leads the court to conclude that "this is direct racial discrimination."[14] Judge Lady Hale clarifies the basic difference between direct and indirect discrimination:

> The rule against direct discrimination aims to achieve formal equality of treatment: there must be no less favourable treatment between otherwise similarly situated people on grounds of colour, race, nationality or ethnic or national origins. Indirect discrimination looks beyond formal equality towards a more substantive equality of results: criteria which appear neutral on their

9 Ibid. at 13.

10 Ibid. at 14.

11 Ibid. at 16. For the Orthodox and Reform definitions of conversion to being Jewish, see ibid. at 14–16.

12 Ibid. at 16.

13 Ibid. at 17.

14 Ibid.

> face may have a disproportionately adverse impact upon people of a particular colour, race, nationality or ethnic or national origins.
>
> Direct and indirect discrimination are mutually exclusive ... The main difference between them is that direct discrimination cannot be justified. Indirect discrimination can be justified if it is a proportionate means of achieving a legitimate aim.[15]

Indirect discrimination can be determined only if the measure has a disparate impact on the affected group. The court cites a number of critical discrimination cases, such as *Birmingham City Council, Ex p Equal Opportunities Commission*, which dealt with a school that preferenced boys over girls,[16] and *James v. Eastleigh Borough Council*, where women at the age of 60 were allowed free entry to swimming facilities, whereas men had to be 65;[17] the House of Lords found both of these policies unconstitutional. Use of the Race Relations Act and equality decisions of the courts seems to be a significant basis for the rendering of free exercise cases. This reflects the constitutional order of the UK: the main source of constitutional rights are long-standing constitutional norms, determined in crucial documents, such as the Magna Carta, parliamentary acts, or decisions of the high courts. And with this, the *JFS* decision provides a strong basis for the protection of individual exercise of religious rights, demonstrating a trend in the UK for preservation of core rights.

What is interesting about the UK decisions is that they often look to the jurisprudence of other countries. While in this contrast between direct and indirect discrimination the court does not cite foreign jurisprudence, it has analogies to United States Supreme Court jurisprudence. For example, if a suspect trait is implicated, such as race or ethnicity, strict scrutiny will apply and the measure will not be legal unless there is a compelling justification that is justified by a narrow tailoring to the end.[18] This is an idea of formal neutrality, meaning the measure is either formally neutral or not formally neutral; if facially discriminatory, the measure strikes out at a particular racial or ethnic group. By contrast, substantive neutrality means the measure is formally or facially neutral, but has an adverse impact on a particular group of people.[19]

---

15 Ibid. at 20 (opinion of Judge Lady Hale).

16 [1989] AC 1155 (discrimination entails less favourable treatment on the ground of sex).

17 [1990] 2 AC 751.

18 *Adarand Constructors, Inc. v. Pena*, 515 U.S. 200, 227 (1995). ("[C]lassifications are constitutional only if they are narrowly tailored measures that further compelling governmental interests.")

19 In United States equal protection analysis, the court utilizes disproportionate adverse impact only if there can be a showing of a discriminatory purpose. *Washington v. Davis*, 426 U.S. 229 (1976).

Comparative law has a vital role to play in evaluating and assessing a country's native legal system. It is important to see how other countries deal with issues that are in common with a native land. Looking only inside your borders can often be too confining. It is better to look outside your borders for better perspectives on issues common to countries.

Williamson v. Secretary of State for Education and Employment: corporal punishment

In *Williamson v. Secretary of State for Education and Employment*, the House of Lords dealt with the issue of corporal punishment, a traditional conservative Christian custom rooted in the Bible, based on the metaphor of spare the rod and spoil the child.[20] The facts involved teachers at an independent Christian school who would stand in the place of parents of the students and render corporal punishment if the student was guilty of some form of misconduct. For these fundamentalist Christians, the rendering of corporal punishment is a core Christian value rooted in the Bible. They brought lawsuits against the school, based on the religious protections rooted in Article 9 of the European Convention for Human Rights—which are also now embodied in the Human Rights Act of 1998—but they lost in all of the lower courts, leading to their appeal of the lawsuit to the House of Lords. The significance of the case lies in its rendering of a fairly clear definition of what constitutes religion meriting protection as a right. In this respect, *Williamson* helps lend coherence to free exercise rights.

Under the Education Act of 1996, corporal punishment is not allowed in schools. The state of the law developed over time, starting with two mothers who objected to their children being subjected to corporal punishment. The European Court of Human Rights upheld their claim under Article 2 of the European Convention of Human Rights.[21] As a consequence of the European Court of Human Rights ruling, the UK changed its law in the Education Act of 1986 by stating that teachers in public schools have no right to render corporal punishment. Then in response to another European Court of Human Rights case, *Costello-Roberts, v. UK*,[22] Parliament changed the law again, mandating that corporal punishment cannot be administered if it is "inhuman or degrading," under the 1993 Education Act, and now applying the law to private schools. The next stage of the development of the law against corporal punishment, in 1998, was that the ban would apply to students at all types of school. The ban would apply to all teachers and staff members, but not to parents. However, Parliament also strictly regulated the degree and manner in which parents can render corporal punishment to their children. Punishment of a child that causes "actual bodily harm" cannot be justified. Any rendering of

20 [2005] UKHL 15, [2005] All ER 1. In Proverbs 13:34, the passage states, "He who spares the rod hates his son, but he who loves him is diligent to discipline him."

21 *Campbell v. UK* [1982] 4 EHRR 293.

22 [1994] 1 FCR 65.

corporal punishment must stop short of actual bodily harm. It is this extension of the law to all schools that became the basis for the case.[23] Corporal punishment of students in schools has not been allowed in Germany, but still is allowed in the US in about 20 states.[24]

The crucial opinion in the case is rendered by Lord Nicholls of Birkenhead. It is common practice in UK judicial decision-making that each of the judges renders their own opinion. Generally, one or two of the judges will issue an important opinion that sets forth important rules of laws. Many of the other judges will simply set out an abbreviated opinion or simply concur.

The House of Lords first goes on to note that European Convention of Human Rights protections, including beliefs and convictions:

> are part of the humanity of every individual. They are an integral part of his personality and individuality. In a civilised society individuals respect each other's beliefs. This enables them to live in harmony. This is one of the hallmarks of a civilised society. Unhappily, all too often this hallmark has been noticeable by its absence.[25]

This illustrates the UK courts' reliance on European court jurisprudence, as many fundamental freedoms are not concretely part of the UK constitutional order. The court then goes on to articulate a relatively clear definition of what constitutes freedom of religion under Article 9 of the European Convention of Human Rights:

> This freedom is not confined to freedom to hold a religious belief. It includes the right to express and practise one's beliefs. Without this, freedom of religion would be emasculated. Invariably religious faiths call for more than belief. To a greater or lesser extent adherents are required or encouraged to act in certain ways, most obviously and directly in forms of communal or personal worship, supplication and meditation. But under art 9 there is a difference between freedom to hold a belief and freedom to express or "manifest" a belief. The former right, freedom of belief, is absolute. The latter right, freedom to manifest belief, is qualified.
>
> This is to be expected, because the way a belief is expressed in practice may impact on others. Familiar instances of conduct shaped by particular religious beliefs are the days or times when worship is prescribed or encouraged, the need to abstain from work on certain days, forms of dress, rituals connected with the preparation of food, the need for total abstinence from certain types of food

23 [2005] UKHL 15, [2005] All ER at 8–9. A 2003 law also placed a ban on childminders, or babysitters, smacking children.

24 Dan Frosch, A Trip to These Principals May Mean A Paddling, *N.Y. Times*, p. A 15 (30 March 2011).

25 Ibid. at 10–11.

> or drink, and the need for abstinence from all or some types of food at certain times. In a more generalized and non-specific form the tenets of a religion may affect the entirety of a believer's way of life: for example, "thou shalt love thy neighbor as thyself." The manner in which children should be brought up is another subject on which religious teachings are not silent. So in a pluralist society a balance has to be held between freedom to practise one's beliefs and the interests of others affected by those practices.[26]

Under the European Convention of Human Rights and the UK Human Rights Act, rights are protected, but subject to democratic concerns for matters such as public safety, public order, health or morals, or protection of rights and freedoms of others.[27] In this respect, UK rights bear some similarity to the rights systems in place in Germany and the USA: rights are not always absolutely protected, but subject to social concerns such as harm to others. At issue here in the case is the difference between freedom of belief (which is generally absolutely protected) and practice or manifestation of belief (which is not absolutely protected and will depend on the competing social or other party interest).

The court goes on next to clarify its role in determining what is a person's religious belief. The court comes up with this principle:

> When the genuineness of a claimant's professed belief is an issue in the proceedings the court will inquire into and decide this issue as a question of fact. This is a limited inquiry. The court is concerned to ensure an assertion of religious belief is made in good faith, "neither fictitious, nor capricious, and that it is not an artifice," … But, emphatically, it is not for the court to embark on an inquiry into the asserted belief and judge its "validity" by some objective standard such as the source material upon which the claimant founds his belief or the orthodox teaching of the religion in question or the extent to which the claimant's belief conforms to or differs from the views of others professing the same religion. Freedom of religion protects the subjective belief of an individual … religious belief is intensely personal and can easily vary from one individual to another. Each individual is at liberty to hold his own religious beliefs, however irrational or inconsistent they may seem to some, however surprising.[28]

Thus, as concerns faith and belief, the individual is entitled to full protection. This standard articulated by the House of Lords is more in line with the German approach to judging freedom of belief. In *Rumpelkammer*, the Constitutional Court determined that "Religious exercise has central meaning for every faith and creed, and must be broadly interpreted in view of its historical content. … The self-understanding of the religious and ideological group should not be disregarded

26 Ibid. at 11.
27 Ibid.
28 Ibid. at 12.

in determining, in the individual case, what qualifies as the exercise of religion and ideology."[29] The British and German definition of religion stand in contrast to the United States approach articulated in *Employment Division, Department of Human Resources of Oregon v. Smith*, where the court stated:

> It is no more appropriate for judges to determine the "centrality" of religious beliefs … in the free exercise field, than it would be for them to determine the 'importance' of ideas … in the free speech field … "it is not within the judicial ken to question the centrality of particular beliefs or practices to a faith, or the validity of particular litigants' interpretations of those creeds.[30]

The US Supreme Court is much less interested in defining religion in comparison to its definition of free speech or equality. In past cases the Supreme Court did set out a definition of religion. In *Wisconsin v. Yoder*, the court took a more conventional, established approach to defining religion. Amish belief was religious because it entailed a theocratic view "of deep religious conviction, shared by an organized group, and intimately related to daily living."[31] A more accommodating definition of religion can be gleaned from *United States v. Seeger*, where the court fixed the standard for judging congressional exemption from military service as "[a] sincere and meaningful belief which occupies in the life of its possessor a place parallel to that filled by … God."

Judge Lord Hope takes issue over the court determining what constitutes religion. In this respect, Lord Hope is more in line with the Supreme Court in *Smith*.[32] For Lord Hope, it is not the job of a judge to determine the essence of religion, essentially echoing the thought of Justice Scalia. Further, it makes no difference under Article 9 of the European Convention of Human Rights as to whether the belief is to be characterized as religious:

> It does not matter whether the claimants' beliefs regarding corporal punishment of children are categorised as religious. Article 9 embraces freedom of thought, conscience and religion. The atheist, the agnostic, and the skeptic are as much entitled to freedom to hold and manifest their belief as the theist. These beliefs are placed on an equal footing for the purpose of this guaranteed freedom.[33]

The court then turns to the next part of religious freedom: manifestation of belief or what might be called free exercise of religion. While everyone:

29 *Rumpelkammer*, 24 BVerfGE 236, 246–48 (1968).
30 494 U.S. 872, 887 (1990) (citation omitted).
31 *Wisconsin v. Yoder*, 406 U.S. 205, 216 (1972).
32 [2005] UKHL 15, [2005] All ER at 57–58.
33 [2005] UKHL 15, [2005] All ER at 13.

> is entitled to hold whatever beliefs he wishes. But when questions of "manifestation" arise, as they usually do in this type of case, a belief must satisfy some modest, objective minimum requirements. These threshold requirements are implicit in art 9 of the convention and comparable to other human rights instruments. The belief must be consistent with basic standards of human dignity and integrity. ... The belief must relate to matters more than merely trivial. It must possess an adequate degree of seriousness and importance ... it must be a belief on a fundamental problem. With religious belief this requisite is readily satisfied. The belief must also be coherent in the sense of being intelligible and capable of being understood. But, again, too much should be demanded in this regard. Typically, religion involves belief in the supernatural. It is not always susceptible to lucid exposition or, still less, rational justification. The language used is often the language of allegory, symbol and metaphor. Depending on the subject matter, individuals cannot always be expected to express themselves with cogency or precision. Nor are an individual's beliefs fixed and static. The beliefs of every individual are prone to change over his lifetime. Overall, these threshold requirements should not be set at a level which would deprive minority beliefs of the protection they are intended to have under the convention.[34]

With these parameters in place, the court goes on to measure whether the infliction of corporal punishment is consistent with religious freedoms. The key question is whether use of corporal punishment is consistent with standards of human integrity and decency. In considering the issue, the court observes that corporal punishment can be justified as a legitimate exercise of religious rights. Then the court has to consider the relevance of section 548 of the Education Act, which bans all corporal punishment in all schools, public or private. Here the court concludes that the ban on corporal punishment is an interference with the parents' religious right. Now the critical question is whether the ban on corporal punishment can be justified. Here what comes into play is article 9(2) of the European Convention of Human Rights, which provides that rights can be limited when "necessary in a democratic society for the protection of the rights and freedoms of others."[35] The court now measures the law against article 9(2) and concludes:

> The statutory ban pursues a legitimate aim: children are vulnerable, and the aim of the legislation is to protect them and promote their wellbeing. Corporal punishment involves deliberately inflicting physical violence. The legislation is intended to protect children against the distress, pain and other harmful effects this infliction of physical violence may cause. That corporal punishment may have these harmful effects is self-evident.

34 Ibid. at 13.

35 Ibid. at 13–18.

> Further, the means chosen to achieve this aim are appropriate and not disproportionate in their adverse impact on parents who believe that carefully-controlled administration of corporal punishment to a mild degree can be beneficial, for this reason, the legislature was entitled to take the view that, overall and balancing the conflicting considerations, all corporal punishment of children at school is undesirable and unnecessary and that other, non-violent means of discipline are available and preferable. On this Parliament was entitled, if it saw fit, to lead and guide public opinion. Parliament was further entitled to take the view that a universal ban was the appropriate way to achieve the desired end. Parliament was entitled to decide that, contrary to the claimants' submissions, a universal ban is preferable to a selective ban which exempts schools where the parents or teachers have an ideological belief in the efficacy and desirability of a mild degree of carefully controlled corporal punishment.
>
> Parliament was entitled to take this course because this issue is one of broad social policy. As such it is pre-eminently well suited for decision by Parliament. The legislature is to be accorded a considerable degree of latitude in deciding which course should be selected as the best course in the interests of school children as a whole.[36]

Thus, in conclusion, the court decides that the ban on corporal punishment does not violate the religious rights of the parents, as it can be justified to protect the best interests of the child. As a free exercise matter, the court decides that while religious belief is protected absolutely, manifestation of belief is subject to the law; religious conduct must be weighed against the law to determine which of the two is weightier. What the case thus settles is that corporal punishment can no longer be practiced in any school, even if on religious reasons. However, parents still may administer corporal punishment to their children at their home, but only if they do not inflict serious bodily or mental harm; if they do that, they will be subject to the law. The importance of *Williamson* is in setting a benchmark for the definition of religion, again demonstrating how the UK is moving more in a direction of establishing constitutional rights and independent judicial review.

Religious Attire: Religious Freedom or Health and Safety

Mandla et al. v. Dowell Lee et al.: male dress attire and health issues

The *Mandla et al. v. Dowell Lee et al.* case is another important development of UK free exercise rights.[37] The case involved an orthodox Sikh who wore long hair under a turban, a Sikh custom. Under the policy of the private school, the wearing

---

36 Ibid. at 18.

37 [1983] 2 AC 548, 1 All ER 1062.

of a turban was not allowed. Therefore, the student was not allowed admittance to the school. This led to a lawsuit instituted under the Race Relations Act of 1976, which has had a dramatic influence on the development of religious rights. The critical question for the court was whether Sikhs qualify as a racial group under the Race Relations Act.

The path-breaking element of the *Mandla* case is its delineation of what is the criterion of determining what is a racial or ethnic group for purposes of the Race Relations Act. The definition of what is a racial or ethnic group set out by Lord Fraser of Tullybelton was quoted in the critical *R. v. Governing Body of JFS and the Admissions Appeal Panel of JFS et al.*, the first religious free exercise case issued by the newly constituted Supreme Court, described above.[38] In the opinion of Lord Fraser:

> a person [may] fall into a particular racial group either by birth or by adherence, and it makes no difference, so far as the 1976 Act is concerned, by which route he find his way into the group. This view does not involve any inconsistency between direct discrimination … and indirect discrimination.[39]

Under this definition of a racial group, the court construes the term racial in a broad cultural and historical sense.[40] The court then goes on to consider whether Sikhs qualify as a racial or ethnic group, concluding that Sikhs do qualify as a group:

> defined by ethnic origins for purposes of the Act … They were originally a religious community founded about the end of the fifteenth century in the Punjab. … But the community is no longer purely religious in character … '[the] Sikhs are a distinctive and self-conscious community. They have a history going back to the fifteenth century' … The result is, in my opinion, that Sikhs are a group defined by a reference to ethnic origins for the purpose of the 1976 Act, although they are not biologically distinguishable from the other peoples living in the Punjab.[41]

With this established, the court now considers whether there has been discrimination on ethnic grounds for the Sikh student, and concludes that there has been discrimination. With discrimination having been established, the next inquiry is as to whether there is any justification present to allow the discrimination. The best justification for the school is that it sought to run a Christian school and the wearing of attire not compatible with Christianity was improper. The court rejects this argument, finding this not to be a proper justification for the no turban rule

38 [1983] 2 AC 548, 1 All ER 1062, at 2; See *R. v. JFS* at 11–12.

39 [1983] 2 AC 548, 1 All ER 1062, at 8.

40 Ibid. at 8.

41 Ibid. at 9–10.

and thus there is no basis on which to deny admission to the Sikh student. No valid justifications of health, safety, or public order are presented. Health or safety justifications can arise in other contexts, most notably wearing a beard or turban while performing work in a factory or other setting, as for example in the *Panesar v. Nestle Co* case, where the health hazards of making chocolate outweighed the religious justifications of wearing a beard.[42] But here there is no valid justification for the no turban rule. Thus the religious rights outweigh the grounds for the school no turban rule. And with that we can see that the UK courts are making progress toward enforcing a person's right to exercise his or her religious practices.

With that said, valid justifications for public health, safety, and public order can justify curtailment of religious freedoms. This was noted in the *Panesar* case, where the wearing of a beard presented too many dangers in making chocolate, and in a wide range of other cases. Many of these cases resemble *Panesar*, where health justifications in the production of a product outweigh the religious justification of wearing a beard. In *Singh v. Rowntree Mackintosh Ltd*, the Employment Appeal Tribunal rejected a Sikh's argument that the religious requirement of wearing a beard justified being able to work and produce the confectionery product.[43] Likewise in *Singh v. Lyon Maiden Ltd*, no credible religious freedom argument could be made for producing ice cream while wearing a beard; health reasons prevail over religious reasons.[44] And in *Mohmed v. West Coast Trains Ltd*, the Employment Appeal Tribunal upheld the dismissal of the Indian of Muslim origin for failing to comply with the beard standard set by the train company, where beards are to be neatly trimmed.[45] In *Mohmed* there might be a less strong reason for justifying limitation of the religious practice, as health justifications may be less convincing. Other cases raised similar concerns over whether religion or health would trump the other. In *Singh v. British Rail Engineering Ltd.*, the Employment Appeal Tribunal upheld the judgment of the Industrial Tribunal that a Sikh was not allowed to wear a turban but instead was supposed to wear a hard hat over the turban, for safety reasons, which he was unable to do; this resulted in the Sikh being demoted to a lesser position.[46]

In *Kingston & Richmond Area Health Authority v. Kaur*, the Employment Appeal Tribunal overruled the decision of the Industrial Tribunal that the Sikh woman was discriminated against based on religion.[47] Under certain religious dress requirements of Sikh women, women are supposed to wear either a sari or a salwer kameez, a form of trousers. The Industrial Tribunal concluded that this was religious discrimination under the Race Relations Act, but the Employment Appeal Tribunal ruled that this did not constitute discrimination, based on religion

42 *Panesar v. Nestle Co.* [1980] IRLR 64, ICR 144.
43 [1979] IRLR 199, ICR 554.
44 [1975] IRLR 328.
45 UKEAT/0682/05/DA (transcript).
46 [1986] ICR 22.
47 [1981] ICR 631, IRLR 337.

under the Race Relations Act. Looking at these facts today, with the 1983 *Mandla* decision, it is most likely that this would constitute discrimination, based on religion, under the Race Relations Act.

The *Dawkins v. Department of the Environment* case presented a complicated question as to whether Rastafarian qualified as an ethnic group under the *Mandla* test.[48] The case involved a Rastafarian who applied for a job as a van driver. He wore dreadlocks, an integral part of being a Rastafarian, but under the company's rule drivers were required to have their hair cut short; accordingly, the company rejected his application for a job. The Industrial Tribunal concluded that the Rastafarian did qualify as an ethnic group under the *Mandla* test, but the Court of Appeals came out the other way, concluding that their history went back only 60 years and this was insufficient to meet the requirement of a long shared history of ethnicity. The length of time to qualify as a group is somewhat of a contested issue: should it be 60, 100 or 200 years, or more, to be sufficient to qualify as a group under the *Mandla* test? How relevant is the length of time the group is together necessary for qualification as an ethnic group? With the dramatic changes in Western society, perhaps 60 years is enough time to qualify, but of course that is a contested issue. Likewise, in *Harris v. NKL Automotive Ltd.*, the Employment Appeal Tribunal upheld the dismissal of a Rastafarian, who wore dreadlocks as part of his system of belief, on the ground that he did not comply with the dress code necessary for drivers.[49]

R. (on the application of Begum) v. Denbigh High: Islamic women dress codes

R. (on the application of Begum) v. Denbigh High School involved a controversy over the school's dress code.[50] The school had a very diverse student population, involving 21 different ethnic groups and 10 religious groups, with Muslims now comprising 79 per cent of the population, having dropped from 90 per cent in 1993. The school is not a faith-bound school, but a school open to all faiths and those with no faiths. The head teacher grew up as a Muslim and lived in India, Pakistan, and Bangladesh and was thus very familiar with Muslim dress customs. Being so aware of Muslim practices, the head teacher drew up the dress code for the school. There were three uniform options, and the one that applied to Muslim, Hindu, and Sikh women was a shalwar kameeze: a combination of the kameeze, a sleeveless smock-like dress with a square neckline, combined with the shalwar, a trouser tapering at the ankles. The student, Shabina Begum, complied with this dress code for the first two years of her education at Denbigh High, as did her sister. But in September 2002, she changed her dress attire, wearing a jilbab, which was not compatible with the school's dress policy. The committee of governors of the school then met and upheld the decision of the head teacher, and advised her

48 [1993] ICR 517, IRLR 284.

49 UKEAT/0134/07/DM (transcript).

50 [2006] UKHL 15.

to return to school, conforming to the dress code, or go to another school which would permit the wearing of the jilbab. She made an application to one school, but it was full. Two other schools would permit the wearing of the jilbab, but she did not apply to them. This led to the lawsuit; which should control: religion or the school dress code? The Court of Appeals ruled in her favor, but the case went to the House of Lords, which concluded that the school policy trumped her religious rights.[51]

Begum then brought her claim for religious and educational rights under the European Convention of Human Rights and the UK Human Rights Act of 1998, but our focus will be on religious rights. The House of Lords sets out the parameters of freedom of religion under Article 9 of the European Convention of Human Rights:

> article 9 protects both the right to hold a belief, which is absolute, and a right to manifest belief, which is qualified.
>
> It is common ground in these proceedings that at all material times the respondent sincerely held the religious belief which she professed to hold. It was not the less a religious belief because her belief may have changed, as it probably did, or because it was a belief shared by a small minority of people. Thus, it is accepted, obviously rightly, that article 9(1) is engaged or applicable. That in itself makes this a significant case, since any religious belief must command respect, particularly when derived from an ancient and respected religion. The main questions for consideration are, accordingly, whether the respondent's freedom to manifest her belief by her dress was subject to limitation (or, as it has more often been called, interference) within the meaning of article 9(2) and, if so, whether such limitation or interference was justified under that provision. [52]

The crucial question now is whether there is justification under Article 9(2) for limitation of the student's religious rights. Common in European constitutional orders is the rule that while rights are protected, they can be limited by countervailing principles, such as, in Article 9(2) "limitations prescribed by law and are necessary in a democratic society … for the protection of the rights and freedoms of others." Here the House of Lords has to measure the Article 9(2) limitation to determine that it is directed to a legitimate purpose and is proportionate in scope and effect.[53] The intensity of the level of review is no higher than in the past. The court "must … make a value judgment, an evaluation, by reference to the circumstances prevailing at the relevant time. … Proportionality must be judged objectively, by

51 [2005] EWCA Civ. 199; [2006] UKHL 15, at pp. 2–6.

52 [2006] UKHL 15, at p. 8.

53 Ibid. at 11.

the court."[54] Lord Bingham concludes that the school's policy cannot be considered disproportionate.[55]

Lord Bingham then goes on to elaborate the proportionality test, looking to guidance in the jurisprudence of the European Court of Human Rights. In citing the European Court, Lord Bingham observes that:

> The court there recognizes the high importance of the rights protected by article 9; the need in some situations to restrict freedom to manifest belief; the value of religious harmony and tolerance between opposing or competing groups and of pluralism and broadmindedness; the need for compromise and balance; the role of the state in deciding what is necessary to protect the rights and freedoms of others; the variation of practice and tradition among member states; and the permissibility in some contexts of restricting the wearing of religious dress.[56]

While the student criticized the school for permitting certain attire, like the headscarf, and that other schools allowed the jilbab while this school did not, the court rejected these assertions. Instead, the court deferred to the school authorities in setting the dress code policies. Lord Bingham concludes that the school was fully justified to devise a uniform policy that respected Muslim beliefs, and thus allowed the appeal and set aside the judgment of the Court of Appeals.[57]

What the case illustrates is that the English courts are moving more in the direction of respecting religious rights, but still may significantly defer to school authorities. School authorities have made a strong effort to respect minority religions, consulting with religious authorities of the particular faith, and then assessing the situation and setting the policy. The goal here is for inclusiveness of the wide range of religious belief within the society.

A range of cases reflect the same concerns; which should prevail: religious practice or school policy? These cases involve both students and teachers. The *R. (on the application of X) v. Head Teachers and Governors of Y School* follows essentially the facts and line of reasoning of the *Denbigh High School* case.[58] Both religious attires were based on the Muslim faith: in *Denbigh High School* it was a jilbab; in *R. (on the application of X) v. Head Teachers and Governors of Y School* it was a niqab—a veil that protects the whole face except for the eyes. Previously, the school had allowed female Muslim students to wear the niqab, including the two older sisters of the 12-year-old student. Her sisters were allowed to wear the niqab from 1995 to 2004, but the school changed the policy in 2006, resulting in the young student not being permitted to attend the school. She had the option to go to another school, about 25 minutes from her home, but she decided not to

54 Ibid. at 13.
55 Ibid.
56 Ibid. at 14.
57 Ibid.
58 [2007] EWHC 298 (Admin); 1 All ER 249, ELR 278.

follow that option. The family claimed a violation of article 9 religious rights under the European Convention of Human Rights. The court rejected this argument, reasoning that the school's policy was justified on the grounds of security, public safety, and protection of the rights of others.[59] A thorn in the case is that the policy previously allowed the wearing of the niqab, but did not now. The real question: does the wearing of a niqab actually present a concern for security, public safety, or the rights of others? But a common practice of courts is to defer to school authorities. This is especially so in the UK and the USA; it is less so in Germany.

Another central case is *R. (on application of Watkins-Singh) v. Aberdare Girls' High School*, which involved a 14-year-old Sikh girl who wore an item of jewelry, a plain steel bangle, known as a Kara, which was only about one-fifth of an inch in width.[60] The school considered the wearing of the Kara to be inconsistent with the school dress code. The student applied for a waiver from the dress code policy, but was denied. Upon reviewing the situation, the school concluded that she would have to be taught in isolation, away from the rest of the students so as not to disturb them. The court, Queen's Bench Division, Administrative Court, concluded that the school's decision not to grant a waiver constituted indirect discrimination under the Race Relations Act and the Equality Act of 2006 on both race and religious grounds.

There is a major difference in the outcome of the *Aberdare Girls' High School* case and a range of other cases that dealt with similar issues, such as the *Denbigh High School* case discussed previously. The crucial difference is the change in UK laws on protection of religion. Most of these earlier cases were decided on the basis of the Human Rights Act of 1998, which essentially mirrored the provisions of the European Convention of Human Rights. But the *Aberdare Girls' High School* case was based on a change in UK law: an amended version of the Race Relations Act of 1976 and the new Equality Act of 2006. These more recent laws provide greater protection of religious rights, leading to better claims to religious freedoms for minorities.

How these earlier decisions, like *Denbigh High School*, would come out as constitutional or unconstitutional under the present UK law would call for a careful assessment of the rule of law as applied to the facts at issue. Among other factors to be considered are the nature, size, and visibility of the religious attire. The Kara is very small, not very visible and unobtrusive. Thus, the Kara is less likely to raise an issue that might provoke discontent, hostility, or insult. By contrast, the niqab and the jilbab are much more visible to an observer. On this basis the court concluded that the student could wear the Kara, as this was much less observable than a niqab or a jilbab.[61] Still, the question is, does the wearing of a niqab or a jilbab actually present any kind of health, safety, or security issue? Which is more important: religious practice or a school dress code?

---

59 [2007] EWHC 298 (Admin); 1 All ER 249, ELR 278, at pp. 424, 428, 451, 465.

60 [2008] EWHC 1865 (Admin); 3 FCR 203.

61 [2008] EWHC 1865 (Admin); 3 FCR 203, at p. 225.

Evaluating the case, the court concluded that this amounted to indirect discrimination under the Race Relations Act of 1976 and the new Equality Act of 2006, on racial and religious grounds, and that the school policy could not be justified under the proportionality test. The wearing of the Kara was a matter of great importance for her genuine belief in religion and race. According to the court, it is important for the school to respect and be tolerant of the religious rites and beliefs of people, no matter what race or belief, in order to have a cohesive and multicultural society.[62]

In *Azmi v. Kirklees Metropolitan Borough Council*, the Employment Appeal Tribunal upheld a claim of the teaching assistant for victimization, but dismissed the appeal for direct and indirect discrimination on the basis of religion and for harassment.[63] Under European Union directives, the UK has implemented the Employment Equality (Religion or Belief) Directive that provides equal treatment in the areas of religion and belief, covering any religion, whether based on a godly or philosophical belief. The facts involved a Muslim teaching assistant who wanted to wear her veil as a matter of her religion. The school told her that she could wear the veil in open areas and when walking around the school, but she could not wear the veil when working with children and with teachers. For the tribunal, the religious claims are outweighed by the need for stability and order in the classroom. The UK decision stands in contrast to the German Constitutional Court decision in which it allowed the Islamic teacher to wear a head veil in the classroom, preferring free exercise of religious rights over classroom order.[64]

The case of *Eweida v. British Airways* involved a devout Christian woman who worked as a part-time check-in agent and regarded the wearing of a plain silver cross as a central element of her religion.[65] Under British Airways rules, employees can wear any item they wish provided it is not visible and underneath their clothing. Exceptions are made only for religious items to be worn on the outside if the item is a mandatory part of the person's religion. This was not the case here. British Airways offered her alternative employment positions where she did not have to wear a uniform and she could wear her cross openly, but she refused this offer. She then brought a claim for discrimination, both direct and indirect, but she was not successful. The employee argued that her case was analogous to the *Aberdard Girls' High School* case, where a Sikh student was allowed to wear the Kara, the small plain steel bangle, but this argument was not successful. A range of other cases involving Sikhs and Muslims wearing religious attire of their choosing were rejected by the courts under education laws. The Employment Appeal Tribunal upheld the judgment of the Employment Tribunal that there was no justification for discrimination, direct or indirect. There was not

62 [2008] EWHC 1865 (Admin); 3 FCR 203, at pp. 226, 227, 228.

63 UKEAT/0009/07/MAA (transcript).

64 BVerfG, 2 BvR 1436/02 (24 September 2003) (hereinafter "*Islamic Teacher's Head Scarf*").

65 UKEAT/0123/08/LA (transcript).

sufficient evidence to demonstrate that she was a member of a group that shared her religious faith.[66]

Sabbath Day: Sabbath or Work

Stedman v. UK: work on day of Sabbath

Stedman v. UK involved a claim by an assistant manager of a travel agency that now required her to work on Sundays, which she considered a day of rest for her family and important for the practice and observance of her Christian religion.[67] She did work Sundays from December 1991 to May 1992, but then decided that she would no longer work on Sundays, claiming violation of her religious rights under article 9 of the European Convention of Human Rights and also a number of other rights, such as family and privacy and discrimination. Under UK law, she did not qualify for the requisite two-year employment term that necessitated a claim for unfair dismissal. She then brought her claim to the European Court of Human Rights, but the court dismissed all of her claims. The court found no basis for violation of her religious, family or right to equal treatment under the non-discrimination principle. Her dismissal was based on her refusal to sign a new contract, not on religious grounds.[68]

Stedman thus sets the basis for the rule of whether religion or work requirements determine which controls. Two other cases deal with the same issue. In *Copsey v. WWB Devon Clays Ltd*, a practicing Christian was required to work on Sundays, as the business demand had picked up considerably.[69] Previously, with business having risen, the claimant Copsey was allowed to work on a six-day basis, and not on Sunday, which he considered to be a day of rest consistent with Christian practices. The company tried to negotiate a range of alternative options for its employees, including Copsey, but these negotiations were to no avail. Both the Employment Tribunal and the Employment Appeal Tribunal dismissed his claim for religious discrimination.

The European Court of Human Rights reconsidered Copsey's claim and decided that his religious rights were involved under Article 9. However, the court concluded that his dismissal could be justified under Article 9(2) because the company had compelling economic reasons for putting in place the seven-day work week. Another case involving the same issue was that of a recently reconverted Jehovah's Witness bus driver who refused to work on Saturday. Here the Industrial Tribunal concluded that his refusal to work on Saturday was a clear

66 Ibid. at pp. 139–141, 147, 153.
67 [1997] 23 EHHR 168.
68 [1997] 23 EHHR 168 pp. 2–6.
69 [2005] EWCA Civ.932, ICR1789, IRLR 811.

breach of his employment contract.[70] And finally, in *James v. MSC Cruises*, a body ruled that requiring a Seventh Day Adventist to work on Saturdays was justifiable on business grounds, entailing no indirect discrimination.[71]

There is a difference in approach to these cases involving the refusal to work on a day of Sabbath between the UK and the United States. In the UK case, the employer attempted much more accommodation of the believer's work schedule. Likewise, this happened in *Sherbert v. Verner*, where the US Supreme Court did recognize that a Seventh Day Adventist could quality for unemployment benefits for refusing to work on her Saturday day of Sabbath.[72] By contrast, in *Braunfeld v. Brown*, the Supreme Court did not recognize the free exercise rights of an Orthodox Jew who wanted to keep his store open on Sunday on the ground that Sunday was a uniform day of rest and thus the Pennsylvania law could be justified.[73] Also interestingly, freedom to practice one's religion is covered more concretely in the US Constitution than in the UK, but that is because the USA has a written constitution. By contrast, the UK does not have a written constitution and instead has a series of customs and written documents, such as the Magna Carta. However, now with the European Convention of Human Rights in place, the courts will give much more deference in the standard of margin of appreciation to the member states than would happen in the USA.

Under the margin of appreciation test, rights will generally have a high status measured against competing purposes in scope and effect. The government must justify its basis for the law with a strong justification. If government can show a strong justification, for example, health or safety, then the rights can be curtailed. We might characterize the margin of appreciation test, which is essentially in substance like the proportionality test, as favoring rights over laws.

Islamic Prayer Ritual

Ahmad v. UK: Islamic prayer ritual

Ahmad v. UK involved a school teacher of the Islamic faith who exited his Friday school day to pray at a mosque, a crucial part of Islamic ritual rites.[74] Ahmad taught from 1968 to 1974 at a school that was too far away from a mosque so he could not attend. In 1974, he taught at a school that was only 15 to 20 minutes from a mosque. He asked for permission from school authorities to attend the mosque, but was told that they could not stop him from going but that he would not be granted a leave to do so. He then took it upon himself to leave school premises on

70 *Esson v. London Transport Executive*, [1975] IRLR 48.

71 Case No. 2203173/05, reported in 157 Equal Opportunities Rev. (2006).

72 374 U.S. 398 (1963).

73 366 U.S. 599 (1961).

74 [1982] 4 E.H.R.R. 126.

Friday afternoon, which had the consequence of disrupting his teaching services for 40 to 45 minutes. School authorities then offered him a four-and-a-half-day teaching schedule, which entailed a reduction in his salary. He also proposed that the Friday school day be reconfigured so that he could attend the mosque, which school authorities were not willing to do. He rejected the offer and then resigned. He was unemployed for nine months, but then the school agreed to take him back for a four-and-a-half-day teaching schedule. He then made appeals to the Industrial Tribunal, Employment Appeal Tribunal and then the Court of Appeals; each of the courts rejected his appeal; the House of Lords refused to hear the appeal.[75]

Ahmad asserted that his religious rights were violated by not being allowed to attend the mosque on Fridays. The European Commission for Human Rights considered his claim, and determined that he may claim a right to manifest his religion "in community with others" under Article 9(1). However, after assessing the facts against Article 9(1), the Commission concluded that there has been no interference with his religious rights. The Commission also considered his claim under Article 14 equality rights, and concluded that he was not treated any less favorably than other members of religious minorities.[76] The Commission upheld the judgments of the UK courts.

A similar situation arose in *Hussain v. London Country Bus Services Ltd.*, where a Muslim who had worked for the company turned to be a more devout Muslim, observing the Muslim ritual of praying at selected times during the day.[77] He started work at six in the evening. Under Muslim practice, he was required to pray at sunset. Sunset, of course, would vary with the time of the year. The problem was that at six many of the buses came in and needed to be serviced and turned around quickly. This disrupted the work pattern at the bus company. The Employment Appeal Tribunal cites the *Ahmad* case, observing that he was to observe the rules set by educational authorities and concludes that Hussain has no basis for a claim of violation of religious rights. The workplace rule for maintenance of buses outweighed religious rights.

Other Cases

I want to finish this chapter by discussing a number of other cases that raise matters of personal religious freedoms. As is common in Western society, most cases concern people who belong to a minority faith. In *Surayanda v. Welsh Ministers*, the matter concerned a bullock (or bull) who was an integral part of the religious faith of the Community of the Many Names of God.[78] Unfortunately, the bull tested positive for bovine tuberculosis. And so the question is which is

75 [1982] 4 E.H.R.R. 126, at pp. 2–3.

76 Ibid. at 9.

77 EAT 750/83 (transcript) (13 March 1984).

78 [2007] EWCA Civ 893 (transcript) (2007).

weightier: the religious faith of the practitioners or the public threat to health. Here there was no choice: the threat to public health was too great and, accordingly, the court ordered that the bull had to be slaughtered. While the religious groups had claims for religious freedoms under Article 9(1) of the European Convention of Human Rights, concerns for democracy, public health, and the rights and freedoms of others under Article 9(2) outweighed this practice of religious faith.

Ritual slaughter is an integral part of Muslim and Jewish faith. Ritual slaughter is permissible in the UK, but subject to health and geographic regulations. In *Hussain et al. v. Secretary of State for the Environment*, the court ruled that ritual slaughter could not be carried out because the chickens were kept live in the backyard of the shop. In order for slaughter of chickens to take place, the owner would have to get permission for a zoning variance.[79] Likewise, in *R. v. Rabbinical Commission for the Licensing of Shochetim*, the appellant argued that the Rabbinical Commission for Licensing had no authority to restrict the Jewish ritual of slaughter to a specific geographic area.[80] The court deferred to the Rabbinical Commission, recognizing their religious authority. Religious bodies should determine religious rules rather than courts.

Several cases involve an employer's dismissal of employees for religious reasons. In *Saini v. All Saint's Haque Centre*, two employees of the Hindu faith worked for an immigration advice center.[81] The center was controlled by adherents of the Ravidassis faith, a group distinct from the Sikh and Hindu community. A feud had simmered between employees of the Ravidassis and Hindu faith. At first, a Hindu manager was in charge. Two Ravidassisians lost their jobs, one for lack of funding and the other because his volunteer services came to an end. Later, the board of directors changed from Hindu to Ravidassisian. With this change, the board terminated the employment of the two Hindus. There was a good argument for dismissing the Hindu manager, as he had displayed lack of competence in managing money. There was not a good argument for dismissal of the other Hindu, an advice worker. The Employment Appeal Tribunal overturned the verdict of the Employment Tribunal, concluding that the advice worker had been discriminated against on religious grounds under the Employment Equality (Religion and Belief) Regulations 2003.

In *Glasgow City Council v. McNab*, the Employment Appeal Tribunal upheld the appeal of the employment tribunal in respect to an atheist who had applied for the position of acting principal teacher of pastoral care, but was turned down by the Roman Catholic school; the school did not even grant him an interview.[82] The problem for the Roman Catholic school was that it was short of teachers

79 23 P & CR 330, 221 EG 627 (Queen's Bench 1971).

80 *The Times* (22 December 1987); *The Independent* (28 December 1987) (transcripts) (Court of Appeal 1987).

81 Employment Appeal Tribunal, UKEAT/0227/08/ET (transcript) (24 October 2008).

82 [2007] IRLR 476 (17 January 2007).

and staff. There were not enough Roman Catholics interested in working for the school. Thus, the church was forced to hire many people who were not of the Roman Catholic faith, including D. McNab, an atheist, who had worked at the school since 1990. However, to obtain a position as principal teacher of pastoral care, the person must be Roman Catholic. Other positions requiring that one be of the Roman Catholic faith include head teacher, principal or assistant principal and teacher of guidance or religious education. The Employment Appeal Tribunal concluded that the position McNab applied for was one both for guidance and pastoral care and that the school had discriminated against him on the basis of religious belief. The Employment Appeal Tribunal further asserted that McNab's guidance of students is different than pastoral care. Pastoral care should be done by Roman Catholics.

In a final case on dismissal of employees over religion, a social worker was dismissed from his job for proselytizing Christianity.[83] The job of a social worker is to give honest and fair guidance to people in need. But the social worker, Chondol, used his job to promote Christianity, spreading the word of God and handing out Bibles. Based on this, he was terminated from his job. He filed a lawsuit based on religious discrimination, but his suit was not successful as the role of a social worker is to be neutral and not faith based. Proselytizing religion is inappropriate for a social worker. A social worker is to act honestly, fairly and openly, and not base any discussion on religion.

A number of cases deal with the critical issue of whether the life of the child is more important than the religious beliefs of the parents. This issue has come up in the UK, Germany, and the USA. The German courts are more protective of religious rights over this crucial issue than the UK and USA courts, as will be discussed later. In the UK cases, the court has ordered that the blood transfusion take place to save the life of the child, trumping the religious beliefs of the parent. In *Jane v. Jane*, the court ordered a blood transfusion for the child, a matter of extreme urgency for the life of the child, over the objections of the mother, a committed Jehovah's Witness.[84] Under the tenets of the Jehovah's Witness faith, the health of the person is to be determined by God; blood transfusions are not permitted. The parents were divorced. The father, concerned about the life of his child, applied for a joint custody order. The recorder determined that a joint custody order was not appropriate and granted sole custody to the father in order to save the life of the child. The mother appealed, but her appeal was struck down; the life of the child was more important than her religious beliefs, the court concluded. Likewise, in *Re L*, the court ordered a blood transfusion for a 14-year-old girl, a committed Jehovah's Witness, in a life-threatening condition.[85] The girl had lived a largely sheltered life, influenced by the Jehovah's Witness faith. The order was

83 *Chondol v. Liverpool City Council*, Employment Appeal Tribunal, UKEAT/0298/08/JOJ (transcript) (11 February 2009).

84 4 FLR 712, 13 Fam. Law 209 (Court of Appeal, Civil Division 1983).

85 [1998] 2 FLR 810, [1999] 2 FCR 524, [1998] Fam. Law 591 (1998).

granted without her consent given her extremely grave situation. For the court, it is more important to save the girl's life than respect her religion.

And in a final case involving the clash between religious faith and the life of children the matter at issue was a conjoined set of girl twins who were born of dedicated Roman Catholic parents.[86] Medical evidence showed that J was the stronger of the twins and she sustained the life of her twin, M, who was a weaker twin. M would not be able to live on her own; her only hope was being conjoined with J. However, over time J too would die with the sustenance she was providing M. Reviewing all the medical data, the court was faced with a tough choice; which should prevail: the life of J or the religious beliefs of the parents? The court concluded that the life of J would have to prevail over the religious beliefs of the parents. Preservation of life was more important than religious tenets.

Observations

Traditionally, the UK courts would defer to Parliament, as the role of the courts was weak under the principle of parliamentary supremacy. But now with the UK adhering to the constitutional orders of the European Union and the European Convention of Human Rights, constitutional norms and rights are getting much more protection. With this movement to constitutionalism, the UK is making significant progress on assuring personal rights to act on religious freedoms.

The Supreme Court's decision in *JFS* demonstrates how the movement toward independent judicial review is a major catalyst for protection of individual rights. In *JFS* the Supreme Court evaluated the standard for what constitutes Orthodox Jewish status, and relied on the important criterion laid out in the *Mandla* case, determining that race status could constitute religious status, as part of a person's ethnicity and nationality involving a shared religion. The *Mandla* case lays out a clear definition under the Race Relations Act as to what qualifies as a racial or ethnic group; shared religious belief and practice falls within the definition of a racial or ethnic group.

Also significant is the *Williamson* case, which involved corporal punishment, where the House of Lords states a fairly clear definition of religion; setting out that belief is absolutely protected, but practice of belief is qualified. The House of Lords sets out an inquiry into a person's religious belief as a way to determine whether the belief or practice qualifies as a religious protection. The House of Lords only wants to do a preliminary inquiry to determine whether it is religious. It does not want to do a full-blown inquiry. But determining what is religious as a matter of law is important to determine the status of rights concerning religious freedom.

With these important principles in place, the UK is making progress toward religious freedom. The UK courts are asserting their influence to see that rights

86 In *re A (Children)*, [2001] Fam 147 (2000).

are protected in order to curtail the democratic process. Still, the courts tend to be deferential to school authorities and employers. Regarding Islamic dress, for example, the court determined that the wearing of a Kara was a religious right, but otherwise generally denied the wearing of religious attire by students, teachers, and employees, instead deferring to authorities. Likewise, the court deferred to school and employee officials not to allow practicing Muslims to engage in faith-required rites of prayer. In sum, while religious rights are growing, there is still significant deference to authorities, mainly in school and work settings.

Chapter 4
Personal Religious Freedom in Germany

The German Basic Law accords broad scope to the freedom to believe or not believe in God or a philosophical tenet, and the freedom to act on such belief through free exercise of religion. This follows from the clear textual mandate of the Basic Law, which states that "freedom of faith … conscience … and creed … shall be inviolable [and that] [T]he undisturbed practice of religion is guaranteed."[1] German constitutional law thus solves straightforwardly central religious protections along lines that required court elaboration in the UK and the USA.[2] Explicit protection of the undisturbed practice of religion was a new development for Germany, different from the situation under the Weimar Republic, where religious practice could be limited by law.[3] The movement toward natural, inalienable rights is attributable to the reaction against Hitler. By anchoring the social order to natural principles of justice, the framers hoped to better contain the vagaries of human passion.[4] These principles animate the broad construction of religious freedoms.

Religious freedoms have a very preferred position in the constellation of values that comprise the German constitutional order. The preference for religion is due in part to textual mandate, as the Basic Law places no constraint on Article 4 freedoms. The Constitutional Court has facilitated this position of high rank as well. Given that the architectonic value of the Basic Law is human dignity and the unfolding of human personality in accordance with it, human values and human capacity stand at the very heart of the constitutional order, as elaborated on by the Constitutional Court. Human spiritual development and transcendence are indispensable elements of personal growth. Fortified by these principles, the Constitutional Court has accorded broad scope to free exercise freedoms.

The preferred position of religion and the correspondingly broad scope accorded it are notable characteristics of the German constitution. When faced with interests of the general law or social order asserted in limitation of religious freedoms, the Constitutional Court has generally preferenced religiously motivated actions. This

---

1 GG art. 4.

2 See, e.g., *Sherbert*, 374 U.S. at 402 ("Government may neither compel affirmation of a repugnant belief, … nor penalize or discriminate against individuals or groups because they hold religious views abhorrent to the authorities … nor employ the taxing power to inhibit the dissemination of particular religious views." (citations omitted)).

3 *Denial of Witness Oath*, 33 BVerfGE 23, 29–30 (1972).

4 Edward J. Eberle, Roger Williams's Gift: Religious Liberty in America, 4 *Roger Williams L. Rev.* 425, 427 (1999) (citing Roger Williams, *Mr. Cotton's Letter Examined and Answered* (1644)), at 18.

dynamic has resulted in a pattern of general accommodation for people of faith, excusing them from the constraints of the general law. The Constitutional Court has not interpreted such freedom as an invitation to disobey the law. The court's motivation, rather, is to relieve a person from the dilemma of trying to obey claims of conscience that conflict with claims of law. The court has been careful to limit accommodation to sincerely motivated religious conduct, and to carve out relief in ways that complement social order.

It is worth observing that the broad, preferred position that religious claims have in German society stands in sharp contrast to the USA under the Supreme Court's controversial ruling in *Employment Division, Department of Human Resources, Oregon v. Smith*.[5] Under *Smith*, obligations of the general law prevail over sincerely motivated religious actions. The two countries' contrast over the scope of personal religious freedom is one of the greatest differences between the laws. We will pursue this contrast later.

First, we need to get a better sense of the scope of German law. German free exercise law has three dimensions. First, German law recognizes personal free exercise liberty which consists of the right to act on chosen tenets. Here we will concentrate on situations where religiously motivated conduct clashes with claims of the general law in order to evaluate an essence of religious freedom and to obtain a sharp contrast with British and American law. Second, the German constitution expressly recognizes conscientious objection from military service,[6] an area covered in British and American law only by laws or legal decisions. Conscientious objectors must perform alternative service for a period equivalent to military service. They might work, for example, in hospitals, schools, or other aids to society. The clause has given rise to significant litigation.[7] Now, however, Germany has gotten rid of conscription in the military.

One significant case on conscientious objection entailed a change in the law that required conscientious objectors to perform 20 months of service in contrast to military inductees who performed 15 months of military service; two judges dissented from the opinion, objecting to the extension of conscientious objection service to 20 months.[8] The reason for this is that conscientious objectors are under a much less severe burden than military personnel.

The USA no longer requires compulsory military service. Present military service is voluntary. When compulsory military service was in place, the US Supreme Court ruled in a number of cases. For example, in *United States v. Seeger*, the court ruled that the draft applicant qualified for the statutory exemption on the

---

5 494 U.S. 872 (1990).

6 GG art. 4(3) and 12(a).

7 See authorities collected in David P. Currie, *The Constitution of the Federal Republic of Germany* (1994), at 250 n. 36.

8 *Conscientious Objector*, 69 BVerfGE 1 (1985).

ground that he believed in goodness and virtue and an ethical creed, with no real belief in God except in a very remote sense.[9]

Third, German law further accommodates religious organizations from claims of the general law on the ground that they have a right to run their own affairs autonomously.[10] Religious organizations enjoy a broad right of autonomy over their affairs. For example, a Catholic hospital could fire a doctor who took a public position on abortion contrary to official Catholic doctrine and not suffer the consequences normally required by labor law.[11] Religious organizations are free to set their own policies, and it is not the duty of the state to intrude into these internal affairs, including matters of employee policies, except if a matter is of great controversy that might trigger an aspect of the constitution. Or a Protestant church could relieve from his duties a pastor because he had been elected as a political representative, a status ordinarily protected by law from impairment.[12] The pastor needs to be dedicated to church matters, not political ones. The church does not want the pastor to serve in both capacities, a matter of church right under the principle of autonomy. The church did not relieve the pastor of his duties, but asked that he take a leave of absence, demonstrating remarkable restraint. Church and state need to respect the autonomy of each. The autonomy of religious bodies to run their affairs is highly developed in Germany and is generally in accord with the development of American law.[13] While the range of free exercise rights in a society can be rich and varied—consisting of people's daily practices, social conventions, habits or customs that are elements of society, as well as court cases at all levels—our lens on free exercise rights will be restricted to the leading decisions of the UK, German and American high courts.

Catholic Religious Charity

Rumpelkammer

The leading case establishing the scope of Article 4 freedoms is the 1968 case of *Rumpelkammer*.[14] The controversy concerned a Roman Catholic youth

9 380 U.S. 163 (1965). The court also recognized the conscientious objector's claim to exemption from the draft in *Welsh v. United States*, 398 U.S. 333 (1970), but rejected the claim in *Gillette v. United States*, 401 U.S. 437 (1971), on the ground that conscientious objection was not available when it relates only to a particular conflict.

10 WRV art. 137.

11 *Catholic Hospital Case*, 70 BVerfGE 130 (1985).

12 *Bremen Pastor Case*, 42 BVerfGE 312 (1976).

13 See, e.g., *Corp. of Presiding Bishop of the Church of Jesus Christ of Latter-Day Saints v. Amos*, 483 U.S. 327 (1987) (exempting church from federal antidiscrimination laws so that church may run autonomously its affairs).

14 24 BVerfGE 236 (1968).

organization that actively sought to practice its faith as a missionary in society, trying to realize the ideal of daily life lived by good deed. At issue was the group's collection of used clothes, paper and other recyclable goods for the purpose of raising money, which it then donated to charitable causes dedicated to the relief of hunger and misery in underdeveloped countries.[15] To further this effort, the group enlisted the pulpit, calling on priests to urge parishioners to donate to the cause. These activities raised the ire of a commercial rag dealer, who complained that the group's activities illegally competed with his business, which suffered.[16] The lower courts agreed, enjoining the youth organization from engaging in its clothing drive.

The Constitutional Court disagreed, overturning the injunction, finding it to be a violation of the group's Article 4 religious guarantees. Freedom to act and practice religion is central to religious belief:

> The article four guarantees of religion—irrespective if the creed is rooted in religious or nonreligious ideological belief—entail not only the inner freedom to believe or not believe, that is to profess a particular creed, or to remain silent or disavow a previously held creed and profess a new one, but also the freedom to engage in ritual acts, to proselytize, and to propagandize. ... Religious exercise has central meaning for each faith, and in view of its historical content, must be interpreted broadly. It includes not only ritualistic acts, like adherence to religious practices such as worship services, church collections, prayer, receipt of the sacrament ... but also religious education, religious and atheistic celebrations and other practices of religious or nonreligious life.[17]

The broad scope of religious freedom elaborated on by the court has its roots especially in the history of religious persecution under Hitler, the court observed.[18]

The wide berth of religious freedom is available on equal terms to all faiths and philosophies, not just to Christian churches, which are dominant in Germany.[19] In practice, German jurisprudence has primarily entertained religious belief. The principle of equality follows from the command of religious and ideological neutrality, which the state is bound by, and the principle of parity of church and creed.[20] Under these tenets, the state cannot favor or disfavor any religion over another, or religion over non-religion. Rather, under the principle of parity,

15 Ibid. at 237.

16 The rag dealer argued that enlisting the authority of the Catholic Church in support of the collection was an unfair business practice. Ibid. at 238–39.

17 Ibid. at 245–46.

18 Ibid. at 245.

19 Ibid. at 246.

20 Ibid.

all beliefs are to be treated equally.[21] Official neutrality and parity of faith and creed are indispensable to the guarantee of religious freedom and are especially pertinent given the increasingly pluralistic nature of German society. An open, pluralistic democratic society is the context envisioned for the exercise of basic rights, including religious rights.[22] In these respects, German society mirrors British and American. Both the German and US courts pitch rights philosophies against the social background of an open, pluralistic, democratic society. The UK courts are also now moving in that direction. The movement toward pluralism will put German religious rights to the test.

Religious freedoms apply to groups as well as to individuals, and protections further encompass organizations such as the youth group at the middle of the *Rumpelkammer* case, which "do not completely, but only partially further the religious or ideological goals of its members."[23] Decisive for the court is that religion be a primary motivation. "The condition [for applicability of Article four freedoms] … is that the purpose of the organization is directed at the achievement of such [a religious or ideological] goal."[24]

In American law, religious rights are one of the few areas where a group dimension to rights is evident.[25] It is much more common the case that rights are conceived in personal terms in the United States, meaning that individual rights will generally prevail over the general law. By contrast, the group dimension to rights is more characteristic of German law,[26] and European law more generally. Under group rights, individual rights are balanced against the community or the social order. Still, what is provocative is that even under US law, sometimes an individual rights approach will be limited based on the general law. A profound example of this is the *Employment Division, Department of Human Resources, Oregon v. Smith* case, which will be discussed later.[27] And even though Germany and most European courts apply a group-oriented approach, the German courts often give higher preference to individual rights in the balance over interests of the social order.

Having set out these broad parameters for religious freedoms, the court next had to apply them to the facts at hand. The court found religious exercise broad in

---

21 Ibid. The principles of neutrality and parity follow from the Weimar period. These principles are even more firmly entrenched in the pluralistic society envisioned in the Basic Law.

22 Ibid. at 248–49.

23 Ibid. at 247.

24 Ibid.

25 See, e.g., *Corp. of Presiding Bishop of the Church of Jesus Christ of Latter-Day Saints v. Amos*, 483 U.S. 327 (1987) (exempting church from federal antidiscrimination laws so that church may run autonomously its affairs).

26 See, e.g., *Auschwitz Lie Case*, 90 BVerfGE 241 (1994) (identity of Jewish people is bound with Holocaust as constituent element of their human dignity; accordingly, such dignitarian rights can limit publication of assertion that Holocaust never occurred).

27 494 U.S. 872 (1990).

practice, as it had in principle. The key question for determination was whether the charitable activity, and its solicitation by pulpit, were religious activities. Because the activities were economic, they were more far afield of conventional religious acts, such as taking of the sacrament, worship, or prayer. Decisive for the court was the religious motivation that inspired the conduct. Collecting clothes and material for charitable purposes, and their solicitation by pulpit, was religious, according to the court, supported by Biblical and Christian teaching.[28] Religion is not just a spiritual exercise. Religion includes the freedom to influence the world around you as well, to act outwardly in accordance with the dictates of your creed.[29]

Necessarily, these determinations entailed a judgment by the Constitutional Court that religious motivation lies at the base of the charitable activity. The court's approach seems quite sensible, for how else is a body to determine whether religious/philosophical freedoms are at issue other than by determining whether the actions under review are religious/philosophical? The Constitutional Court has straightforwardly gone about the business of determining what is or is not religious. The matter-of-fact course of the Constitutional Court contrasts with that of the US Supreme Court, which has often expressed discomfort at judging what is or is not religious. As the court in *Smith* states, "we have warned that courts must not presume to determine the place of a particular belief in a religion or the plausibility of a religious claim."[30]

The court saw its obligation as assessing religion or philosophical acts on their own terms. To do this, the court applied neutral, generally applicable constitutional criterion. However, the court emphasized that fair consideration must be given to the understandings of the believers at issue.[31] This is all the more important in a pluralistic society, where a range of disparate beliefs are practiced. If the religious or philosophical belief under review is not evaluated on its own terms, there is a danger that its vision will be lost among the multitude of voices apparent in pluralistic democracy. Further, there is danger that the vision will be drowned by the hegemony of dominant views that are likely to crystallize as social convention or norms, making it difficult to get one's tenets communicated or respected. Viewing religion or philosophy from the perspective of the believer is an important tenet of religious liberty. It is a perspective not notably present in contemporary United States law under *Smith*.

The court determined the activities to be religious, and therefore within the ambit of Article 4 protection. Being able to act on one's beliefs is an important part of religion. "Religious exercise has central meaning for every faith and creed,

---

28 24 BVerfGE at 248

29 Ibid.

30 See, e.g., *Smith*, 494 U.S. at 887.

31 24 BVerfGE at 247–48. "The self-understanding of the religious and ideological group should not be disregarded in determining, in the individual case, what qualifies as the exercise of religion and ideology." Ibid. at 247.

and must be broadly interpreted in view of its historical content."[32] Engaging in charitable activities is one way of realizing faith in daily life. For the court, this was decisive, even if such charitable activities might be viewed as standing somewhat at the outer bound of Article 4 freedoms, beyond more conventional religious rites. For its purposes, the Constitutional Court deliberately left open determination of the bounds of religious freedoms, preferring to determine what is protected on a case-by-case basis, an approach more in keeping with the vicissitudes of an open, pluralistic society.[33] There is always danger in judging freedoms by the past. Looking backwards can distort views of the present. With respect to religion, this might have a suffocating effect on new views of the world beyond.

Having determined that the charitable activities were protected, the court next moved to the second part of its methodology, application of a general balancing of interests test. This test involves a review of the lower court's decision to ascertain whether the lower court has given due regard to the rights at issue. Because religion is defined as an integral component of the constitutional order, it must be given especially significant weight. The Constitutional Court does not like to substitute its judgment for that of the lower courts. It prefers to review the lower court decision only to see whether appropriate weight was given to constitutional values. However, to the extent the court performs a balance or emphasizes the worth of a constitutional value, some second-guessing is inevitable. Under all circumstances, the lower court must re-perform the general balancing of interests upon remand in accordance with the court's instructions.

Performing this balance, the court compared the claims of religion against the competing demands of the businessman faced with unwelcome competition to determine which was weightier in the circumstance. It was no contest. The preferred value of religion in the constitutional order took precedence. Hence, the court lifted the injunction on the charitable activities. The marketplace had to yield to the preferred value of religion and adjust accordingly. No person has a right to participate in the market as they would like.[34]

Our review of *Rumpelkammer* reveals the main principles of German law. First, Article 4 freedoms are broadly construed. Inner freedom protects the interior world of the spirit. Outer freedoms guarantee the ability of a person to act on faith. The ability to influence the world through religiously motivated action is central. Second, the protections of religious freedoms are equally open to all, religious or non-religious belief, majority or minority creeds. Official neutrality and parity of creed help to assure fair consideration of religion/philosophy on its own terms, and also helps assure a level playing field in the competition among beliefs for influence. Third, the Constitutional Court must determine, through constitutional interpretation, what is or is not religious or philosophical for purposes of Article 4. Fourth, once an activity is determined to be religious and the claimant's exercise

32 24 BVerfGE at 246.

33 24 BVerfGE at 249.

34 Ibid. at 251.

thereof is burdened, religious rights must be balanced against the claim or claims of the social order asserted in limitation. In performing this balance, the court gives wide preference to religion consistent with its place as a preferred value in the constellation of values that comprise the constitutional order. Fifth, it is thus clear that religious activities will be presumptively protected and that their accommodation will generally occur in the social order as a sign of due respect for their importance. This methodology has wide implications.

Viewed in comparison to American law, the methodology of *Rumpelkammer* is much more akin to the approach of the Supreme Court under *Sherbert v. Verner*[35] than *Employment Division, Department of Human Resources, Oregon v. Smith.*[36] Similar to *Rumpelkammer*, the Supreme Court under *Sherbert* must first determine that the activities at issue are religiously motivated and that the legal measure under review burdens the exercise of those freedoms. Once it is determined that religious freedoms are at issue and that they are burdened, then they are to be preferred and ordinarily will prevail unless the state can demonstrate an overriding or compelling reason. Under the German methodology, this balance is achieved pursuant to the general balancing of interests test, with preference being given to fundamental rights, including religion. Under *Sherbert*, the court employs strict scrutiny analysis.[37] While the methodologies of the two courts have some connection to each other, they are not similar. Both courts grant broad protection to rights and rights can be trumped only if there is an overriding interest. The US strict scrutiny standard is more stringent than the German balancing of interests test. However, under the German test, fundamental rights will often trump social or legal interests. But with the *Smith* case, US free exercise rights get more diminished protection than the German system. The courts also differ in the range of their application of the methodologies. Under *Sherbert*, the Supreme Court has only rarely granted an accommodation. As the rule of *Sherbert* was crafted in the context of a state unemployment scheme, several cases addressing unemployment likewise resulted in accommodation under the *Sherbert* approach.[38] In addition, *Wisconsin v. Yoder*, employed generally the *Sherbert* approach in deciding that the Old World Amish could be excused from sending their children to school beyond the eighth grade despite Wisconsin state law requiring attendance through high school.[39] And finally, in

35 374 U.S. 398 (1963).

36 494 U.S. 872 (1990).

37 *Sherbert*, 374 U.S. at 403, 407 (burdens on free exercise of religion "may be justified by a 'compelling state interest in the regulation of a subject within the State's constitutional power to regulate … ' [and] that no alternative forms of regulation would combat such abuses without infringing First Amendment rights.") (citations omitted).

38 See *Frazee v. Illinois Dept of Employment Security*, 489 U.S. 829 (1989); *Hobbie v. Unemployment Appeals Comm'n*, 480 U.S. 136 (1987); *Thomas v. Review Board*, 450 U.S. 707 (1981).

39 *Wisconsin v. Yoder*, 406 U.S. 205 (1972).

McDaniel v. Paty, the court upheld a free exercise challenge by an ordained Baptist minister who wanted to serve as a delegate to the state's constitutional convention.[40] The Constitutional Court has been far more accommodating of religion, as we shall see.

As in the sharp contrast in approach between *Sherbert* and *Smith*, the approach of the Constitutional Court aligns much more with *Sherbert* than *Smith* for essentially the same reasons that the two Supreme Court cases differ. First, unlike *Smith* and like *Sherbert*, the Constitutional Court accords religious freedom preferred status through the methodology it employs to gauge the relative importance of the values at issue. Because religious freedoms are valued as preferred manifestations of human dignity, the Constitutional Court is unwilling to subject them to the vagaries of the political process. By contrast, the *Smith* court is willing to allow the political process to arbitrate the range of permissible religiously grounded action because conduct, religious or otherwise, is subject to the limitations of the general laws.[41] Thus, general laws circumscribe religious freedom.

Second, because religious freedoms are preferred in Germany, the general law must yield and the social order must accommodate religious practices. Thus, under the methodology of the Constitutional Court, there is no place for application of neutral, generally applicable laws over and above religious freedom, the approach of *Smith.* There is a world of difference between an approach that carves out religious freedom as a haven amidst the wide expanse of general laws and one that insists upon obedience to general laws, notwithstanding the demands of inner conscience. We might say the German approach accords high respect to the dictates of conscience, whereas the *Smith* approach forces a conflict between the demands of law and faith.

No doubt, the specific textual mandate of religious freedom in the two constitutions reasonably preferences religion. Thus, a person acting pursuant to religious conviction should be excused from trying to satisfy claims of law and conscience. The approach of *Sherbert* and the German Constitutional Court is in line with Madisonian thinking. There is much more to say about these general approaches to claims of conscience. But we are getting ahead of ourselves. We need to examine further German law to gain greater insight into its contrast with American law.

---

40 435 U.S. 618 (1978).

41 *Smith*, 494 U.S. at 890 ("It may be fairly said that leaving accommodation to the political process will place at a relative disadvantage those religious practices that are not widely engaged in, but that unavoidable consequence of democratic government must be preferred to a system in which each conscience is a law unto itself or in which judges weigh the social importance of all laws against the centrality of all religious beliefs.").

Blood Transfusion

The degree to which German law is willing to accommodate a person's exercise of religious freedom is perhaps best illustrated by the *Blood Transfusion Case*.[42] The facts are heart-rending, posing a stark choice between the claims of conscience and law. A married couple were members of a dedicated evangelical brotherhood that relied on God to take care of all their worldly problems. Consistent with this belief, the group refused medical treatment as a practice, putting their faith in God. After the wife had her fourth child, she had severe blood loss. A blood transfusion was recommended. After discussion among themselves and consultation with doctors, the couple decided to forego the blood transfusion, placing their faith in God to heal her. The woman was fully conscious and understood the consequences of her decision up until the moment she died, due to loss of blood.[43]

The husband did not act to hospitalize or otherwise seek medical treatment for his wife. He wanted to respect his wife's wishes. The state brought charges of neglect against the husband. He was convicted and was sentenced to eight months in prison.[44] The stark question for the Constitutional Court was whether such obviously religiously motivated action could be limited by concerns of health and life, mediated here by the criminal law. As with *Rumpelkammer*, *Blood Transfusion* is a landmark case, and it is worthwhile to study the court's construction of religious freedom.

Religious freedoms are particularly valued manifestations of human dignity and, therefore, are to be broadly construed in the German constitutional order, as we have learned:

> In a state anchored to human dignity as the ultimate value, and in which individual self-determination is likewise acknowledged as a common value, freedom of belief guarantees individuals a protected sphere against state incursion, in which people can freely form their lives according to their beliefs. In this way, freedom of belief is more than religious tolerance, i.e., mere tolerance of religious or nonreligious conviction. Religious freedoms embrace not only the inner freedom to believe or not believe, but also the outer freedom to manifest faith in life, to profess, and to proselytize. Also included is the right of individuals to orient their whole lives on the lessons of faith and their inner convictions.[45]

The Constitutional Court's estimation of the value order as centered on human dignity facilitates the central focus of German law: nourishing the ideal of men and women as self-responsible, free personalities developing within the social order.[46]

42 32 BVerfGE 98 (1971).

43 Ibid. at 99.

44 Ibid.

45 Ibid. at 106.

46 Ibid. at 107–08.

The role of religious rights within this strategy is to enable people to unfold human capacity according to the needs of inner conviction and spirit. Religious rights are especially valued in this regard, as they constitute some essential part of the innermost soul of men and women.

The high valuation of religious freedom can be acknowledged in another regard as well. Unlike most of the basic rights contained within the Basic Law, Article 4 religious freedoms are textually unbounded, a status few rights have.[47] Thus, as a matter of constitutional architecture, individual religious freedoms constitute part of the very essence of the German Basic Law's value order.[48] Under this construct, the interests of the general law will ordinarily yield to the preferred constitutional value of religion.

In view of these principles, the result of *Blood Transfusion* is predictable. There was no real question that the husband's conduct (and for that matter the wife's) was religiously motivated and, therefore, within the ambit of Article 4 religious freedoms. Contra-poised against the preferred value of religion was the limitation of the criminal law. The court recognized that this placed the husband in a difficult, seemingly irresolvable, conflict of conscience. "He was put in a situation that tested the limits, in which the general legal order posed a conflict with the command of his personal beliefs, and he felt the obligation here to follow the higher command of conscience."[49] In view of the centrality of man and woman developing freely according to the dictates of human dignity, precisely such a conflict is one that the constitutional order is designed to remove. "All state power must respect to the utmost degree religious conviction. … Thus, criminal law must yield, when its application leads to a concrete conflict between … legal obligations and a command of conscience that places the person in mental distress over being labeled a criminal that predominantly stigmatizes him socially and therefore violates his human dignity."[50] Accordingly, the requirements of criminal law must be suspended in situations where they pose direct conflicts with religious convictions.[51]

47 Note again that the main communication freedoms of Article 5 are limited by "the provisions of general laws, … protection of young persons, and in the right to personal honor." GG art. 5(2). By contrast, artistic and scientific freedoms, like religion, are unlimited by the text. GG art. 5(3).

48 32 BVerfGE at 108.

49 Ibid. at 109. The Supreme Court framed the relevant conflict similarly. "The ruling forces her to choose between following the precepts of her religion and forfeiting benefits, on the one hand, and abandoning one of the precepts of her religion in order to accept work, on the other hand." *Sherbert*, 374 U.S. at 404.

50 32 BVerfGE at 109.

51 Despite the Constitutional Court's statements that criminal laws must be suspended in the face of religious conviction, it is doubtful such will always be the case. Criminal laws yet apply to religious actors, and it is unrealistic to think that all criminal laws will be suspended in favor of conscience motivated action. See 1 *Das Bonner Grundgesetz, Prämbel, Artikel* 1 bis 19, 519–20 (Christian Starck, ed.).

Applying these teachings, the Constitutional Court released the husband from any criminal sanction, finding that the lower court had not adequately respected the freedoms of Article 4. The couple appreciated the physical danger the wife was in. Nevertheless, they believed God would take care of them. Their religious conviction must be respected.[52] Moreover, the decision was one the wife made with full awareness; it was unfair to punish the husband for her decision. "A marriage consists of two autonomous people each with the right to free unfolding of personality."[53] Ultimately, the decision was hers, and hers alone, to make.

Measured against British and American law, *Blood Transfusion* is a sharp contrast with prevailing British and American authority over blood transfusions. In most cases, American courts order hospitals to administer blood transfusions to religious believers, like Jehovah's Witnesses.[54] Likewise, British courts generally will order blood transfusions to save the life of the person notwithstanding the religious beliefs of the patient.[55] There are a few cases where American courts will respect the religious rights of the person.[56] The German approach in *Blood Transfusion* also contrasts with the Supreme Court's approach in *Smith*. *Blood Transfusion* and American cases pose exactly the same conflict: religious conviction juxtaposed against life and religious conviction juxtaposed against obligations of the criminal law. The Constitutional Court resolves the conflict exactly opposite of the Supreme Court and most American lower courts. The weight of American authority overrides religious conviction in favor of life. In *Smith,* the Supreme Court determined that religious conviction is no excuse for disobeying the law, especially the criminal law.[57] Thus, the Supreme Court brushed over the religious motivation of the conduct, fearing otherwise that "conscience [will be] … a law unto itself."[58] The court seems to prefer law and order—security and predictability—to the unpredictable and disruptive influence that exercise of religious rights can have. Thomas Jefferson feared the irrationality and zeal of religion as well. He preferred rational religion, like Unitarianism, his ideal of sensible religion. Jefferson called the idea of the holy trinity "unintelligible

52 32 BVerfGE at 110.

53 Ibid.

54 See, e.g., *Application of Georgetown College*, 331 F.2d 1000 (D.C. Cir. 1964) (court signed order allowing hospital to administer blood transfusion to Jehovah's Witness, over her and her husband's objections for religious reasons); *J.F.K. Memorial Hospital v. Heston*, 58 N. J. 576, 279 A.2d 670 (1971) (state authorized to perform operation and blood transfusion to Jehovah's Witness, despite lack of consent, to save life).

55 4 FLR 712, 13 Fam. Law 209 (Court of Appeal, Civil Division 1983) (court granted custody to father to allow him to authorize blood transfusion to save life of child).

56 See, e.g., *Public Health Trust of Dade County v. Wons*, 541 So. 2d 96 (Fl. 1989) (court held state violated religious rights of Jehovah's Witness in administering blood transfusion over person's objections).

57 *Smith*, 494 U.S. at 879.

58 494 U.S. at 879.

Athanasian jargon."[59] Consistent with the position of John Locke, the general law should prevail over religious conviction in the social order. As a matter of personal choice, a religious person should follow the dictates of conscience and pay the price for disobeying the law. In essence, the message is: go to jail for conscience, as the husband in *Blood Transfusion* was prepared to do.

By contrast, we can now see that the Constitutional Court unravels the conflict exactly opposite. In situations of conflict, religious freedoms are to be preferred to the extent possible over the obligations of the general law, including those of the criminal law, so that a person can freely pursue his destiny as empowered by his inalienable rights. Contrasted with *Smith*, *Blood Transfusion* is all the more remarkable in that the nature of the conduct sought to be discouraged was so much more severe. A human death, albeit resulting from the victim's own will and non-action of the actor, is far more serious than a man's use of peyote. We might use this contrast to illustrate the lengths to which German law is willing to accommodate religious conviction, especially when viewed against the weight of British and American authority. Conversely, we might observe how skittish the Supreme Court seems over giving religion its proper due, perhaps fearing too much the disorder that might be unleashed within society by religious conscientious objection.

In all respects, *Blood Transfusion* fits the pattern of German law and brings into central focus the conflict that can arise between claims of conscience and claims of law. As a matter of methodology, a claimant must show that his or her religion is burdened. Once a burden on religion is demonstrated, accommodation must be made within society unless strong considerations suggest otherwise. In *Rumpelkammer*, the accommodation affected the marketplace. In *Blood Transfusion*, accommodation affected the criminal law. We will soon review other illustrations of accommodating religious conviction, including with respect to judicial process, political qualification and laws respecting animals. Suspension of the general law illuminates the point of German law: human beings are to be accorded high respect in the pursuit of their dignity—which they fundamentally determine—especially over affairs of the soul. Respect of human being is one essence of constitutional democracy.

Denial of Oaths

The pattern of granting people motivated by religious conviction accommodation from requirements of the general law is further evident in a set of cases where people refused to take oaths that ordinarily were required as qualifications to perform duties under the law. In *Denial of Witness Oath*,[60] an evangelical priest refused to be sworn in as a witness to a court proceeding because of his conviction

59 Timothy Hall, *Separating Church and State: Roger Williams and Religious Liberty* 130 (1998) (citations omitted).

60 33 BVerfGE 23 (1972).

that the Bible prohibited the taking of oaths. To swear an oath was to blaspheme God. In a similar manner, in the *Bavarian Official Oath Case*,[61] a man elected as an alternate representative to local government in Bavaria refused to be sworn in under the required oath because of his religious conviction as well. In both cases, the Constitutional Court accommodated the objectors, realizing that compelling the oath constituted coercion of conscience. The approach of the court is along the lines of the seminal Supreme Court case of *West Virginia State Board of Education v. Barnette*,[62] where the court recognized, upon second thought,[63] that forcing the pledge of allegiance on unwilling believers was a cardinal violation of a free democratic order.

Protection against compelled oaths is built into the architecture of the Basic Law, as in the United States Constitution.[64] The design of both charters grants broad relief from the requirement of taking oaths, usefully obviating a case-by-case assessment of these issues. Article 140 of the Basic Law incorporates the Weimar constitutional provision that no one can be compelled to render a religious oath against his or her will.[65] Articles 56 and 64(2) of the Basic Law declare that the federal president, chancellor and federal ministers, respectively, assume office upon taking an oath, but that the oath can be religious or non-religious. Release from the taking of prescribed oaths is thus very much in accord with the design of the Basic Law.

Denial of Witness Oath

In *Denial of Witness Oath*, there was no doubt that the pastor's refusal to take the oath was religiously motivated. The pastor felt that taking the oath was a violation of Jesus's teaching in the Sermon on the Mount.[66] The Constitutional Court thus had little difficulty in determining that his decision not to take an oath was a central aspect of religious freedom guaranteed in Article 4. Each person is free to follow his or her own beliefs and act on them. Religious freedom is not limited by the Basic Law. It can only be limited by human dignity and the value order. The core values of the German constitution are designed to protect minority religious or non-religious sects. The Basic Law is even more protective of religious rights than the Weimar Constitution, where ordinary law can sometimes limit religious freedom.

---

61 79 BVerfGE 69 (1988).

62 319 U.S. 624 (1943).

63 *Minersville School District v. Gobitis*, 310 U.S. 586 (1940) *o.r. in Barnette*, 319 U.S. 624 (1943).

64 U.S. Consti. Art. VI cl. 3 ("no religious Test shall ever be required as a Qualification to any Office or public Trust under the United States").

65 GG art. 140 incorporating WRV art. 136(4).

66 33 BVerfGE at 28.

The conflict posed was between religious conviction and assurance of truth, solemnity, and fairness in the judicial process, which the required oath was designed to facilitate.[67] The interests of civil justice are unquestionably important. Yet, the court concluded that the values of religious conviction are more important. Thus, the court, in a 5-2 decision,[68] ruled that religious objectors must be exempted from the necessity of taking oaths. "The state must allow an exception here, in order to fulfill the guarantee of the [Article 4] right, to avoid placing the person in an unavoidable conflict in his spiritual-moral existence as an autonomous person between state commands [of law] and commands of faith."[69]

In Justice von Schlabrendorff's dissent, he argued that while there was no textual limitation for taking or not taking an oath, the common good could act as a limit to not taking an oath.[70] Denying an oath violates the basis of the common good. The oath is designed to serve truth and trust for the state, and is to be binding. For Justice von Schlabrendorff, belief is deep and metaphysical and he thinks that the pastor states a major misunderstanding of the Sermon on the Mount.[71] Justice von Schlabrendorff believes that Germany has a long tradition of belief in God.[72]

The exemption is available to anyone motivated by genuine religious or ideological conviction. "The state is not qualified to judge the correctness or falsity of anyone's religious conviction."[73] Rather, the state must be neutral and tolerant with respect to claims of religion or ideology. "The command of official tolerance in questions of faith and ideology applies especially to minorities and sects, which experience shows are not ordinarily given much due."[74] Thus, the court ordered the legislature to enact a law allowing for conscience-motivated exemptions.

In its methodology and result, *Denial of Witness Oath* fits the pattern of German law, as we have observed. Once the court determined that the motivation of the pastor was religious, it identified the conflict as one between religious freedom and obligations of the law. With the conflict in full view, the court takes the next step and accommodates religious practice against the claims of the general law. In the case, the pastor must be exempted from the general requirement that witnesses in judicial proceedings render an oath prior to testifying in order to relieve the pastor from the conflict. Freed of the conflict, the pastor can then act fully on the dictates of conscience.

---

67 Ibid. at 30.

68 The dissent reasoned that the rendering of an oath was an indispensable element of the constitutional order, binding the oath-taker and the state to principles of justice and God, and therefore necessary to the administration of justice. Taking of the oath was thus to be preferred over the religious convictions of the pastor. Only those sects that had a long-standing history of dispensation from the taking of oaths should be excused. Ibid. at 35–43.

69 Ibid. at 32.

70 Ibid. at 36.

71 Ibid. at 37–38.

72 Ibid. at 41.

73 Ibid. at 30.

74 Ibid. at 32.

Bavarian Official Oath

The *Bavarian Official Oath* case builds on the principle of *Denial of Witness Oath*. Like that case, the elected official felt commanded by religious scripture not to participate in an oath that was required as part of the ceremony to assume political office.[75] He had been elected to serve as an alternate representative to a Bavarian state office. He wanted to serve in office, but was denied that privilege because of his refusal to take the oath.[76]

The Constitutional Court resolved the dilemma, on a 5-3 basis, along the lines of its resolution in *Denial of Witness Oath*. It is a cardinal violation of the German constitution to place a person in the position of choosing fidelity to conscience or law. Animated by the seminal value of human dignity, the only reasonable course is to remove the dilemma by suspending the legal requirement that caused it, allowing the person to follow freely the claims of conscience. Accordingly, the requirement of taking the oath prior to assuming office must be suspended so that the man can follow his conscience and his political career. Besides, alternative means were available to attest to a representative's belief in the constitutional order.[77] Thus, granting an accommodation was not difficult. United States law comes out similarly. In *McDaniel v. Paty*, the court struck down law prohibiting ministers from serving as delegates to constitutional convention.[78]

Islamic Ritual

Ritual Slaughter

Ritual Slaughter[79] involved a Turkish citizen of Sunni Orthodox Muslim faith who had lived in Germany for the last 20 years as one of the many guest workers (*Gastarbeiter*) who populated Germany during its labor shortage after the Second World War and contributed to the economic miracle (*Wirtschaftswunder*) of West Germany. He was descended from one of these guest workers, inheriting a butcher shop from his father.[80] Free exercise rights are not confined to citizens, but apply to aliens as well. He desired to practice his craft of butchering according to his belief in Islamic slaughter rites for which he had a dedicated clientele. According to his

75 The court had no difficulty determining his religious conviction. 79 BVerfGE at 76.

76 Ibid. at 70–71.

77 The representative was prepared to confirm the substance of the oath in a ceremonial way, without actually having to take the oath. Ibid. at 77.

78 *McDaniel v. Paty*, 435 U.S. 618 (1978).

79 104 BVerfG 337 (2002).

80 Ibid. at 340.

belief, it is necessary to slaughter animals quickly and painlessly. The Islamic rite is akin to kosher butchering (*schächten*).[81]

The problem for the butcher was that the craft of butchering, like so many aspects of German and European Union life, was heavily regulated. Germany recently incorporated into the Basic Law a provision empowering the state to protect natural foundations of life, including animal life. The provision, Article 20a of the Basic Law, provides: "Mindful also of its responsibility toward future generations, the state shall protect the natural bases of life by legislation and, in accordance with law and justice, by executive and judicial action, all within the framework of the constitutional order." The German law reflected high regard for the welfare of animals, if such a thing may be said about the act of slaughtering.

Under the German law, animals were to be stunned first, and then killed as a way of making death as painless as possible. The Turkish butcher refused to comply with the law, viewing it to be contrary to Islamic teaching. The law had contemplated just such circumstances, carving out exceptions for those motivated by religion. The people contemplated by such accommodation, in fact, were Jewish and Islamic believers.[82] However, to get such an accommodation, it was necessary first to acquire permission from relevant religious authorities. The Turkish butcher had no such official permission. The Turkish butcher had obtained permits in the past to engage in ritual butchering. However, these permits were granted before the law went into effect and before the decision of the Federal Administrative Court enjoining the practice. Under the law, accommodations could be granted when religious authorities determined that the ritual was mandatorily required by the religion. In this altered legal situation, officials would not grant the permit.[83]

Evidence indicated that prevailing Sunni opinion did not require that meat be prepared according to the rite the Turkish butcher practiced.[84] The Federal Administrative Court deferred to a lower appellate administrative court opinion, which relied on the opinion of a Sunni expert in Cairo for its determination that the rite desired by the Turkish butcher was not required as a matter of faith. According to this expert, Muslims consumed meat whether or not prepared pursuant to the ritual. According to the Muslim council in Germany, however, the rite was required. The Muslim council in Germany believed that the proper interpretation of the expert from Cairo was that the rite could be dispensed with in an emergency.

---

81 Ibid. at 338.

82 Kosher butchering (*schächten*) was previously widely exempted from the general law in Germany that animals first be stunned prior to being slaughtered. With the rise of Nazism, these exemptions were removed as part of the persecution of Jews. After the Second World War, there was only piece-meal, state-by-state regulation of slaughter, although the practice was widely tolerated. The federal law of 1986 at issue in *Ritual Slaughter* was the first countrywide treatment of the issue in modern times. *Ritual Slaughter*, 104 BVerfGE at 338.

83 Ibid. at 339–41.

84 Ibid. at 340–41.

Muslims do not organize themselves into a hierarchical structure which can set and manage policy for the religion as a whole. The lack of organizational hierarchy makes it difficult for European countries, such as Germany and France, which are accustomed to negotiating with representatives of a religion to reach accords.[85] In Germany, a representative of the religion is needed to form a public corporation, determine religious instruction in the public schools or other religious matters.[86] Lacking official permission, German authorities and courts enjoined the butcher from practicing his craft according to his chosen creed.

Ritual Slaughter thus raised a number of important issues for religious freedom in Germany. First, the case involved a Muslim, and thus illustrated how free exercise freedoms are accorded broad protection in contemporary Germany, including for minority religions, especially non-Christian ones. Second, the case involved the practice of Islam, a growing force in Germany, but yet a minority religion in relation to the predominantly Christian character of the country. Third, the case also involved a diversity of views within the Islamic community, forcing the Constitutional Court to confront a range of beliefs over what Islam is. In view of the increasingly pluralistic nature of German society, these were extremely crucial questions in need of an answer.

The German Constitutional Court has been extremely solicitous of minority religious groups, including Muslims. This appears to be a contrast with the US Supreme Court, which has not always been so solicitous of minority religious groups, as in, for example, the *Smith* case. But within German society there has sometimes been contention against minority groups, including Muslims, who have wanted to adhere to their Islamic practices and not integrate all the way into German society. This is especially the case of Muslims who lived in Islamic lands in the countryside and not in the city. With the 11 September 2001 terror attack in the US, there is even more contention now, leading to a rise in Islamic terrorism.

Because enjoining his craft in his chosen way impeded his personal freedom, Article 2 personality rights were at issue as well as Article 4 free exercise claims. Article 2 personality rights are always available as a catch-all for dimensions of personal freedom not captured by more specific basic rights.[87] Likewise, because the prohibition impacted on his profession, Article 12 occupational freedoms were at stake as well. However, the Constitutional Court applied the plain language of the article to hold that occupational freedoms applied only to Germans. The court

85 Katherine Pratt Ewing, Legislating Religious Freedom: Muslim Challenges to the Relationship between "Church" and "State" in Germany and France, *Daedulus*, at 5–6 (22 September 2000).

86 Gerhard Robbers, Religious Freedom in Germany, 2001 *B.Y.U.L.* 643, 657.

87 The case of *Eppler*, 54 BVerfGE 148, 153 (1980), cemented the view that Article 2 always exists as a reserve of personal freedom to protect activities that do not fit in the more particular enunciation of freedoms in the Basic Law. For development of this idea, see Eberle, *supra* note 18, at 62–63.

then valued the occupational freedom issue under the Article 2 personality right catch-all.[88]

Centrally, however, *Ritual Slaughter* concerned free exercise rights, and that is how the Constitutional Court evaluated it. The court cut to the chase. At issue here was the ability of the Muslim butcher to practice his creed according to his belief. Individual exercise of religious belief is a core manifestation of the personal vision of human existence that emanates from the ultimate constitutional value of human dignity. So viewed, what is important is that the personal vision prevail, not technical legal requirements. Thus, for the court it was less significant that the butcher had not obtained required permissions from religious authorities. More significant was the underlying religious motivation for the butcher's actions.

Further, preparation and consumption of meat prepared according to this Islamic rite was a central religious experience for a whole community of believers formed by the butcher and his customers. The butcher and his customers fervently believed in this ritual butchering as central to their daily lives. It was important to recognize the religious convictions of these believers so that they might live life according to their creed, even if other Muslims believed differently. In so doing, the Constitutional Court recognized a diversity of belief within the Islamic community.[89]

Recognition of alternative, and competing, communities of faith, even within a particular religion, is an important principle of religious freedom. First, the principle acknowledges the validity of belief from the perspective of the believer, as compared to the body that hierarchically or organizationally may stand to administer the faith. The orientation toward individual belief seems more in keeping with principles of religious freedom and individual rights. Second, providing for the possibility of competing communities of faith facilitates an open contest for multiple claims of truth and conviction to set forth their tenets. The success on earth of any creed will be determined by how many adherents it attracts. Third, competition between communities of faith is, by definition, open to the new and the different. Minorities or dissenting voices thereby encounter a more hospitable environment. They have a better chance of advancing their claims and achieving success by the strength of their creeds. This is in keeping with the origins of religion, most of which had their start in a position of dissent, gaining success later. In these respects, the Constitutional Court has designed an approach sensitive to minorities' exercise of religious liberty.

Facilitation of diversity of religious faith logically serves to protect religious freedom as well. Guaranteeing every person the ability to believe what they like and to act on such belief engenders broad respect for religious liberty. Vigorous religious rights will act as a bulwark against government, as citizens will voice objection to government curtailment of liberty. In a country of diverse religious

88 *Ritual Slaughter*, 104 BVerfGE at 346.

89 *Ritual Slaughter*, 104 BVerfGE at 354.

beliefs, it will be hard for any one group to impose its beliefs on another.[90] James Madison advocated diversity in religious belief as security for civil rights and as security for peace and stability in a republic. "A religious sect may degenerate into a political faction in a part of the Confederacy; but the variety of sects dispersed over the entire face of it must secure the national councils against any danger from that source."[91] Madison repeated the idea in Federalist No. 51: "In a free government the security for civil rights must be the same as that for religious rights. It consists in the one case in the multiplicity of interests, and in the other in the multiplicity of sects."[92] Madison's theory for protection of religious liberty thus parallels his theory for protection of the republic against factions, as he famously developed in Federalist No. 10.

It was not always so in Germany. Authorities sometimes treated Islam as a threat to society because of their perception that the religion was fundamentalist, antidemocratic and hostile to human rights, especially the equality of women. Germans feel especially vulnerable to perceived threats in view of their past history of political instability during the Weimar democracy, which aided the rise of totalitarian Nazism. These perceptions may help explain authorities' reluctance to facilitate public practice of Islam, such as the building of recognizable mosques, public broadcasting of calls to prayer through loud speakers, and freedom of Muslim women and girls to cover themselves.[93] Yet, courts have also accommodated Muslims from social strictures. For example, courts have allowed Muslim women and girls to wear head scarves in the classroom (unlike in France and Turkey) and exempted girls from compulsory school activities such as gym and swimming classes.[94] The Constitutional Court has also ruled that a woman of Islamic faith cannot be denied a position as a public school teacher because she desires to wear a head scarf while teaching, as discussed more fully next.[95] The integration of Muslims into German society is a forefront issue. Within this context of historical German and European treatment of Islam, *Ritual Slaughter* stands out in bold relief as a landmark case on religious liberty, recognizing the principle of religious equality—that liberty applies equally to majority and minority practitioners, in deed as well as in word. The German principles of respect for diverse beliefs had immediate application in the case. Whether a practice is absolutely required as a matter of religious belief is less a question to be determined by religious officials.

---

90 Michael McConnell, The Origins and Historical Understanding of Free Exercise of Religion, 103 *Harv. L. Rev.* 1409, 1515–16 (1990).

91 *The Federalist No. 10* (J. Madison).

92 Ibid.

93 Ewing, *supra* note 85, at 3–4, 7–8. The experience is much the same in France. Ibid.

94 Ibid. See also Ingrid Brunk Wuerth, Private Religious Choice in German and American Constitutional Law: Government Funding and Government Religious Speech, 31 *Vand. J. Transnat'l L.* 1200–1201 (1998).

95 BVerfGE, 2 BvR 1436/02 (24 September 2003).

The question is much more to be answered within the context of a concrete community of believers.[96] Mere subjective belief is insufficient. The community must demonstrate to the court's satisfaction that the practice is required by their beliefs.[97] Given their sincerity and dedication to ritual slaughter, the court was well satisfied that the butcher and his customers constituted a community that acted according to creed.

Posing the question in this fashion, the court resolved it in the now common pattern of free exercise law that we have become familiar with. Given the clash between exercise of religious freedom and the constraints of the general law, the proper resolution is recognition and respect of religious practices even if that requires accommodation of the general laws. It is improper for the state to deny legitimate religious claims just because they deviate from accepted practice.[98] The Constitutional Court was careful to note the important state interest in preventing needless cruelty to animals. Animals are accorded high respect in Germany. The purpose of the law was to recognize animals as mutually living beings, not just objects.[99] Ethical treatment was the goal. However, the religious practice at issue had to be given fuller consideration than had been the case by the lower courts under the general balancing of interests test. The impact of the law was severe. Without any exception, the butcher would not be able to practice his craft according to his creed. His customers would also have difficulty obtaining meat sanctified according to chosen ritual. Thus, the Constitutional Court concluded, Article 2 personality rights, in conjunction with the more specific protections of Article 4, had been violated.

In a sense, accommodation of the Turkish butcher was less of a leap than in the cases previously reviewed. The law recognized a range of exceptions from the general requirement that a person first stun animals before killing them, most of which were geared to Jewish and Islamic believers. Accommodating the butcher could as well fit within the pattern already recognized within the law. Moreover, the court noted that the authorities could have given fuller consideration to the second alternative listed in the law, which granted some discretion to parties trying to fulfill the aims of the law in making death as painless and quick as possible.[100]

But in another sense the case did represent a leap. The Constitutional Court had the prescience to recognize the inherently personal nature of the convictions at issue. The court respected the choices of the Turkish butcher and his customers on their own terms as they defined their belief. Recognition of such personal conviction was more important than belief as defined by religious or secular authorities. Validating the personal quest for faith is central. Thus, we can see

96 *Ritual Slaughter*, 104 BVerfGE at 353–54.

97 Ibid. at 354–55.

98 Ibid. at 355.

99 Ibid. at 351.

100 Ibid. at 353–55.

the approach of the court is one especially sensitive to the dilemma of individual existence, including the demands of conscience.

Ritual Slaughter contrasts with *Smith* over the process of accommodation of religion. In *Smith*, the Supreme Court viewed the democratic process as the main avenue for accommodation of religious belief.[101] Viewing *Ritual Slaughter* under this construct, one would be led to argue that democratic decision-makers had made all the accommodations they desired in the law already enacted. The Federal Administrative Court evaluated the case on this basis. Hence, the Turkish butcher ought to seek political relief, not judicial relief, as in *Smith*. In contrast to the Supreme Court, however, this solution was not adequate to the Constitutional Court. Religious freedoms are too precious, and arguably too fragile, to be entrusted to the political process. It is instead the core of the judicial function to safeguard these rights, especially when exercised by minorities. Minorities, more than majorities, need judicial solicitude precisely because minorities operate under laws made by majorities. Minorities are thus much more likely to run afoul of convention than majorities. In view of these concerns, the Constitutional Court's decision was all the more remarkable in that it further carved out religious freedom in the polity notwithstanding the significant accommodation already rendered in the statute.

Notably, German law has been stable and consistent well over a 40-year period, in contrast to the ebb and flow of American law, from *Sherbert* to *Smith*. Fidelity in service of basic human rights is desirable in a world undergoing severe change caused by forces such as computerization, globalization, multiculturalism, and terrorism. A second lesson of *Ritual Slaughter* is that these freedoms apply to all, minority religions as well as majority. In this respect, the case is notable in its solicitude for the Turkish minority in Germany, which has often felt like second class citizens. Indeed, the Turkish butcher was a minority believer within a minority faith. Looking forward, *Ritual Slaughter* would seem to signal that Germany is equipped to deal with the demands of minorities to equal religious liberty. In these respects, Germany seems more attuned to demands of a multicultural society, a likely product of globalization. By contrast, *Smith* would seem to signal the opposite, recognizing that minority religions will likely suffer under democratic rule while majority religions prosper.[102]

Islamic Teacher's Head Scarf

The Constitutional Court rendered another important decision on free exercise freedoms, ruling 5-3 in a hotly contested case that an Afghani-born woman of acquired German citizenship, Fereshta Ludin, could not be denied a teaching position in the public schools because of her religious conviction to wear a

101 494 U.S. at 890.
102 494 U.S. at 890.

head scarf while performing her duties. *Islamic Teacher's Head Scarf*[103] is a long and complicated decision, involving a constellation of rights that include Article 4 religious rights of students and parents, Article 6 parental rights, Article 7 educational rights and Article 33 guarantees of equality in qualification and treatment (including with respect to religion or philosophical view) as a civil servant, in addition to the prospective teacher's Article 4 free exercise rights. Because *Islamic Teacher's Head Scarf* further substantiates the Constitutional Court's proactive empowerment of free exercise freedoms, especially in relation to Germany's rising minority Islamic population, it is in keeping with trends evident in *Ritual Slaughter* of making the society more inclusive.

The basis for the Constitutional Court's decision was that religiously compelled dress, such as the wearing of a head scarf, was a matter of personal free exercise of religion which government, therefore, could not use as a basis to deny qualification to the civil service (which public school teachers are) under Article 33, at least in the absence of an underlying law that appropriately took into account the range of rights and considerations at stake in this complicated issue.[104] In this respect, *Islamic Teacher's Head Scarf* underscores the continuing flowering of free exercise freedoms in Germany, especially with respect to minority religions such as Islam, a major concern of the court.[105] On this point, *Islamic Teacher's Head Scarf* is of a similar tenor to *Ritual Slaughter* and also of another recent decision in which the Constitutional Court ruled that a Turkish shop assistant had been wrongly dismissed for expressing a desire to wear a head scarf, again for religiously compelled reasons, at work in the perfume section of a department store.[106] Wearing a head scarf is an intimate aspect of religious expression. Religious belief can sometimes take precedence over affairs of daily life. It is a choice people are often forced to make. Which is more important: religion or integration within the society? Yet, because the court predicated its ruling on the technical point that no law undergirded authorities' decision to deny Ludin the teaching position, and further stated that a law that properly considered relevant rights and interests at issue could result in denial of teaching positions to people wearing religiously compelled dress, *Islamic Teacher's Head Scarf* was a quite limited victory for religious freedom, although a victory indeed for Ludin. At present, in fact, the German *Länder* of Baden Württemberg and North-Rhein Westfalia do not allow head scarfs to be worn in the classroom. Most other German *Länder* allow the wearing of head scarves in the classroom.

---

103 BVerfG, 2 BvR 1436/02 (24 September 2003) (hereinafter "*Islamic Teacher's Head Scarf*").

104 Ibid. at 8.

105 Ibid. at 16 ("A regulation that prohibits teachers from displaying overtly their membership in a particular religious community or adherence to beliefs ... is clearly in tension with especially pronounced growing diversity of religion in society").

106 BVerfG, 1 BvR 792/03 (30 July 2003) (chamber decision) (hereinafter "*Turkish Sales Clerk's Head Scarf*").

The mixed nature of the decision can perhaps best be read as a tentative attempt to resolve this contentious issue in respect to the far-reaching role of Islam in Western, German society. Islam is relatively new to Germany, and more broadly Europe, and occidental society is adjusting to this new phenomenon. Many Germans are anxious about Islam, not knowing quite how to integrate people of Middle Eastern faith with Western culture. Germany is in the process of working out how Islamic minorities can express their identity in secular western European society. Germans' multifaceted view of Islam is reflected in the different perceptions as to what wearing a head scarf represents. Wearing a head scarf could be interpreted variously as a political expression of Islamic fundamentalism, especially in contrast to the secular West; a cultural statement of ethnic identity expressing longing for the distant homeland; a traditional dress that honors familial ties; a modern statement of self-determination and identity; a symbol of subordination of women to men under Islamic law; or a religious observance.[107] The court chose for the latter, valuing the dress as religiously compelled based upon Ludin's association of the head scarf with her Islamic identity.[108]

The disputed nature of the ruling left the court open to heavy criticism, with justification. While it is beneficial for constitutional democracy to engage its citizens through democratic deliberation over the meaning of the constitution as much as possible, fundamental rights are not ordinarily thought to be subject to the majoritarian process of democracy. In this respect, *Islamic Teacher's Head Scarf* approximates to a degree the line of thinking present in *Smith.*[109] Given the complex of rights at stake in *Islamic Teacher's Head Scarf*, however, there may be greater justification for caution and deference in the case as compared to *Smith.*

It is quite possible that the Constitutional Court acted timidly out of respect for the democratic process, not wanting to substitute its judgment for democratic deliberation and decision over such a newly emerging issue as the role of Islam in German society. It is also possible the court was meek in reaction to serious and sustained criticism unleashed in response to the court's controversial decisions in *Soldiers are Murderers II*[110] and *Krucifix II.*[111]

The majority's recognition of the prospective teacher's free exercise freedoms seemed to be based on an attempt to understand the spiritual world of Islamic

107 Ibid. at 13–14. The dissent viewed wearing of the head scarf as mainly a symbol of subordination of women to men and, therefore, inconsistent with the equality guarantee of Article 3. Ibid. at 29.

108 Ibid. at 3, 8. In rejecting Ludin's application for a teaching position, school officials of Baden-Württemberg reasoned that display of a head scarf was a political symbol of cultural separation from Western society as well as a religious symbol. Ludin instead valued the head scarf as an expression of her personality and of her religious faith. Ibid. at 3.

109 494 U.S. at 890.

110 22 EuGRZ 443 (1995) (protected expression to call soldiers murderers) affirming in substance, *Soldiers are Murderers I*, 45 NJW 2943 (1994) (chamber decision).

111 93 BVerfGE 1 (1995) (Bavarian required display of crucifix in public schools unconstitutional in face of complaint).

believers. Recognition of Islamic belief acknowledges the emerging role Islam now plays in German society. In turn, these developments led the court to reassess civil service rules and state neutrality obligations in religious affairs. Left open was how multiculturalism would change church-state relations.

Traditionally, the state is under an obligation of neutrality in matters of religion out of concern that state support of particular religious/philosophical views will be coercive to individuals partaking of state benefits. This principle of neutrality and corresponding posture of official restraint animates the German civil service. The German civil service is conceived as an intermediary between the state and citizens, a facilitator of citizens' rights under the positive dimension of freedom characteristic of the German constitutional order. For these reasons, civil servants are traditionally viewed as neutral agents of the legal order and, therefore, not able to exercise full basic rights in their official capacity. Proactive exercise of rights by civil servants, it is feared, would coerce or undermine citizens' exercise of their freedoms. On this view, Ludin could justifiably be denied a position as a teacher, for her exercise of free exercise rights would fundamentally violate civil service norms of neutrality and restraint, as the dissent argued.[112]

But the majority saw it differently. Requiring abstinence from religiously compelled dress out of concern that display of religious conviction would coerce students and undermine parental choice was asking too much of Ludin. She did not totally sacrifice her religious freedoms at the school door. These freedoms are fundamentally to be determined from the perspective of the religious community she is a part of, echoing the fundamental principle of *Ritual Slaughter* that religious freedoms are to be judged from the perspective of the believer's community of faith.[113] The court also recognized that acceptance of growing religious diversity in society might call for readjustment of legal concepts, such as stricter neutrality in the obligations of members of the civil service. Her community of belief viewed wearing head scarves as religiously compelled. It was therefore untenable to place her in a position of choosing her religion or her job.[114] As the court observed, "A regulation that prohibits teachers from displaying overtly their membership in a particular religious community or adherence to beliefs ... is clearly in tension with especially pronounced growing diversity of religion in society."[115]

These principles follow from the growing diversity among religions in German society and the way such diversity affects the classroom.[116] School is the place for exposure to a marketplace of ideas and beliefs. "Schools are no refuge, in which eyes are to be closed from the reality of a pluralistic society. Rather, schools have the mission to prepare youth for what they will encounter in society."[117] Learning

112 *Islamic Teacher's Head Scarf*, 2 BvR 1436/02 at 20–25.

113 Ibid. at 11; accord *Ritual Slaughter*, 104 BVerfGE at 353–55.

114 Ibid. at 10–11. Accord, *Sherbert*, 374 U.S. at 404.

115 *Muslim Teacher's Head Scarf*, 108 BVerfGE 282, 310 (2003).

116 *Islamic Teacher's Head Scarf*, 2 BvR 1436/02 at 16.

117 Ibid. at 6.

to appreciate difference, respect alternative beliefs and achieve toleration as building blocks to realization of integration of diverse people within society are important objectives in constitutional democracy.[118] True, overt display of religious observance in the classroom, especially controversial dress such as display of a head scarf, could create conflict between teachers and students, or among students, or among students and parents. But to the mind of the court, it was better to see whether, in fact, such conflict develops and then resolve it, as compared to presuming it will occur and prohibiting such dress out of such fear.[119]

Underlying the court's reasoning would appear to be acknowledgment of Islam as a religion, which the court seemed especially eager to respect given its minority status in Germany. Because Islam is a minority faith, there might be less danger that overt displays of its observance in classrooms would coerce students. These factors seem to be an implicit basis by which the majority distinguished *Krucifix II*. There is something fundamentally different between official accommodation of a minority belief within a majoritarian Christian culture (*Islamic Teacher's Head Scarf*) as compared to state sponsorship of the majority faith (*Krucifix II*), the display of a crucifix in the classroom, or so the court seemed to be saying.

The court distinguished the case from *Krucifix II* on the basis that *Islamic Teacher's Head Scarf* involved an individual's exercise of religion (and therefore was also less likely to be attributed to state sponsorship) in comparison to the state sponsorship of religion in *Krucifix II*, and on the basis that a head scarf could be subject to multiple interpretations, only being a religious symbol when worn by a believer, in comparison to the cross, which always had the religious meaning of Christianity.[120] Not surprisingly, this distinction was not convincing to the dissent.[121] In fact, while the majority made the case for distinguishing the two decisions, the decisions were much alike. First, in both cases students had no choice but to be confronted with the symbols. Second, a teacher's display of plausibly religious dress might reasonably be attributed to state sponsorship as well, although indirectly. Third, many observers would view a head scarf as a religious symbol.

Necessarily, the court's emphasis on personal freedom and sectarian diversity, even within public classrooms, called for some reconception of the role the state

---

118 Ibid. at 11–12.

119 Ibid. at 17. The court reasoned that if conflicts over the wearing of religious garb in schools arise, then it makes sense to require proof that wearing religious garb influences students. Ibid. at 14–15. The dissent valued the situation differently, viewing display of a head scarf as fraught with such conflict. Ibid. at 25–26. See *Lee v. Weisman*, 505 U.S. 577, 588 (1992) ("The potential for divisiveness is of particular relevance here [prayer after graduation] … because it centers around an overt religious exercise in a secondary environment where … subtle coercive pressures exist and where the student had no real alternative which would have allowed her to avoid the fact or appearance of participation.").

120 Ibid. at 13.

121 Ibid. at 27.

plays with respect to religion and, derivatively, civil service obligations. Rather than strict separation of church and state, more characteristic of the laciest tradition in France, the Constitutional Court envisioned the state role to be "not a distant, absent role ... but rather a respectful, nourishing neutrality"[122] that accords "equality to the beliefs of all believers, understanding the attitudes advanced [by people] on equal terms."[123] Thus, even schools are "open for religious activity under the principle of an ... overlapping, open and respectful neutrality."[124] Concretely in the case, this meant that a prospective teacher could not be refused a position out of hand for religious conviction to wear certain dress. Likewise, this more flexible principle of neutrality filtered into civil service obligations.[125]

Yet, the court also recognized that the phenomenon of multiculturalism might result ultimately in a stricter separation of church and state in order to prevent discord in society.[126] Whether this would come to be or not would depend on how events unfolded. The contingencies at play in the issue would appear to be a factor in the court's preference to have the democratic process be the forum initially to forge some workable accommodation of the competing rights and interests at stake. In the case, the absence of such a law determined the outcome.[127] Thus, at bottom, we can see that *Islamic Teacher's Head Scarf* is a tentative step in determining the role of Islam in Germany. The case does not resolve definitively the issue of permissible religious garb in official forums, an additional point of contention to court observers.

One concern over Islam is the nature of the faith. Is Islam too extreme and fundamentalist and do those values ask for blind adherence to religious doctrine? Is Islam antidemocratic in nature? Does that pose a threat to a free and democratic basic social order? Any religious group that poses a threat to a democracy and acts in a militant and violent way does not get free exercise rights or recognition as a religious group. One example of such a case is the *Kalifstaat*, which is covered in the German chapter on church-state relations.[128] Concerns might also arise with other out of the mainstream religions, such as Hare Krishnas, the Unification Church (known as the Moonies) or other fringe religious groups like OSHO, which is covered in the German chapter on church-state relations.

122 Ibid. at 4.

123 Ibid. at 11.

124 Ibid. at 6.

125 Ibid. at 10. Not surprisingly, the dissent took issue with the majority's conception of neutrality in church-state relations, and how this affected civil service obligations. Ibid. at 20–24.

126 Ibid. at 16–17.

127 Baden-Württemberg, the German Land at issue in the case, had considered but determined not to enact such a law. Ibid. at 30 (dissent).

128 BVerfG, 1 BvR 536/03 (2 October 2003).

Similar trends are apparent with respect to Jehovah's Witnesses[129] and the Baha'i.[130] Each of these religions is somewhat exotic when viewed against the traditional Christian culture. Their favorable treatment attests to the growing climate of hospitality toward minority creeds and the correspondingly vigorous state of religious liberty in Germany.

Observations

Personal religious freedom in Germany is highly valued. The Constitutional Court has been highly protective of people's personal religious freedom, according the freedom to all people, regardless of ethnicity or religious creed. In the *Rumpelkammer* case, the court preferred Catholic youth who wanted to obtain used clothes to donate to charities over the business interests of a rag dealer. In *Blood Transfusion*, the court ruled that the dedicated evangelical Christian husband was allowed, constitutionally, to allow his wife not to accept a blood transfusion as part of religious conviction, leading to her death.

The Constitutional Court has also been extremely accommodating of minority religions. A main focus has been members of the Islamic faith. In *Ritual Slaughter* the court ruled that a Turkish citizen of Sunni Orthodox Muslim faith could be allowed to perform ritual slaughter of animals as part of his religious faith. Under the German law, Jews and Muslims are allowed exemptions under the slaughter law. In the past, the Turkish butcher had gotten exemptions, but did not get one under the current law. Still, the court ruled in his favor, allowing ritual slaughter. And in *Islamic Teacher's Head Scarf*, the court ruled that the Islamic woman was allowed to wear a head scarf in the classroom where she taught. At present, most German states still allow Muslim women teachers to wear the head scarf, with the exception of Baden Württemberg and North-Rhein Westfalia.

We might say personal religious freedoms are extremely highly valued in Germany. These root values form the basis of fundamental freedom and the securing of democratic values. This reflects emanations of the core value of the German constitutional order, human dignity and its unfolding of personal freedom. Germany is very tolerant of people's exercise of religious freedoms.

We might say Germany is a model for religious freedom.

129 *Jehovah's Witness*, 102 BVerfGE 370 (2000) (ruling that religion could not be denied public corporation status under Article 137 of Weimar Constitution on ground participation in voting not requisite to prove loyalty to democratic order).

130 *Baha'i*, 83 BVerfGE 341 (1991) (ruling that Article 4 self-autonomy allows Baha'i religion to rule itself as it likes, even when supreme religious authorities outside Germany order affairs differently than communities within Germany).

Chapter 5
Personal Religious Freedom in the United States

In the United States, free exercise of religion has been upheld as a constitutional right only rarely. It started with *Sherbert v. Verner* (1963), where the court upheld the free exercise rights of a devout Christian who refused to work on Saturdays because of her faith and was then denied unemployment benefits in South Carolina. The court ruled that this was a violation of her free exercise rights, as she was motivated by religious beliefs. The court applied the conventional strict scrutiny analysis, calling for the law to survive constitutionality only if it serves a compelling interest and is tightly tailored to effectuate that compelling interest.

Ironically, in the beginning of its fundamental rights jurisprudence, the court has tended to treat free exercise rights under other constitutional provisions, such as first amendment free speech protections. Prior to the incorporation of the Free Exercise Clause into the Fourteenth Amendment, making it applicable to the states, the court employed implied rights to protect religious freedom that were impacted by state government. For example, in *Pierce v. Society of Sisters*, the court ruled that a state cannot mandate public school attendance when parents desire to send children to private school in order to read German so that parents can engage their children in the reading of the Bible and other religious work.[1] And in *Meyer v. Nebraska*, the court ruled that a state cannot mandate teaching of only English in schools, as other languages are also necessary so that parents can communicate with their children over religious matters.[2] With the incorporation of free exercise rights into the Fourteenth Amendment, thereby making them applicable to the states, the court has frequently treated the activity at issue as a free speech matter.[3] The critical case illustrating this trend is *Cantwell v. Connecticut*,[4] which dealt with a Jehovah's Witness, Jesse Cantwell, who played a phonograph record that attacked the Roman Catholic faith as he walked down the sidewalks in New

---

1 268 U.S. 510 (1925).

2 262 U.S. 390 (1923).

3 310 U.S. at 303:

The fundamental concept of liberty embodied in [the Fourteenth] Amendment embraces the liberties guaranteed by the First Amendment. The First Amendment declares that Congress shall make no law respecting an establishment of religion or prohibiting the free exercise thereof. The Fourteenth Amendment has rendered the legislatures of the states as incompetent as Congress to enact such laws.

4 310 U.S. 296 (1940).

Haven, Connecticut. Likewise, in *West Virginia v. Barnette*,[5] the court also treated the refusal of students of the Jehovah's Witness faith to perform the compulsory flag salute and pledge of allegiance to the flag as a free speech matter and not a free exercise of religion matter. The court based its ruling on free speech because "To sustain the compulsory flag salute we are required to say that a Bill of Rights which guards the individual's right to speak his own mind, left it open to public authorities to compel him to utter what is not in his mind."[6] The court went on to state a core principle of American constitutional law, especially relating to rights:

> If there is any fixed star in our constitutional constellation, it is that no official, high or petty, can prescribe what shall be orthodox in politics, nationalism, religion, or other matters of opinion or force citizens to confess by word or act their faith therein. If there are any circumstances which permit an exception, they do not now occur to us.[7]

There are a range of other cases along these lines during this genre, favoring free speech over free exercise of religion.[8]

Free Exercise as a Preferred Fundamental Right

The genesis of free exercise jurisprudence is the principle of equality. While the Free Exercise Clause clearly states "that Congress shall make no law … prohibiting the free exercise thereof,"—which should be interpreted to protect a person's practice of religious acts—the court has started with an equality approach, which then gets rejuvenated in *Employment Division, Dep't of Human Resources, Oregon v. Smith*.[9] In *Reynolds v. United States*, the court observed that "Laws are made for the government of actions, and while they cannot interfere with mere religious belief and opinions, they may with practices."[10] Here the case dealt with Mormons (called the Church of Jesus Christ of Latter-Day Saints), in Utah, which was not yet a state, and the issue was polygamy, which was a religious ritual of the Mormons. For the court, polygamy is a crime. But the court makes a strong distinction between belief and action premised on belief. For the court, "Congress was deprived of all legislative power over mere opinion, but was left free to reach

5 319 U.S. 624 (1943) o.r. *Minersville v. Gobitis*, 310 U.S. 586 (1940).

6 Ibid. at 634.

7 Ibid. at 642.

8 See, e.g., *Chaplinsky v. New Hampshire*, 315 U.S. 568 (1942) (Jehovah's Witness convicted for making offensive statement to policeman after being arrested—considered fighting words—although he was proselytizing the Jehovah's Witness faith before a crowd that got unruly being annoyed by the speech).

9 494 U.S. 872 (1990).

10 98 U.S. 145, 166 (1879).

actions which were in violation of social duties or subversive of good order."[11] With longstanding legal proscriptions against polygamy in the United States and the United Kingdom, the court stated that it was "impossible to believe that the constitutional guaranty of religious freedom was intended to prohibit legislation in respect to this most important feature of social life."[12] "*Reynolds* remained the Supreme Court's authoritative interpretation of the Free Exercise Clause for many years."[13]

The issue of crimes of bigamy and polygamy came up again in the case of Mormons, in *Davis v. Beason*, 133 U.S. 333 (1890), which dealt with the territory of Idaho, which was not yet a state. Targeting minority religious groups seems a common occurrence under United States law, which the Supreme Court almost always upholds. The court in *Beason* simply repeats the rules of *Reynolds*: religious belief can be protected, but not conduct based on religion that violates the laws of the general order. Again, for the court, marriage is simply to be between one man and one woman; not one man with multiple wives. The principle of equality stays in free exercise jurisprudence until the case of *Sherbert v. Verner*.

Sherbert v. Verner

Sherbert v. Verner was a landmark case in fundamental rights jurisprudence, establishing free exercise rights as core freedoms that can be circumscribed only if the standard of strict scrutiny can be met. *Sherbert* is reflective of the Warren Court approach to interpreting the Constitution under the theory of *Carolene Products*: if government acts to address general socio-economic policies, the court will defer to government under a rational basis test.[14] On the other hand, if government acts

11 Ibid. at 164.

12 Ibid. at 165. Ronald J. Krotosznski, Jr., If Judges Were Angels: Religious Equality, Free Exercise, and the (Underappreciated) Merits of Smith, 102 *Nw. L. Rev.* 1189, 1200 (2008).

13 Ibid. at 1200.

14 In the United States, the theoretical foundation for sliding scale review is the famous theory of Justice Harlan Stone set forth in footnote 4 of *United States v. Carolene Products Co.*, 304 U.S. 144, 152–53 n. 4 (1938). Under this theory, measures involving general socio-economic measures are subject to only light brush judicial review on the theory that they entail the formation of public policy that is the province of the political process and, therefore, not appropriate for the judiciary in so far as there is no glaring inequality or lack of justification for the law. Under the formulation of Justice Stone, the purpose of the measure must be "at least debatable" for the court to uphold it. In modern law "at least debatable" has been translated into law as a standard demanding simply that "a legislation classification must be sustained if the classification itself is rationally related to a legitimate governmental interest" and the means employed are so rationally related.

to impede a fundamental right, then strict scrutiny will attach.[15] The theory of *Carolene Products* yields a fairly predictable set of legal results.

Sherbert is a crucial case because the woman, a Seventh-Day Adventist, was forced to choose between working on Saturday, a policy her employer had recently implemented, or honoring the Saturday as her day of Sabbath, which was normal for Seventh-Day Adventists. She chose for her faith, leading to termination of her employment. She then applied for unemployment benefits under South Carolina law, but was denied because she lacked good cause to refuse suitable available work. Most other states allowed observance of the workers' Sabbath to be good cause for obtaining unemployment benefits.

The court invalidated the South Carolina law. According to the court:

> The door of the Free Exercise Clause stands tightly closed against any governmental regulation of religious *beliefs* as such. ... Government may neither compel affirmation of repugnant belief, … nor penalize or discriminate against individuals or groups because they hold religious views abhorrent to the authorities, … nor employ taxing power to inhibit the dissemination of particular religious views.[16]

The Supreme Court recognized the significance of the conflict she faced, as the law in effect impeded the observance of her religion. The court determines that the effect of her dismissal from work impedes her religious freedom and disqualified her from obtaining unemployment benefits:

> The ruling forces her to choose between following the precepts of her religion and forfeiting benefits, on the one hand, and abandoning one of the precepts of her religion in order to accept work, on the other hand. Governmental imposition

---

15 Under *Carolene Products*:

There may be a narrower scope for operation of the presumption of constitutionality when legislation appears on its face to be within a specific prohibition of the Constitution, such as those of the first ten amendments, which are deemed equally specific when held to be embraced with the Fourteenth Amendment …

It is unnecessary to consider now whether legislation which restricts those political processes [such as voting, expression, and political association] which can ordinarily be expected to bring about repeal of undesirable legislation, is to be subjected to more exacting judicial scrutiny under the general prohibition of the Fourteenth Amendment than are most other types of legislation …

Nor need we enquire whether similar considerations enter into the review of statutes directed at particular religious, [or] national, [or] racial minorities [;] whether prejudice against discrete and insular minorities may be a special condition which tends seriously to curtail the operation of those political processes ordinarily to be relied upon to protect minorities, and which may call for a correspondingly more searching judicial inquiry [304 U.S. at 144, 152–53 n. 4 (1938)].

16 374 U.S. at 402.

> of such a choice puts the same kind of burden upon the free exercise of religion as would a fine imposed against appellant for her Saturday worship.[17]

The Supreme Court under *Sherbert* must first determine that the activities at issue are religiously motivated and that the legal measure under review burdens the exercise of those freedoms. As the court observes "to condition the availability of benefits upon … [her] willingness to violate a cardinal principle of her religious faith effectively penalizes the free exercise of her constitutional rights."[18] There is also a dramatic contrast between the Seventh-Day Adventist and normal Christians. While the Seventh-Day Adventist was not allowed to obtain unemployment benefits for refusing to work on Saturdays, normal Christians, under South Carolina law, are allowed to be excused from work on Sundays in times of national emergency. Essentially, this reflects religious discrimination; favoring of majority religions over minority ones.[19]

It is thus critical that government be neutral and fair to people of all religious beliefs. Favoring one religion over another is a clear violation of the cardinal principles of religious freedom. South Carolina is not allowed to force a worker to abandon religion in favor of work. For the court, "no State may 'exclude individual Catholics, Lutherans, Muhammadans, Baptists, Jews, Methodists, Non-believers, Presbyterians, or the members of any other faith, *because of their faith, or lack of it*, from receiving the benefits of public welfare legislation.'"[20]

Once it is determined that religious freedoms are at issue and that they are burdened, then they are to be preferred and ordinarily will prevail unless the state can demonstrate an overriding or compelling reason. As the court states in *Sherbert*, burdens on free exercise of religion "may be justified by a 'compelling state interest in the regulation of a subject within the State's constitutional power to regulate … ' [and] that no alternative forms of regulation would combat such abuses without infringing First Amendment rights."[21] In *Sherbert*, the state could not demonstrate any compelling reason to justify the denial of unemployment benefits to Sherbert, resulting in invalidation of the governmental measure. Fraud did not play a role. In this respect, the ruling differs from *Braunfeld v. Brown*, where the court recognized that Sunday was a uniform day of rest and that the state goal could not be accomplished in any other way. Accordingly, the Orthodox

17 *Sherbert*, 374 U.S. at 404.

18 Ibid. at 406.

19 Ibid.

20 Ibid. at 410 (citing *Everson v. Board of Education*, 330 U.S. at 16).

21 *Sherbert*, 374 U.S. at 403, 407 (citations omitted). Justice O'Connor expressed the qualities of strict scrutiny aptly. *Smith*, 494 U.S. 872, at 894 (O'Connor, concurring in judgment) ("we have respected both the First Amendment's express textual mandate and the governmental interest in regulation of conduct by requiring the government to justify any substantial burden on religiously motivated conduct by a compelling state interest and by means narrowly tailored to achieve that interest.") (citations omitted).

Jewish merchant lost his case.[22] For the court, Braunfeld was impeded to a degree in his business income, but the burden on his religion was less severe than for the Seventh-Day Adventist; she faced no choice: maintain her faith or lose her job. Now, however, with the *Sherbert* case, there might be a stronger argument that Braunfeld should win his case on free exercise grounds. *Sherbert*, in a sense, has devitalized *Braunfeld.*[23]

Sherbert is also significant because it recognizes that free exercise rights protect not only freedoms to believe in a deity and practice religious rights associated with the religion, but also freedom to act on religiously motivated actions, such as refusing to work on a day of Sabbath, as in *Sherbert.* What this demonstrates is that the court is applying free exercise rights in a straightforward textual manner; free exercise of religion means the right to act on religiously rooted beliefs. The approach of *Sherbert* results in a broad interpretation of personal religious freedoms, protecting religious belief and conscience, the practice of religious rite, and conduct that is religiously motivated. Under this rule of *Sherbert*, the law does not have to selectively target a person based on religion. The law can simply be neutral and of general applicability. Thus, if the general, neutral law at issue impedes the right of the believer to carry out her faith, the court will strike down the law unless government can demonstrate a compelling interest in justifying the law. *Sherbert* thus follows the conventional theory of *Carolene Products.*

Nevertheless, despite the broad interpretation of free exercise rights under *Sherbert,* the Supreme Court has only rarely granted accommodations of religious beliefs and practices. Most of these cases mirror the facts of *Sherbert*—denial of unemployment benefits based on religious belief.[24] The only other notable case is *Wisconsin v. Yoder* (1972), where the court ruled that the Amish could remove their children from public school after eighth grade based on religious convictions. The United States Supreme Court, thus, has only ruled in six free exercise cases for recognition of free exercise of religion as a fundamental right. The approach of *Sherbert v. Verner* appears to be based on the philosophy of Roger Williams[25]

22 366 U.S. 599 (1961).

23 Paul G. Kauper, The Warren Court: Religious Liberty and Church-State Relations, 67 *Mich. L. Rev.* 269, 275 (1968).

24 As the rule of *Sherbert* was crafted in the context of a state unemployment scheme, several cases addressing unemployment likewise resulted in accommodation under the *Sherbert* approach. See *Frazee v. Illinois Dept of Employment Security*, 489 U.S. 829 (1989); *Hobbie v. Unemployment Appeals Comm'n*, 480 U.S. 136 (1987); *Thomas v. Review Board*, 450 U.S. 707 (1981).

25 "By persecution for cause of conscience, I … mean either for professing some point of doctrine which you believe in conscience to be the truth, or for practicing some work which you believe conscience to be a religious duty." Perry Miller, *Roger Williams: His Contribution to the American Tradition* 114 (1965) (quoting from excerpt of Williams' *The Bloody Tenet, of Persecution, for Cause of Conscience*).

and James Madison,[26] both of whom argued for protection of religiously inspired conduct.

Wisconsin v. Yoder

The only other seminal case protecting free exercise of religion is *Wisconsin v. Yoder*,[27] which dealt with a Wisconsin law that mandated that children must attend school until they are 16 years of age. Here the case dealt with the Amish, a religion of the Anabaptist faith that resulted from the 30 Years War in Europe during the seventeenth century. For the Amish, they desired to remain separate from the modern world so that they could preserve their simple, common religious way of life. Important, of course, was that the Amish be self-sufficient and independent. To do this, it was necessary that the Amish receive training in reading, writing and math so that they could read Biblical works and carry out their manual tasks in order to support their livelihood.

In this respect, the court determined that the Amish were a highly successful unit of society, even when outside the mainstream. The Amish seem to follow the thought of Thomas Jefferson, who emphasized that education was a bulwark of a free people against tyranny and the virtues of the Jefferson ideal of a "steady yeoman."[28] Alternatively, we might say Jefferson got his ideal from the Amish or some other old community groups. The Amish wanted to take no part in modern technological developments, such as automobiles, telephones, computers, etc. Thus, the Amish wanted their children to go to public schools, but only until a certain age when they had acquired these skills. The Amish did not want their children to go to school until the age of 16, the requirement of the Wisconsin law, as that would expose their children to too much of the modern world; religion was more important than material success. Being aloof from the world is central to their faith. The Amish are interested in a life of goodness and community welfare, not a life of intellect or competition. And the Amish did not want their children to be subject to peer pressure, as that would harm their emotional development.[29]

Faced with this, the court had to determine whether religious freedom was at issue under the Free Exercise Clause and then which of free exercise freedom or

26 "The Religion then of every man must be left to the conviction and conscience of every man; and it is the right of every man to exercise it as these may dictate. This right is in its nature an unalienable right. … It is unalienable also, because what is here a right towards men, is a duty towards the Creator. It is the duty of every man to render to the Creator such homage, and such only, as he believes to be acceptable to him. … This duty [to the Creator] is precedent both in order of time and degree of obligation, to the claims of Civil Society … therefore that in matters of Religion, no man's right is abridged by the institution of Civil Society." [*Memorial and Remonstrance*, cited in *Everson*, 330 U.S. at 64.]

27 406 U.S. 205 (1972).

28 Ibid. at 222, 225.

29 Ibid. at 210–11.

the state law would prevail. First, the court had to determine whether religious beliefs were at issue of a significant enough nature to trigger free exercise rights. The court observed that long before the need for universal formal education, the "Religious Clauses had specifically and firmly fixed the right to free exercise of religious beliefs, and buttressing this fundamental right was an equally firm, even if less explicit, prohibition against the establishment of any religion by government."[30] To qualify for free exercise freedoms, the belief "must be rooted in religious belief."[31] Then evaluating the Amish belief, the court determined that it did merit treatment under the Free Exercise Clause:

> [W]e see that the record in this case abundantly supports the claim that the traditional way of life of the Amish is not merely a matter of personal preference, but one of deep religious conviction, shared by an organized group, and intimately related to daily living. That the Old Order Amish daily life and religious practice stem from their faith is shown by the fact that it is a response to their literal interpretation of the Biblical injunction from the Epistle of Paul to the Romans, "be not conformed to this world … ." This command is fundamental to the Amish faith. Moreover, for the Old Order Amish, religion is not simply a matter of theocratic belief … the Old Order Amish religion pervades and determines virtually their entire way of life, regulating it with the detail of the Talmudic diet through the strictly enforced rules of the church community.[32]

The Amish way of life is to be a "church-oriented community, separated from the outside world and 'worldly' influences."[33] And as with *Sherbert v. Verner*, actions are protected by the Free Exercise Clause, not just beliefs.

Yoder is also seminal because the court sets forth a definition of religion that is crucial to determine the meaning of the Free Exercise Clause, as noted above: a "deep religious conviction, shared by an organized group, and intimately related to daily living."[34] A more accommodating definition of religion can be gleaned from *United States v. Seeger*, where the court fixed the standard for judging congressional exemption from military service as "[a] sincere and meaningful belief which occupies in the life of its possessor a place parallel to that filled by … God."[35] So the court has at least offered some tentative definitions as to what constitutes religion under the Free Exercise Clause.

30 Ibid. at 214.

31 Ibid. at 215.

32 Ibid. at 216. The court analogizes the Amish to "Jefferson's ideal of the 'sturdy yeoman' who would form the basis of what he considered as the ideal of a democratic society." Ibid. at 225–26.

33 Ibid. at 217.

34 Ibid. at 216.

35 *United States v. Seeger*, 380 U.S. 163, 176 (1965).

The case of *United States v. Ballard* is another attempt at trying to ascertain the meaning of religious belief.[36] This case dealt with the "I Am movement," which used the mail system to distribute literature on the "I Am movement," which many thought was fraudulent. The question here is the religion truthful or false. Justice Douglas proclaimed that "Heresy trials are foreign to our Constitution."[37] For the court, it remanded back to the district court, not allowing a judgment to be made on the religious beliefs, but allowing a jury to determine subjective good faith. Judge and jurors should not inquire into religious truth which ill serves freedom of conscience. However, subjective good faith can be considered and allows for arguments about fraud, which allows the conviction to stand. The real question is whether an average juror can distinguish between subjective belief and plausibility of religious belief.[38] In dissent, Justice Jackson observed, "If we try religious sincerity severed from religious verity, we isolate the dispute from the very considerations which in common experience provide its most reliable answer … any inquiry into intellectual honesty in religion raises profound psychological problems."[39] Jackson goes on to say: "But the real harm is on the mental and spiritual plane."[40]

The definitions of religion rendered by the UK and German courts seem to be much more precise and predictable than that of the Supreme Court. But this likely reflects the Supreme Court's hesitation to intrude into religious matters. On the other hand, since the First Amendment straightforwardly states that "Congress shall make no law … prohibiting the free exercise of religion," there is a strong textual argument for the Supreme Court, and other courts, to render a meaning of free exercise of religion, including religiously motivated actions. After all, the job of courts is to interpret the law.

Based on this assessment, the court determined that the state compulsory attendance law until age 16 interfered and "contraven[ed] the basic religious tenets and practice of the Amish faith, both as to the parent and the child."[41] As the court states:

> The impact of the compulsory-attendance law on respondents' practice of the Amish religion is not only severe, but inescapable, for the Wisconsin law affirmatively compels them, under threat of criminal sanction, to perform acts undeniably at odds with fundamental tenets of their religious beliefs. … Nor is the impact of the compulsory-attendance law confined to grave interference with important Amish religious tenets from a subjective point of view. It carries with

36 322 U.S. 78 (1944).

37 Ibid. at 86.

38 Ronald J. Krotosynski, Jr., The Apostle, Mr. Justice Jackson, and the "Pathological Perspective" of the Free Exercise Clause, 65 *Wash. & Lee L. Rev.* 1071, 1079–81 (2008).

39 322 U.S. at 93 (Jackson, J., dissenting).

40 Ibid. at 94.

41 406 U.S at 218 (citations omitted).

> it precisely the kind of objective danger to the free exercise of religion that the First Amendment was designed to prevent. As the record shows, compulsory school attendance to age 16 for Amish children carries with it a very real threat of undermining the Amish community and religious practices as they exist today; they must either abandon belief and be assimilated into society at large, or be forced to migrate to some other and more tolerant region.[42]

Having evaluated the religious claims of the parents against the state compulsory education attendance law, the court determined that a claim could be made under the Free Exercise Clause.

Here the court evaluated the law and determined that it was "neutral on its face," not selective or discriminatory.[43] The court then went on to say that:

> A regulation neutral on its face may, in its application, nonetheless offend the constitutional requirement for governmental neutrality if it unduly burdens the free exercise of religion. … The Court must not ignore the danger that an exception from a general obligation of citizenship on religious grounds may run afoul of the Establishment Clause, but that danger cannot be allowed to prevent any exception no matter how vital it may be to the protection of values promoted by the right of free exercise.[44]

What *Yoder* illustrates is that the court can be very protective of free exercise freedom. *Yoder* follows *Sherbert*: the law does not have to be religiously discriminatory. The law can be neutral; and if neutral, the law places a burden on religious believers, who can then make a case to protect their rights under the Free Exercise Clause. *Yoder* also further follows the *Sherbert* case by subjecting the government law to an exacting, high standard. While the court in *Yoder* does not apply the conventional strict scrutiny as in *Sherbert*, the standard approximates the strict scrutiny standard, but with a different word choice. The court calls for government to prove the constitutionality of the measure by proving that "only those interests of the highest order and those not otherwise served can overbalance legitimate claims to the free exercise of religion."[45] The court states the exacting level of scrutiny in a different manner:

> Where fundamental claims of religious freedom are at stake, however, we cannot accept such a sweeping claim; despite its admitted validity in the generality of cases, we must searchingly examine the interests that the State seeks to promote by its requirement for compulsory education to age 16, and the

42 Ibid. at 218 (citations omitted).
43 Ibid. at 220 (citations omitted).
44 Ibid. at 220–21 (citations omitted).
45 Ibid. at 215 (citations omitted).

impediment to those objectives that would flow from recognizing the claimed Amish exemption.[46]

Applying the high level of strict scrutiny, the court determined that the state could not meet its objectives and thus allowed the Amish children to be exempt from the compulsory school attendance law. Instead, the state law constituted a severe intrusion into family decisions over education and religion.[47] The family decisions should prevail over the state law, as personal family and religious matters are crucial to the development of a child and the structure of a family. Thus, what we can conclude is that the court has been relatively stingy in its protection of free exercise rights. The dramatic change in free exercise law is evident in our discussion of *Smith*, which follows next.

Free Exercise as Right under Neutral Principle

Employment Division, Dep't of Human Resources, Oregon v. Smith

The Supreme Court's 1990 decision in *Employment Division, Dep't of Human Resources, Oregon v. Smith* was a controversial decision as it altered the landscape with respect to free exercise rights.[48] The controversy in the case was that two employees, Alfred Smith and Galen Black, worked at a private drug rehabilitation center. Both of them were Native American (or Indian) and ingested peyote, a controlled substance, for sacramental purposes at a ceremony of their Native American Church. The religious rite of ingesting peyote is a long shared history and practice in Native American life. Under Oregon law, however, peyote was treated as a controlled substance. Most other states in the United States allowed peyote to be used by Native Americans for religious purposes. After the *Smith* decision, Oregon also allowed use of peyote by Native Americans for religious purposes.

After the two were fired from their job, they applied for unemployment benefits, but were denied on the ground that the cause was misconduct.[49] The case went through the Oregon state court system, with both the Court of Appeals and the Supreme Court concluding that the employees' free exercise rights had been violated.[50] This led to the case going before the United States Supreme Court, which had looked into the case earlier, and sent it back to the Oregon courts.[51] The Oregon Supreme Court reconsidered its decision, and affirmed that it was a

46 Ibid. at 221 (citations omitted).

47 Ibid. at 231.

48 494 U.S. 872 (1990).

49 Ibid. at 874.

50 Ibid. at 874–75.

51 *Employment Division of Oregon v. Smith*, 485 U.S. 660 (1988) (*Smith I*).

violation of free exercise rights.[52] This now led to the court's dramatic change in free exercise law.

The core basis of the outcome of the *Smith* decision was that the conduct at issue was prohibited by law.[53] Yet there are a range of court decisions where the actions at issue are prohibited by law, but the court nevertheless found the actions at issue are constitutionally protected. For example, in *Yoder* the Wisconsin law mandated that students must attend school until the age of 16. If a student did not comply with the compulsory school attendance law, a criminal penalty would attach. However, the Amish did not want their children to attend school until the age of 16 because they were concerned it would interfere with their religious beliefs, as discussed previously. In *Texas v. Johnson*, the Texas law made it an offense to burn the American flag, but the court found the law to be unconstitutional and the act covered as protected free speech.[54] With this case before it, the court altered the landscape for free exercise law.

First, the court changed the definition of what free exercise of religion means. According to the court:

> The free exercise of religion means, first and foremost, the right to believe and profess whatever religious doctrine one desires. Thus, the First Amendment obviously excludes all "governmental regulation of religious *beliefs* as such." … The government may not compel affirmation of religious belief … punish the expression of religious doctrine it believes to be false … impose special disabilities on the basis of religious views or religious status … or lend its power to one or the other side in controversies over religious authority or dogma …

But the "exercise of religion" often involves not only belief and profession but the performance of (or abstention from) physical acts: assembling with others for a worship service, participating in sacramental use of bread and wine, proselytizing, abstaining from certain foods or certain modes of transportation.[55]

What this definition of free exercise shows is that those rights cover only belief, profession of religious doctrine and acts of religious doctrine. In sum, religiously inspired conduct is no longer free from the constraints of the general law. Under *Smith* now, the court has gone back to the origins of free exercise jurisprudence, which starts with the *Reynolds v. United States* case, meaning only belief is protected and not conduct inspired by religion.[56] As the court states, "We have never held that an individual's religious beliefs excuse him from compliance with an otherwise valid law prohibiting conduct that the State is free to regulate."[57]

52 *Smith II*, 494 U.S. at 875–76.

53 Ibid. at 876.

54 491 U.S. 397 (1989) (Justice Scalia joined the majority).

55 *Smith*, 494 U.S. at 877 (citations omitted).

56 98 U.S. 145 (1878).

57 Ibid. at 878–79.

What have been obliterated are acts inspired by religion that are part of daily life, even if regulated by the general law. In this respect, *Smith* is a dramatic contrast with *Sherbert* and *Yoder*, which validated acts inspired by religion that are governed by the general law.

The second major change in free exercise law is the court's recalibration of what is protected under the Free Exercise Clause. The approach of the court in *Smith* is now a hybrid approach: free exercise rights are no longer protected under the Free Exercise Clause. Essentially, the court is ignoring a textual interpretative approach. Instead, these religious freedoms must be conjoined with other basic rights. As the court states:

> The only decisions in which we have held that the First Amendment bars application of a neutral, generally applicable law to religiously motivated action have involved not the Free Exercise Clause alone, but the Free Exercise Clause in conjunction with other constitutional protections, such as freedom of speech and of the press … [acts like licensing system for religious and charitable solicitation, *Cantwell v. Connecticut*, 310 U.S. at 304–307; flat tax on solicitation of religious ideas, *Murdock v. Pennsylvania*, 319 U.S. 105 (1943); right of parents to direct their children's education, *Pierce v. Society of Sisters*, 268 U.S. 510 (1925) and *Yoder*]. Some of our cases prohibiting compelled expression, decided exclusively upon free speech grounds, have also involved freedom of religion. [*Wooley v. Maynard*, 430 U.S. 705 (1977), invalidating compelled display of license plate slogan that offended religious belief] … And it is easy to envision a case in which a challenge on freedom of association grounds would likewise be reinforced by Free Exercise concerns. …
>
> The present case does not present such a hybrid situation, but a free exercise claim unconnected with any communicative activity or parental right. … Respondents argue that even though exemption from generally applicable criminal laws need not automatically be extended to religiously motivated actors, at least the claim for a religious must be evaluated under the balancing test set forth in *Sherbert v. Verner* … Under the *Sherbert* test, governmental actions that substantially burden a religious practice must be justified by a compelling governmental interest. … Applying that test we have, on three occasions, invalidated state unemployment compensation rules that conditioned the availability of benefits upon an applicant's willingness to work under conditions forbidden by his religion … We have never invalidated any governmental action on the basis of the *Sherbert* test except the denial of unemployment compensation.[58]

Ironically, *Smith* also involves denial of unemployment benefits. If free exercise rights were triggered, as in *Sherbert*, why would they not also be triggered in

58 Ibid. at 881–83 (citations omitted).

Smith? But essentially what the court in *Smith* has done is buried the *Sherbert* test, a test of strict scrutiny that conventionally applies to fundamental rights.

With these two major changes in free exercise law, we have a different approach to free exercise rights. Free exercise rights will get a substantially reduced degree of protection, in comparison to free speech rights and other rights. In fact, free exercise rights will mainly be protected under free speech or a hybrid approach to rights, combining freedom of religion with some express or implied right. Religious speech will generally be protected highly. But religious conduct will get less protection. At present, we might say that personal religious freedoms are better protected in Germany and, now, quite likely also in the UK.

Another change in free exercise law is the application of the criminal law. Many free speech matters are also governed by criminal law, but unless government can demonstrate a clear and present harm, free speech will presumptively prevail. The law at issue in *Smith* was a criminal law. However, the law at issue in *Yoder* was also a criminal law. Both laws were general and of neutral applicability. Nevertheless, in *Smith* the court asserted that criminal laws placed obligations on all citizens, including religious believers, even when they are generally applicable neutral laws. This means that the *Smith* test is essentially rooted in equal protection norms, like neutrality compared to non-neutrality. Conduct is to be measured against the general law at issue. If it is neutral, the general law will prevail over the religiously motivated behavior of the person. If the law is non-neutral, targeting people of religious faith, the people's religious rights will likely prevail. Thus, effectively, *Smith* has dramatically altered free exercise jurisprudence.

What this now means is that the court is willing to allow the political process to arbitrate the range of permissible religiously grounded action because conduct, religious or otherwise, is subject to the limitations of the general laws.[59] Thus, general laws circumscribe religious freedom. The approach of *Smith* differs over how to treat religiously induced conduct. Such conduct is permissible only to the extent it is within the scope of the law. When religiously inspired action collides with generally applicable neutral laws, neutral laws predominate.[60] Under the rule of *Smith*, therefore, the scope of religious action is determined by the democracy through the enactment of its laws. Law controls more than religion, an approach opposite of *Sherbert.* In fact, we can now see a difference in perspective. The approach of *Sherbert*, like German law, is oriented toward the believer; religious duties control more than the law. *Smith* is oriented toward the law; law determines the range of religious freedom. The scope of religious freedom depends significantly on which perspective controls. The controversy of the *Smith* decision led Congress to pass the Religious Restoration Freedom Act, under its Fourteenth Amendment power, which was designed to restore strict scrutiny as the applicable test to judge free exercise

59 *Smith*, 494 U.S. at 890.

60 *Smith* is in line with *Reynolds v. United States*, 98 U.S. 145 (1879) and also the famous position of neutrality advocated by Philip Kurland. See Philip Kurland, *Religion and the Law* 22 (1962).

claim. However, in *Boerne v. Flores*, the court struck down the congressional law as unconstitutional, invoking its power of independent judicial review, notwithstanding the fact that section 5 of the Fourteenth Amendment specifically grants power to Congress to enforce the amendment.[61]

Under *Smith*, personal religious freedom can fairly accurately be calibrated along a dichotomy of belief (protected)/action (unprotected), unless allowed by the polity. The *Smith* rule tends to apply a bright-line rule; protection or non-protection depends largely on whether the religious exercise is characterized as belief or action. *Smith* thus follows the thought of Thomas Jefferson. In this respect the *Smith* rule promotes clarity in the law, in comparison to the messiness sometimes associated with balancing regimes. Under the particular balancing regimes of *Sherbert* and the German Constitutional Court, however, the rule of law has been fairly predictable. Under *Sherbert*, the court applies conventional strict scrutiny analysis, as is common when fundamental rights are involved. Strict scrutiny can be categorized as a categorical rule: free exercise rights will presumptively prevail unless government can make out a compelling reason for restricting the right. Thus, the benefits of a categorical rule are in promoting stability in the law.

We might say the German approach accords high respect to the dictates of conscience, whereas the *Smith* approach forces a conflict between the demands of law and faith. John Locke posed the conflict in a way similar to Justice Scalia in *Smith*.[62] Like Roger Williams, Locke attempted to protect religious liberty by separating the jurisdictions of government from religion to the extent possible so that the two would not intrude upon each other's realm. "I esteem it above all things necessary to distinguish exactly the business of civil government from that of religion and to settle the just bounds that lie between the one and the other."[63] However, when faced with a conflict between the two, government would prevail:

> The private judgment of any person concerning a law enacted in political matters, for the public good, does not take away the obligation of that law, nor deserve a dispensation. … Those things that are prejudicial to the commonwealth of a people in their ordinary use, and are therefore forbidden by laws, those things ought not to be permitted to churches in their sacred rites. Only the magistrate ought always to be very careful that he does not misuse his authority, to the oppression of any church, under pretense of public good.[64]

---

61 521 U.S. 507 (1997).

62 For careful consideration of the thought of John Locke, see Timothy L. Hall, Roger Williams and the Foundations of Religious Liberty, 71 *B.U.L. Rev.* 455, 490–95 (1991); McConnell, *supra* note 14, at 1430–1436. For careful consideration of the thought of Roger Williams, see Edward J. Eberle, Roger Williams' Gift: Religious Freedom in America, 4 *Roger Williams Univ. L. Rev.* 425 (1999).

63 John Locke, *A Letter Concerning Toleration* 18 (originally published 1689) (Prometheus Books 1990) (hereinafter "Letter of Toleration"). See ibid. at 18–19, 32, 47, 56.

64 *Letter of Toleration*, see ibid. at 59, 48–49.

And Locke had a decisive influence on Thomas Jefferson, who largely echoed the position of Locke concerning accommodation of religious conduct. "[T]he opinions of men are not the object of civil government, nor under its jurisdiction … it is enough for the rightful purposes of civil government for its officers to interfere when principles break out into overt acts against peace and good order."[65] "The legitimate powers of government extend to such acts only as are injurious to others."[66] "[T]he legislative powers of government reach actions only, and not opinions … [M]an … has no natural right in opposition to his social duties."[67] Jefferson largely conceived freedom as belief and opinion, and not acts, which civil government was free to regulate. Based upon Jefferson's distinction between beliefs (protected) and actions (unprotected), the Supreme Court decided *Reynolds v. United States*, holding that Mormons were not excused from polygamy laws.[68]

There are major differences between the meaning of religious freedom between Locke and Jefferson. For Locke, toleration is a means of securing the tranquility of the state. For him, religious freedom applied only to Protestants. He did not endorse toleration for Roman Catholics, Jews or Atheists. For Jefferson, enlightenment was to be done through exercise of reason and saw mandatory religious duties as fundamentally inconsistent with a process of truth-seeking through rational investigation. Jefferson endorsed religious freedom for all groups, any sect, including all Christians, Jews, Atheists and others. Jefferson was committed to complete and total freedom of belief. Jefferson did not accept Locke's approach of toleration; he totally rejected it. For Locke, freedom of conscience is a means to political stability. For Jefferson, religious freedom is self-actualization and not a means to a political end. In this respect, Jefferson applies a much broader approach of religious freedom than Locke. But part of the problem for Locke is that he is writing his materials in the seventeenth century, using a pseudonym, as there is ongoing conflict in England over religion and politics, a highly contentious atmosphere.[69]

Like Locke and Jefferson, Justice Scalia envisions religious freedoms as encompassing the freedom to believe what you like.[70] However, religiously

---

65 Thomas Jefferson, A Bill for Establishing Religious Freedom, reprinted in *Thomas Jefferson: Writings* 347 (Merrill D. Peterson, The Library of America 1984) (hereinafter *Thomas Jefferson Writings*).

66 Thomas Jefferson, *Notes on the State of Virginia* 159 (W. Peden ed. 1955) cited in McConnell, *supra* note 14, at 1451.

67 Letter from Thomas Jefferson to Nehemiah Dodge and Others, a Committee of the Danbury Baptist Association, in Connecticut (1 January 1802), reprinted in *Thomas Jefferson Writings*, *supra*, at 510.

68 *Reynolds v. United States*, 98 U.S. 145, 164 (1878), holding that Mormons were not excused from polygamy laws. For careful consideration of Jefferson's thought, see Hall, *supra* note 62, at 495–505; McConnell, *supra* note 14, at 1430–31, 1449–1452.

69 Email from Ronald J. Krotosznski, Jr. to Edward J. Eberle (30 March 2011).

70 *Smith*, 494 U.S. at 877 ("free exercise of religion means, first and foremost, the right to believe and profess whatever religious doctrine one desires …).

grounded conduct is limited by law. When faced with that situation, Locke advocated that a person should follow his or her conscience and accept the consequences of breaking the law:

> [O]bediance is due in the first place to God, and afterwards to the laws. ... "What if the magistrate should enjoin any thing by his authority, that appears unlawful to the conscience of a private person?" ... I say, that such a private person is to abstain from the actions that he judges unlawful; and he is to undergo the punishment, which is not unlawful for him to bear; for the private judgment of any person concerning a law enacted in political matters, for the public good, does not take away the obligation of that law, nor deserve a dispensation. ...
>
> Who shall be judge between them? I answer God alone; for there is no judge upon earth between the supreme magistrate and the people. ... You will say then the magistrate being the stronger will have his will, and carry his point. Without doubt."[71]

Smith is an outcropping of Lockean thought. Locken and Jeffersonian thought contrast with the thought of James Madison, who argued that a person acting pursuant to religious conviction should be excused from trying to satisfy claims of law and conscience:

> The Religion then of every man must be left to the conviction and conscience of every man; and it is the right of every man to exercise it as these may dictate. This right is in its nature an unalienable right. ... It is unalienable also, because what is here a right towards men, is a duty towards the Creator. It is the duty of every man to render to the Creator such homage, and such only, as he believes to be acceptable to him. ... This duty [to the Creator] is precedent both in order of time and degree of obligation, to the claims of Civil Society ... therefore that in matters of Religion, no man's right is abridged by the institution of Civil Society.[72]

---

71 John Locke, *A Letter Concerning Toleration*, *supra* note 63 at 59, 61.

72 *Memorial and Remonstrance*, cited in *Everson*, 330 U.S. at 64. At times, Madison expressed quite radical positions. Early in his public life, Madison posited that government should be able to limit religious liberty only when "the preservation of equal liberty and the existence of the state are manifestly endangered." Timothy Hall, *Separating Church and State: Roger Williams and Religious Liberty* 135 (1998). Later in life, Madison expressed similar thoughts. Religious rights should prevail "in every case where it does not trespass on private rights or the public peace." Letter from James Madison to Edward Livingston (10 July 1822) in 9 *The Writings of James Madison* 98, 100 (G. Hunt ed., 1901) *cited in* McConnell, *supra* note 14, at 1464. For detailed consideration of Madison's thought, see Hall, *supra* note 62, at 505–13; McConnell, ibid., at 1453–55, 1464.

Another factor worth considering in assessing approaches to free exercise is promotion of the legal value at issue. Here the legal value is the constitutionally guaranteed right of religious freedom. Comparing the scope of freedom under *Sherbert*, and under German law, as compared to *Smith*, it is fair to say that the *Sherbert* and German approach is more protective of religious freedom. Naturally this would follow from an approach that protects actions as well as belief, as compared to an approach that largely protects only belief.

Conversely, it is also illuminating to measure the approaches from the perspective of how well they facilitate freedom's opposite: social order. Consideration of order is a relevant concern because constitutional democracy protects ordered liberty,[73] not liberty *per se* or unlimited liberty. Religion is fundamentally a spiritual, mystical phenomenon over which the believer has little, if any, control. If God commands, there is little to do but obey. Or, alternatively, a person's inner conscience determines their faith and path in life. Either way, each person's conscience—the path to God—has the potential to be a law unto itself, as Justice Scalia aptly observed in *Smith.* "To make an individual's obligation to obey such a law contingent upon the law's coincidence with his religious belief, except where the State's interest is 'compelling'—permitting him, by virtue of his beliefs, 'to become a law unto himself' … contradicts both constitutional tradition and common sense."[74]

Multiplying conscience by people, any society would have difficulty securing common peace when faced with a multitude of consciences. These motivations were a factor in *Smith.*[75] "Any society adopting such a system [strict scrutiny regime] would be courting anarchy, but that danger increases in direct proportion to the society's diversity of religious beliefs, and its determination to coerce or suppress none of them." It is fair to say that the rule of *Smith* favoring religious actors' compliance with generally applicable law favors order more than the *Sherbert* and German regime where elements of disorder are inevitable—the disorder resulting from religiously inspired conviction. However, while concern that promotion of disorder will unravel society is sound as a theoretical matter, in practice this has been a diminished concern under the particular regimes of *Sherbert* and the German Constitutional Court.

Few free exercise challenges have been successful under *Sherbert*, resulting in minimal conscientious objection. In fact, American law has settled on accommodation in only three sets of cases. One instance is the unemployment context, which has resulted in several cases under the *Sherbert* approach.[76]

73 *Palko v. Connecticut*, 302 U.S. 319, 325 (1937).

74 494 U.S. at 885 (citing *Reynolds v. United States*, 98 U.S. 145, 167 (1879)).

75 Ibid. at 888. Early Americans were concerned that accommodations would lead to anarchy as well. McConnell, *supra* note 14, at 1447.

76 See *Frazee v. Illinois Dept of Employment Security*, 489 U.S. 829 (1989); *Hobbie v. Unemployment Appeals Comm'n*, 480 U.S. 136 (1987); *Thomas v. Indiana Employment Security Review Board*, 450 U.S. 707 (1981).

Thomas v. Indiana Employment Security Review Board is another example of free exercise rights.[77] Here the case dealt with a Jehovah's Witness who had previously worked in a factory which fabricated steel for a variety of industrial uses. Now this foundry was closed, and Thomas was transferred to another factory engaging in the production of weapons. As a Jehovah's Witness, he objected to production of weapons for war. He quit his job and applied for unemployment benefits, but was denied. The court ruled in his favor, observing that religiously motivated beliefs prevail over work in military production.

The second important instance is suspension of compulsory high school attendance in *Wisconsin v. Yoder*,[78] based on religious belief and where the court employed generally the *Sherbert* methodology. And finally, in *McDaniel v. Paty*, the court upheld a free exercise challenge by an ordained Baptist minister who wanted to serve as a delegate to the state's constitutional convention.[79] The Tennessee Constitution barred ministers from serving in such official posts, a law with a long history rooted in the English and early American experience.[80] In the present day, the practice of barring ministers from official positions is mainly gone. Accordingly, the court held it was a violation of the minister's free exercise rights to deny him the right to serve as a delegate. Thus, it appears at present that law prevails over freedom, order prevails over disorder, under the current approach of the Free Exercise Clause.

Since the language of free exercise protects straightforwardly free exercise of religion, the purpose of the clause would seem self-evidently to guarantee religious practice. While allowing religious practice consistent with the law is better than the alternative, it is not much of a step for the democracy to tolerate religious exercise consistent with its general laws. Democracy controls more than religion. Obviously *Sherbert*, the German approach and *Smith* all promote this. In constitutional democracy, however, democracy does not control all. The Constitution does. The acid test of free exercise, accordingly, is to what extent it protects religious practice when such practice conflicts with legal obligations. This dilemma poses for society the hard question of which of the two is preferable.

Sherbert and *Smith* offer alternative solutions to this dilemma. Under *Sherbert*, legal obligations can be suspended in favor of religious practice.[81] Freed from the obligations of the law, a person is then free to act upon God's will. We can see again that the *Sherbert* approach, like the German approach, is rooted in the view that God's claims are superior to society's. Accordingly, the proper role for a society based on religious freedom is to get out of the way and defer to a person's pursuit of divine will. We might say the purpose of free exercise, in this view,

77 450 U.S. 707 (1981).

78 406 U.S. 205 (1972),

79 435 U.S. 618 (1978).

80 Ibid. at 623–25.

81 The best example of this in American law is *Yoder*, where the court excused from mandatory high school attendance the Amish.

is to recognize and empower a person to act on the liberty to follow religious conviction. Free exercise rights, like other rights, delimit democracy.

Smith comes out oppositely. Under *Smith* the dilemma of whether to follow conscience or law is resolved by mandating submission to the law over conscience. We might recall that the *Smith* approach follows the tenets of John Locke[82] and Thomas Jefferson. Under this view, the role of the polity is to be tolerant and equal. All faiths are to be tolerated. All faiths are to be treated equally by officials. All faiths are equal because they are open to all people and all people, no matter what faith, must comply with the law. People of faith are equal to people of non-faith. No exceptions are to be made from the law.

However, *Smith* additionally advocates that the law itself might reasonably favor or disfavor one religion over another or religion over non-religion, although on formally neutral terms. Whatever official favoritism exists must be manifest in effect, not language. *Smith* advocates formal neutrality, not substantive neutrality. This is the meaning of Justice Scalia's statement that:

> It may fairly be said that leaving accommodation to the political process will place at a relative disadvantage those religious practices that are not widely engaged in; but that unavoidable consequence of democratic government must be preferred to a system in which each conscience is a law unto itself or in which judges weigh the social importance of all laws against the centrality of all religious beliefs.[83]

Under *Smith*, religious majorities are likely to profit through the power they hold in the political process. Political representatives will tend to curry favor with dominant elements of their constituency. The law will tend to reflect the interests of these majorities. Thus, it is less likely religious majorities will be placed in the position of choosing conscience or law. For example, Catholics were allowed to drink wine in order to perform the communion ritual commonly as an exemption from the 1919 Eighteenth Amendment to the United States Constitution that prohibited use of alcohol; the Twenty-first Amendment in 1933 repealed the Eighteenth Amendment. That fate is one to be faced mainly by religious minorities, who lack the clout to influence the political process.

And it is clear that the court has not generally favored minority religions. The Supreme Court has rejected accommodations for Jews several times. In *Braunfeld*

---

82 *Smith*'s idea of non-discrimination is grounded in Locke:

Whatsoever is lawful in the commonwealth, cannot be prohibited by the magistrate in the church. Whatsoever is permitted unto any of his subjects for their ordinary use, neither can nor ought to be forbidden by him to any sect of people for their religious use. … But those things that are prejudicial to the commonwealth of a people in their ordinary use, and are therefore forbidden by laws, those things ought not to be permitted to churches in their sacred rites. [John Locke, *A Letter of Toleration*, *supra* note 59, at 48–49.]

83 494 U.S. at 890.

v. Brown, the court did not allow the Jewish merchant to open on Sundays because of the uniform day of rest.[84] In *Goldman v. Weinberger*, the court deferred to the military, not allowing a Jewish serviceman to wear the yarmulke, a symbol of his faith.[85] The court has also rejected religious accommodations for Muslims. In *O'Lone v. Estate of Shabazz*, the court refused to allow Muslim prisoners to attend a weekly congregational service mandated by the Koran out of prison security concerns.[86] However, in contexts like prison, schools and the military, the court will generally defer significantly to authorities and apply a relatively light degree of judicial scrutiny.

And the court has also been relatively intolerant of Native Americans, as we saw in *Smith* and also with *Lyng v. Northwest Indian Cemetery Protective Association*, where the court allowed the federal government to permit harvesting of trees and road construction in a national forest, effectively obliterating the sacred rituals of Native Americans and leaving them in a difficult situation to determine how to practice their religious faith.[87] In fact, in *Lyng*, the government's activities restrained Native American's religious practices more than the religious activities at issue in *Sherbert* and *Yoder*.[88] What this demonstrates is that the political process determines which of majority religions or minority religions has favor; the end result is the favoring of majority religions.

The court has also rejected free exercise claims for the Church of Scientology. There is certainly a much stronger case that the Church of Scientology should not have free exercise rights, as scientologists do not demonstrate a clear religious affiliation and money seems to play a major role. In *Hernandez v. IRS Commissioner*, the court ruled that auditing sessions should not be treated as charitable contributions for personal income tax purposes.[89] For the court auditing session "payments are not deductible" because "these payments were part of a quintessential quid pro quo exchange: in return for their money, petitioners received an identifiable benefit, namely, auditing and training sessions."[90] In her powerful dissent, Justice O'Connor stated that "the IRS cannot constitutionally be allowed to select which religions will receive the benefit of past rulings."[91] The issue is that many people do not view Scientology as a legitimate religion and not on parity with mainstream religions. The court seems to favor religions that have been in place a long time. However, Judaism, Islam and Native Americans are religions that have had a long tradition, and yet the court has rejected most of their free exercise rights. Minority religions tend not to get religious protection.

84 366 U.S. 599 (1961).
85 475 U.S. 503 (1986).
86 482 U.S. 342 (1987).
87 485 U.S. 439 (1988).
88 Ibid. at 467 (Brennan, J., dissenting).
89 490 U.S. 680 (1989).
90 Ibid. at 691.
91 Ibid. at 704 (O'Connor, J., dissenting).

Viewed another way, we can see clearly that the choice between *Sherbert* and *Smith* is one between a society preferring conscience and a society preferring law. The choice, starkly, is between religion and order. Under *Sherbert* and the German approach, religion is king. Under *Smith*, law is king.[92] Law circumscribes religious freedom. Viewed differently, *Sherbert* and the German approach place a premium on liberty whereas *Smith* emphasizes the equality obtained from subjecting everyone to generally applicable neutral laws. *Smith* is ultimately grounded in law and order. We might think of law and order as the price to be paid for religious tolerance in a manner similar to John Locke.[93]

Interpretatively, there are plausible reasons for either the approach of *Sherbert* or *Smith* under the Constitution. Textually viewed, however, the evidence favors *Sherbert* because the American text specifically enumerates free exercise. The language choice is not toleration, belief or equality. Rather, the text singles out religious exercise as a preferred freedom.[94] The language "free exercise" strongly connotes action, not mere belief. The framers deliberately choose the language "free exercise" over "rights of conscience," which more naturally would suggest only thought or belief.[95] The Constitution itself does not distinguish between belief and action. A generally applicable neutral law can impinge on religious freedom as much as a non-neutral law targeting religion.[96] American law demonstrates both varieties.[97] The German text is even clearer; both belief and action are specifically

92 "The civil power can either change everything in religion, according to the prince's pleasure, or it can change nothing." John Locke, *A Letter of Toleration, supra* note 63, at 49.

93 Locke desired to separate affairs of the church from state as much as possible to minimize discord in society. He advocated toleration of all beliefs, except for Roman Catholics (because of their allegiance to the Pope) and atheists (because they could not be trusted to keep their word), as a way further of defusing the tension between church and state. However, he advocated parliamentary supremacy as the way to resolve disputes between church and state and he did not favor accommodation of religiously grounded action. Thus, we might observe that advocacy of toleration was as far as Locke was willing to go for the cause of religious liberty. He advocated a much more moderate position than Roger Williams or James Madison. Likely, Locke feared pushing the cause of religious freedom too far, out of concern it would trigger a backlash. See ibid. and notes *supra* 96, 99.

94 *Smith*, 494 U.S. at 901–02 (O'Connor concurring in judgment) citing McConnell, Accommodation of Religion, 1985 *S. Ct. Rev.* 1, 9.

95 McConnell, *supra* note 14, at 1488–89.

96 Ibid. at 894; *Yoder*, 404 U.S. at 220 ("A regulation neutral on its face may, in its application, nonetheless offend the constitutional requirement for governmental neutrality if it unduly burdens the free exercise of religion.") (citations omitted).

97 Compare *Sherbert* (neutral state unemployment compensation law violates religious freedom by placing believer who refused on religious grounds to work Saturdays in position of choosing religion or job) with *Church of the Lukumi Babalu Aye v. City of Hialeah*, 508 U.S. 520 (1993) (City's ban on animal sacrifice for ritualistic purposes targeted Santeria religion).

enumerated.[98] Thus, in Germany there is stronger textual support for a broad scope to religious freedom, one that encompasses both faith and deed.

Under *Smith*, the court reads the text to protect belief and action to the extent action is not circumscribed by the law. Because generally applicable laws apply to all equally, religion is no more a subject of neutral laws than status, gender or speech. Thus, any effect on religion is incidental, which the court is willing to accept as a price to be paid for adherence to a system of formally neutral laws.[99]

Whether the rule of *Sherbert* or *Smith* obtains has consequences for the role of a court in constitutional democracy as well. The *Sherbert* rule demands a more delicate and complicated judicial role. It is much more demanding to determine whether an accommodation is required (*Sherbert*) than to refuse accommodation as a matter of policy (*Smith*). Before a court can determine whether an accommodation is required, moreover, it must first decide whether the actions at issue are religious and, if so, whether they are burdened.

The rule of *Smith* tactfully avoids most of these difficult inquiries. Under *Smith*, the main judicial determinant is whether the law at issue is neutral. If it is, then it will be upheld. If it is not, then the law will be presumptively unconstitutional because it targets religion. Thus, we can see how the *Smith* rule insulates a court from most of the hard questions. This is a major impetus for the rule of *Smith*. In fact, the rule of *Smith* would seem to be grounded in a desire to minimize the role of the judiciary. By avoiding balancing tests in favor of bright-line rules, judicial discretion is minimized. Cabining judicial discretion likely lies at the root of *Smith*. Interestingly, *Smith* is grounded in a view of legislative supremacy, not unlike John Locke.[100]

Finally, in comparing the rule of *Smith*—based on religious equality—to *Sherbert*—based on religious conduct—a study by Wybraniac and Finke shows that members of majority religions bring fewer claims and win more of them than do minority religions. *Smith* had the effect of lowering success rate across the board and reducing the disparity between majority and minority religious groups. The Ninth Circuit was less biased against minority religions as compared to the other federal circuit courts and tended to rule more in minorities' favor.[101]

---

98 GG art. 4.

99 *Smith*, 494 U.S. at 877–78. But see Gedicks, The Normalized Free Exercise Clause, 75 *Ind. L.J.* 77 (2000) (arguing that *Smith* adopts a rational basis standard of review and thus "contradicts the Court's Speech Clause doctrine governing [incidental] burdens on speech occurring as the result of otherwise legitimate government regulations of conduct or the time, place, or manner of expression.").

100 McConnell, *supra* note 14, at 1435.

101 Ronald J. Krotosynski, Jr., If Judges Were Angels: Religious Equality, Free Exercise, and the (Underappreciated) Merits of *Smith*, 102 *Nw. L. Rev.* 1189, 1248–49 (2008).

Church of the Lukumi Babalu Aye, Inc v. City of Hialeah

With the new *Smith* rule in place, free exercise claims must now be evaluated under the standard of whether the law at issue is neutral or non-neutral. If the law is neutral, the court will not apply strict scrutiny but rational basis. If the law is non-neutral, the court will apply strict scrutiny. This standard came to a head in *Church of the Lukumi Babalu Aye v. City of Hialeah*, which concerned practitioners of the Santeria religion who, as their religious rite, engaged in the sacrifice of animals, a practice in effect since the nineteenth century.[102] Animal sacrifice has a long religious tradition, going back at least as far as the Old Testament of the Bible. Unhappy with this action, the city of Hialeah passed an ordinance that forbade the killing of an animal for sacrifice, defined as "whoever … unnecessarily or cruelly … kills any animal," which was interpreted for religious purposes, with sacrifice being defined as "to unnecessarily kill … an animal in a … ritual … not for the primary purpose of food consumption."[103] The city ordinance allowed for the slaughter, hunting and killing of animals for food consumption, eradication of insects and pests and euthanasia if necessary.[104] In essence, the city targeted the Santeria religion, allowing animal killings in most other instances, including for the Jewish Kosher ritual.

As the court reviewed the ordinance, it concluded that the ordinance at issue appeared neutral on its face, but that it nevertheless was discriminatory because it targeted the Santeria religion. As the court stated, "The Free Exercise Clause protects against governmental hostility which is masked as well as overt," concluding that the city had as its object the suppression of the central element of the Santeria faith.[105] Essentially, the court felt this was a form of "religious gerrymandering" that was designed to target the Santeria religion.[106]

With this determination in mind, the court concluded that the ordinance was not neutral, but non-neutral, specifically targeting the Santeria religion based on conduct motivated by religious belief. With that conclusion, the court applied the strict scrutiny standard. In applying the standard of strict scrutiny, the court concluded that the city could not justify the measure either by a compelling governmental interest nor a narrow tailoring in pursuit of the governmental interests. As the court stated, "To satisfy the commands of the First Amendment, a law restrictive of religious practice must advance 'interests of the highest order' and must be narrowly tailored in pursuit of those interests."[107] Accordingly, the ordinance was struck down as unconstitutional.

102 508 U.S. 520 (1993).
103 Ibid. at 551–53.
104 Ibid. at 537.
105 Ibid. at 534.
106 Ibid. at 535.
107 Ibid. at 546 (citations omitted).

Thus, what *Church of Lukumi* indicates is that free exercise rights can still be protected, but only if the measure at issue is non-neutral. Effectively, the court has shifted the constitutional practice of religious practices out of the Free Exercise Clause and into the equal protection clause. Any neutral measure will be upheld; a non-neutral measure will be evaluated under strict scrutiny, which will generally result in the measure being held unconstitutional. In *Church of Lukumi*, the court significantly draws upon equal protection law. The court cites Justice Harlan's use of equality jurisprudence under an Establishment Clause test: "neutrality in its application requires an equal protection mode of analysis."[108] Neutrality is a core principle of religious freedoms and other rights. The court goes on to employ other equal protection norms, including neutral measures that nevertheless can be documented to be discriminatory based on evidence, such as historical background, legislative or administrative history, unequal application of the norm and so on. This form of equal protection doctrine is based on the *Washington v. Davis* case, which involved an entrance exam for admission to the Washington, D.C., police force.[109]

In *Cutter v. Wilkinson*, the court upheld the Religious Land Use and Institutionalized Persons Act (RLUIPA), which was enacted to prohibit state or federal government from placing any substantial burden of religious exercise of people confined in institutions.[110] This law, like the Religious Freedom Restoration Act, was designed to restore the strict scrutiny standard that had been rendered dead by *Smith.* The court found that the law applied equally to all religions.

What we can conclude here is that free exercise rights have effectively lost any sense of vitality, in comparison to other core constitutional rights, and instead are treated as a matter to be covered under equality norms or other rights. If the law is neutral, only a hybrid approach (combining freedom of religion with another right) will apply. If the law is non-neutral, then equal protection will apply. Under both these norms, strict scrutiny will apply. What we have here now is significantly diminished protection of free exercise of rights. We might even say that the Free Exercise Clause is now a dead letter.

Compelled Pledges and Oaths

West Virginia State Board of Education v. Barnette

As with the German Constitutional Court, in the seminal Supreme Court case of *West Virginia State Board of Education v. Barnette*,[111] the court recognized, upon

108 Ibid. at 540 (citing *Walz v. Tax Comm'n of New York City*, 397 U.S. at 696) (Harlan, J., concurring).

109 426 U.S. 229 (1976).

110 544 U.S. 709 (2005).

111 319 U.S. 624 (1943).

second thought,[112] that forcing the pledge of allegiance on unwilling believers was a cardinal violation of a free democratic order. Freedom to believe what you like is a core aspect of a person's inner being, entailing matters like religion, philosophy or thought. In *Barnette*, the people involved were Jehovah's Witnesses of which a crucial part of their faith was to follow God; God's will was superior to law enacted by government. For the Jehovah's Witnesses, a flag was like an image and must be secondary to God. The problem with a compulsory flag salute is that it requires "affirmation of a belief and an attitude of mind."[113] This is like a form of censorship, which cannot be instituted unless there is a clear and present danger to people or society. A compulsory flag salute entails no clear and present danger. Instead, students are free to speak or not speak their minds.

It is simply not appropriate for government to compel people to speak or not speak what is in their minds or to "invade the sphere of intellect and spirit."[114] As the court goes on to say about the essence of the Bill of Rights:

> The very purpose of a Bill of Rights was to withdraw certain subjects from the vicissitudes of political controversy, to place them beyond the reach of majorities and officials and to establish them as legal principles to be applied by the courts. One's right to life, liberty, and property, to free speech, a free press, freedom of worship and assembly, and other fundamental rights may not be submitted to vote; they depend on the outcome of no elections.[115]

Thus, what we can conclude is that minority religions can follow their religious tenets and be protected from the coercion of laws. Although what is interesting is that many of these protections for minority religions reside in free speech, and not in religious freedoms. This began in the era before the seminal *Sherbert v. Verner* case, and now with *Smith* yet in place we note the diminished protection for free exercise freedoms. It would be good for the court to protect minority religious freedom the same way it protects minorities' free speech rights.

Torcaso v. Watkins

The only other piece of text in the United States Constitution that covers religion is the religious test oath, which states that "no religious Test shall ever be required as a Qualification to any Office or public Trust under the United States."[116] Compelled oaths is also built into the architecture of the Basic Law. In *Torcaso v. Watkins*, the court found it unconstitutional for Maryland to deny a person a place as an official

112 *Minersville School District v. Gobitis*, 310 U.S. 586 (1940) *o.r. in Barnette*, 319 U.S. 624 (1943).

113 Ibid. at 633.

114 Ibid. at 642.

115 Ibid. at 638.

116 U.S. Consti. Art. VI cl. 3. See *Torcaso v. Watkins*, 367 U.S. 488 (1961).

notary public office for refusing to take an oath affirming belief in God required by the Maryland constitution.[117] The man was an atheist. Thus, belief in God was not in accord with his beliefs. For the court this was an easy call: a person simply cannot be forced to make a declaration in the belief of a God.

Torcaso can be thought of as based on the simple rule that no person can be discriminated against on religious grounds in the taking of a public office.[118] Religion embraces a wide variety of beliefs—whether religious, non-religious, ethical or philosophical. There is broad protection for freedom of conscience.[119] For Justice Black, "Among religions in this country which do not teach what would generally be considered a belief in the existence of God are Buddhism, Taoism, Ethical Culture, Secular Humanism and others."[120] The Maryland religious test invades a person's freedom of belief. The point of the Constitution is to put people beyond the reach of compelled belief. Nobody should be forced to profess belief or disbelief in religion.[121] Religious freedom is crucial to the core values of a democracy. Compulsion of belief undermines a person's integrity and democracy.

Earlier cases before the *Smith* case show how the court was willing to accord broad protection to religious beliefs. *U.S. v. Seeger* is a crucial case, dealing with a federal statute on conscientious objection, which had a significant bearing on *Torcaso.* For the court, ethical beliefs parallel standard beliefs in God, both are moral duties. In both *Torcaso* and *Seeger*, religion embraces a wide variety of beliefs, ethical and religious. For the first amendment, no preference may be given to one belief over another, whether religious or non-religious.[122]

Observations

Religious freedom is one of the central values of fundamental rights in the Western world. The United States is a country founded on religious freedom. What is interesting, if not ironic, about the United States is that the idea of religious freedom is mainly covered in rights not rooted in the Free Exercise Clause. For example, early court cases, notably in the beginning of the twentieth century, were rooted in notions of implied fundamental rights and not free exercise; these cases included *Pierce v. Society of Sisters* and *Meyers v. Pierce*. On the other hand, it would be fair to argue that the Free Exercise Clause was not incorporated into

117 367 U.S. 488 (1961). The issue of exempting religiously motivated people from required oaths arose in early, pre-constitutional America. McConnell, *supra* note 14, at 1466–68.

118 Paul G. Kauper, The Warren Court: Religious Liberty and Church-State Relations, 67 *U. Mich. L. Rev.* 269, 273 (1968).

119 Ibid. at 269, 274.

120 *Torcaso*, 367 U.S. at 495 n. 11.

121 Ibid. at 495.

122 Paul G. Kauper, *supra* note 118, at 274.

the Fourteenth Amendment until *Cantwell v. Connecticut*. The first actual use of the Free Exercise Clause to protect personal religious freedom was *Sherbert v. Verner*, in 1963. And even under *Sherbert,* the court ruled for free exercise rights in only three instances: unemployment benefits, which included four court cases; compulsory education up to the age of 16; and a Tennessee constitution provision that barred a minister from serving as a delegate.

With the change in law under *Smith*, free exercise rights have effectively been rendered a dead letter. Personal religious freedoms can now only be sustained if a free exercise of religion claim can be conjoined with another right, usually an implied right that can now be characterized as a "hybrid;" or under equality norms, which call for consideration of whether the law is neutral or non-neutral. An interesting question posed: is the court being faithful to textualism? After all, free exercise of religion is clearly set out in the Constitution and means not just belief but also conduct based on belief. Will the court at some point change its interpretation of the Free Exercise Clause? Isn't religious freedom one of the core human rights in Western society?

Chapter 6
Church-State Relations in the United Kingdom

As we know, the United Kingdom has an established state church, the Church of England, a model that has increasingly lost favor in Europe. On the other hand, many European countries, such as Spain or Portugal, might no longer technically set forth in their constitution that there is an established church, but nevertheless, the Catholic Church, the main religion in the two countries, acts effectively as a de facto state church.

Under the established church approach of the UK, the government often controls significant elements of the state church. For example, the prime minister will often select the bishops and archbishops for the Church of England and then they will be approved by the monarch. Generally, the state will publicly acknowledge the existence and importance of religion, but it does not require conformity to any particular belief. Under the current British established church, religious officials do not play a major role in government. Religious authorities can act in government capacities, generally in the House of Lords, where bishops and religious members of the House of Lords can participate in parliamentary debates, but there is no requirement for compliance with religious doctrine. The crown holder acts in both a political and religious authority, as head of state and head of the church. However, there is still a significant element of establishment in England. The canon law of England is the law of the land and is enforced. Civil courts will thus have jurisdiction over church matters, although the courts try to be cautious in taking on these cases.[1]

Today, the established church in the UK is much less strict and instead more open; it plays a significantly lesser role in government, politics and society than in the past. The UK is also now providing a much more open approach to alternative religions, whether Christian, Jewish, Muslim, Hindu or others. There is much less discrimination against other religions, as compared with the past several centuries. Religious institutions have much more autonomy today than in the past and English society is much more tolerant of alternative religions. So we might say that the UK has an established church, but not an established religion.[2]

---

1 Judith D. Fischer and Chloe J. Wallace, God and Caesar in the Twenty-first Century: What Recent Cases Say About Church-State Relations in England and the United States, 18 *Fla. J. Int'l L.* 485, 490–93 (2006).

2 Ibid. at 513.

Trading on Sunday used to be severely restricted under the Shops Act of 1950. The Sunday Trading Act of 1994 repealed many of the provisions of the 1950 Shops Act. Under the current Sunday Trading Act, restrictions are now in force only for large shops. Large shops may not be open unless they are granted an exemption from the law or they are occupied by people who have observed their Sabbath day like, for example, the Jewish Sabbath, traditionally a Saturday. This part of UK law is still a contrast with US constitutional law, where business goes on as usual on Sundays.

Under the Education Act of 1944, as amended by the Education Reform Act of 1988 and the School Standards and Framework Act of 1998, religious education is part of every school's curriculum. The law requires every state-funded school to provide a daily act of collective worship. The act of worship is mainly to be of a Christian character, although it does not have to be of any particular Christian denomination. Parents may request their children to be excused from the religious teachings. For non-Christians, the religious education is considered to be quite meaningless. Still, there is much opposition to this law. In fact, only about a quarter of secondary schools comply with the law requiring religious education. This is mainly due to lack of support from teachers and the government's unwillingness to attract controversy.[3] In some respects, the UK system seems more in tune with the German system as compared with the US system. However, clearly the UK does not adhere and enforce the law as dedicatedly as the Germans.

Public holidays follow the Christian calendar. Under the Slaughterhouse Act of 1974, animals—cattle, sheep, goats, swine and horses—may only be slaughtered instantaneously by means of a mechanical instrument. The Slaughter Poultry of 1967 applies to fowl. Provided there is no unnecessary suffering, Jews and Muslims are exempt from the law insofar as they follow their religious ritual. The UK law seems in accord with the German approach to the slaughtering of animals.

Concerning church-state relations, there is little law in the UK. This may have much to do with the fact that there is a long relationship between church and state and that the government controls certain aspects of the church, including appointing the Archbishop of Canterbury, the leader of the Church of England. In the recent past, the UK did not have a strong form of independent judicial review. However, today, the UK is moving much more toward a model of independent judicial review. The UK cases covered in this chapter do not entail significant or controversial issues of church-state relations, in comparison with the German and American approach. These are matters of relatively small import, such as questions of tax exemption, repairing a church building or admissions standards to religious schools.

3 Ibid. at 513.

Tax Exemption, Church Repair, School Admission Standards

Gallagher v. Church of Jesus Christ of Latter-Day Saints

Gallagher v. Church of Jesus Christ of Latter-Day Saints involved a Mormon church that was assessed taxes.[4] Under English law, a church can be exempt from taxes insofar as worship is conducted open and to the public. In the case of the Mormon church, only members who were recommended after conforming to Mormon doctrine were allowed in. Non-Mormons and other Mormons were not allowed in.[5] The case had come out the same way previously 40 years ago in *Church of Jesus Christ of Latter Day Saints v. Henning*, with the court determining that a church had to perform the sacred functions of religious rites in order to qualify for the tax exemption.[6] Thus, there was no change in UK law; the rule of *Henning* in assessing tax valuation remains in place.

The Mormons were not being taxed on account of their religion. Rather, their religion prevented them from allowing Mormons who did not subscribe to Mormon doctrine and other members of society from entering the church and thus they did not qualify for any public benefit. According to the House of Lords, not allowing the public to attend church services was justifiable and within the margin of appreciation under the European Convention of Human Rights; thus, the Mormon Church could not quality for a tax break.

The House of Lords accorded a wide level of appreciation to Parliament in determining what constitutes sufficient public benefit to quality for a tax benefit.[7] The church allowed certain of its buildings to be open to the public, such as a reception area, the grounds area and the stake center, where public worship can be conducted, and which had a chapel, multi-purpose hall, with meeting rooms, an office, a baptistry among other spaces. However, the temple cannot be connected to the stake center, as the temple is separate from the center.[8] A temple or church is a place of worship, unlike a reception area or a stake center. Thus, there was not sufficient justification to qualify for the tax benefit. Further, the House of Lords determined that even if this case involved indirect discrimination—that is, while the law is neutrally applied, it may have a disparate impact on its application—Parliament would still have wide discretion in determining whether the Mormon church was entitled to the tax benefit.[9]

4 [2008] UKHL 56; 4 All ER 640, p. 185.

5 Ibid. at 194.

6 [1963] 2 All ER 733, [1964] AC 420.

7 Ibid. at 197.

8 Ibid. at 198.

9 Ibid. at 197.

Aston Cantlow et al. v. Wallbank and another

Aston Cantlow et al. v. Wallbank and another involved a dispute over repair of the chancel of the church.[10] The defendants were the lay rectors or impropriators of the rectorial land and under common law were responsible to repair church property, such as the chancel at issue here. The Chancel Repairs Act of 1932 calls upon the freehold owners of the land to be responsible for repairs. Under the law, the duty of the lay rector is to repair church buildings, a corollary of the rector's right to receive tithes. This is the equivalent of a quid pro quo; ownership of the land requires the duty to repair the land.[11] This quid pro quo concept of property law is reflective of a society that has long disappeared, a relic of the past that might no longer be acceptable, but yet remains in place.[12]

The case went through the different levels of courts. The lay rectors recognized that they had no cause of action or defense, except for a claim under the 1998 Human Rights Act.[13] Going before the Court of Appeals, the court determined that the church council could not recover the cost of chancel repairs on the ground that the church council was a public authority under the Human Rights Act of 1998 and thus could not act in a manner incompatible with the rector's rights under the Human Rights Act, including an element of discrimination. Essentially, this resulted in a windfall for the lay rectors.[14]

Much now depended on assessment of the status of the parochial church council. As examined by the House of Lords, core public authorities for purposes of section 6 of the 1998 Human Rights Act are those bodies, national or local, which perform the function of administering and protecting UK citizens. Acts of a core authority must be compatible with the Convention for the Protection of Rights, which is essentially codified in the Human Rights Act. If the entity, such as here the church council, is a public authority, it cannot bring a claim under the Human Rights Act.[15]

In assessing the church council, the House of Lords determined that the mere fact the Church of England is an established church was not enough for it to qualify as a core public authority. In assessing whether an entity is a public authority, the factors to be considered include whether the body is publicly funded, is exercising statutory powers, is taking the place of central or local government or is providing a public service.[16] According to the House of Lords, the Church of England is not a department of state and has no juridical personality. Only the ecclesiastical courts are the part of the Church of England that qualify as a core public authority.

---

10 [2003] UKHL 37, 1 AC 546.

11 [2003] UKHL 37, 1 AC 546, at p. 5.

12 Ibid. at 7.

13 Ibid.

14 Ibid. at 5.

15 Ibid. at 5, 10.

16 Ibid. at 11.

Moreover, the church council receives no public funding; the main source of its money comes only from its worshiping communities. The members of the church council are volunteers and receive no payment for their services. Members of public authorities are typically paid for their functions.

The main role of the church council is to promote the mission of the church and discharge financial responsibilities in respect of the church and its maintenance. Essentially, this consists of a church body engaged in self-governance and promotion of its affairs. Thus, the church council does not consist of a public body that would engage the responsibility of the state under the European Convention.[17] Accordingly, the House of Lords characterizes the functions of the church council as essentially private, pastoral and spiritual, aiding the carrying out of the church mission.[18]

Section 6 of the 1998 Human Rights Act draws a distinction between core public authorities and hybrid authorities whose acts must be compatible with the Act unless the nature of the act is private. Parliament has not indicated that church councils should be public authorities. Determining the status of the entity—hybrid or private authority—is a fine line. The House of Lords reasons that the only public interest element involved is attending church services, marriage and burial. None of this is sufficient to characterize the church council as public. The church council entering into a contract with a builder to repair the church cannot be characterized as a public function. Likewise, a church council enforcing the 1932 Chancel Repair Act does not qualify as a public act. That is no more a public act than enforcement of the restrictive covenant.[19]

In making this determination, the House of Lords concludes that the church council is a hybrid authority. As a hybrid authority—a combination of a public and private authority—the church council is not totally disabled from convention rights.[20] Accordingly, the church council can take action against the rector for repair of the chancel as a private act under section 6(5) of the Human Rights Act. A major function of the church council is to maintain the fabric of the parish church. Thus, the primary duty of the rector is to maintain the conditions of the buildings on church premises.[21]

As in this case, where the rector has not maintained the repair of the chancel, the church council can take action under the Chancel Repair Act of 1932 to recover the costs of repair. In doing so, the church council is enforcing a private law obligation that rests with the rector. Liability to repair the chancel runs with the land and is enforceable against the owner of the land. In doing so, the church council was performing its function of making sure that the church would be repaired and maintained in good condition. That liability attaches to ownership

17 Ibid. at 12.

18 Ibid. at 6.

19 Ibid. at 12.

20 Ibid. at 11.

21 Ibid.

of the land and is unrelated to church membership confirms that enforcement is a private act.[22]

In further assessing the case, the House of Lords determined that there was no interference under Article 1 of the First Protocol to the Convention in respect to the rector's ownership of the land and obligation to repair church buildings. A landowner who has this obligation must honor the obligation and cannot rely upon discrimination under Article 14 of the Convention. Ownership of the land requires the duty to maintain the land. Acts under the 1932 Chancel Repair Act are not discretionary. Under the Act, there are two requirements: to serve a notice of repair and, in default, to sue for the statutory debt. As a charity, the church council has an obligation to bring in funds and oversee maintenance of church properties.[23] Being a lay rector is not a characteristic that triggers discrimination.[24] Thus, the lay rector cannot claim rights under the Human Rights Act and instead must comply with English law on the right to maintain the property.

What this case shows is that much of the function of the church is to be left to church authorities to determine the status, wellbeing and dimensions of the church. Church autonomy is key. The role of government, even in the UK with its established church, is to leave most of the affairs of the church to the church itself. In this respect, we might characterize this approach as moving somewhat in a direction of separation of church and state. The established function of the church is relatively limited, involving matters like the crown holder being required to be a Protestant, bishops and other church members being members of the House of Lords, and other small matters.

Regina v. Bishop Challoner Roman Catholic Comprehensive

Regina v. Bishop Challoner Roman Catholic Comprehensive involved a voluntary aided comprehensive Roman Catholic girls' school that adopted an admissions policy that gave priority to children who were baptized as Roman Catholics and practicing Christians.[25] The school had an excellent educational reputation. There were more applicants for admission than could be accommodated. The concern of the school was that if the school was oversubscribed, the quality of the education would suffer. Under section 6 of the 1980 Education Act, as amended by the 1988 Education Reform Act, local education authorities are to comply with the preferences of the parent of a student. However, under section 6(3), school authorities do not have to comply with the parents if it would disrupt the provision of efficient education.[26]

22 Ibid. at 6–7.
23 Ibid.
24 Ibid. at 7.
25 [1992] 2 AC 182 (House of Lords).
26 [1992] 2 AC 182 (House of Lords), at pp. 5–6.

In the case at hand, a Hindu and a Muslim student applied for admission, but were denied because they did not satisfy the admission criteria of the school, which required Roman Catholic or Christian faith. This is designed to preserve the Catholic character of the school.[27] The parents appealed to the school committee and the different courts, and the appeals were rejected. The case went before the House of Lords, which upheld the decisions of the lower courts. According to the House of Lords, it is important for the voluntary school to preserve its mission as a Catholic school and to assure a quality education. Taking in too many students might detrimentally affect the educational process. Thus, the House of Lords concluded that given the oversubscription of the school, it falls within section 6(3)(a) of the Education Act and thus there was no duty on the school to give preference to the students' application. Efficient education outweighs oversubscription.[28] What this case indicates is that substantial deference must be given to school authorities to determine the mission of the school. In essence, a strong element of religious autonomy is crucial to determine the mission of a school.

Other Cases

R. v. Bishop of Stafford involved a longstanding dispute between the clergyman, Reverend Raymond Owen, and the laity in the parish.[29] There was a lot of tension between the pastor and the parish. The bishop reviewed the situation and determined, after various consultations, that the parish was best served if the clergy's term was not extended so that the tensions could be resolved. The clergyman took issue with this, believing that the ruling was made improperly and unfairly, and filed an appeal to the courts. The court looked at the review process and determined that the bishop had acted properly and consistently with the rules. The court determined that is was not its business to regulate religious matters. As the court stated:

> the court is hardly in a position to regulate what is essentially a religious function—the determination whether someone is morally and religiously fit to carry out the spiritual and pastoral duties of his office. The court must inevitably be wary of entering so self-evidently sensitive an area, straying across the well-recognized divide between church and state.[30]

This statement by the court reveals a movement toward separation of church and state, a loosening of the idea of an established church. This also demonstrates how courts are more inclined to stay out of the affairs of the church.

27 Ibid. at 10.

28 Ibid. at 12–14.

29 Court of Appeal (Civil Division) (2000) (transcript).

30 Ibid. at 6.

In *R. v. Registrar General*, the court dismissed an appeal by the Church of Scientology on the ground that the chapel where it conducted its mission did not qualify as a place of worship.[31] The court then reviewed the case in accordance with the law that grants a religion a place of worship. As observed by the court, the word religion connotes a place of worship and is principally for religions that believe in a God. As the court defines the term:

> We have had much discussion on the meaning of the word "religion" and of the word "worship," taken separately, but I think that we should take the combined phrase, "place of meeting for religious worship" as used in the Act of 1855. It connotes to my mind a place of which the principal use is as a place where people come together as a congregation or assembly to do reverence to God. It need not be the God which the Christians worship. It may be another God, or an unknown God, but it must be reverence to a deity. There may be exceptions. For instance, Buddhist temples are properly described as places of meeting for religious worship. But, apart from exceptional cases of that kind, it seems to me the governing idea behind the words "place of meeting for religious worship" is that it should be a place for the worship of God.[32]

Then reviewing Scientology, the court determines that this is a philosophy of man's existence, and not a religion. There is nothing about belief in a deity or God, just the spirit of man. Thus, with this review, the court dismissed the appeal of the Scientologists as it did not qualify under the Place of Worship Act.

In *R. v. Lancashire County Council*, the Queen's Bench held that under the existing educational policy, the non-denominational Highfield School could deny admission to a Roman Catholic student because the school was oversubscribed.[33] Local education authorities have a duty to contribute to the spiritual, moral, mental and physical development of the community by providing good education. The value of good and efficient education is more important than admitting more students than the school could deal with. Priority also had to be given to students within the locale of the school. *R. v. Lancashire County Council Ex Parte* involved the same controversy as the case above: good and efficient education is more important than oversubscription of students, which would hamper education.[34]

In another case involving a different dimension of religion, *Board of Governors of St. Matthias Church of England School v. Crizzle*, the Employment Appeal Tribunal allowed the appeal of the religious school over requiring the headmaster to be Roman Catholic because the religious identity of the school was more important than efficient education.[35] The Industrial Tribunal had ruled that there

31 [1970] 2 QB 697, 3 All ER 886, 3 WLR 479.

32 Ibid. at p. 6.

33 [1995] ELR 33.

34 [1994] ELR 478.

35 [1993] ICR 401, IRLR 472.

was indirect discrimination under the Race Relations Act in that Ms Crizzle, who was an Asian Roman Catholic but not a communicant, was denied the position. For the school, participation in Roman Catholic ritual is critical to being a headmaster. The Employment Appeal Tribunal overruled this decision, determining that the religious element of the school was crucial. In this respect, there are similarities and differences between *Lancashire County Council* and *Crizzle.* The similarity is that the courts want to defer to school officials over the policy in place. In the case of *Lancashire County Council*, efficient education is key; in *Crizzle*, religion is key. In this respect, courts defer to school officials. The difference is over the objective: in *Lancashire County Council*, the objective is education; in *Crizzle*, it is religion.

In *Regina v. Chief Rabbi of the United Hebrew Congregation of Great Britain*, the court rejected the appeal of the rabbi who had been dismissed for having affairs with members of his congregation.[36] The court determined that this was a religious matter, and it was no business of the court or the state to intrude into purely religious matters.

R. v. Secretary of State for Education involved a complaint by mothers of two boys who objected to the fact that their sons were exposed to Christian elements in the school's curriculum.[37] The school allowed non-Christian elements to be permitted in collective worship so long as the worship did not exclude Christian elements. Both secular and religious elements were conjoined. The court upheld the judgment of the Secretary of State for Education on the ground that the practice at the school was a multi-faith collective worship not preferring one religion over another. Under the 1988 Education Reform Act, non-Christian elements can play a role, but the main focus must be on Christian character.

Observations

Oddly, there is not much UK jurisprudence on church-state relations. Why this is so is an interesting question. Is it because the UK is an established church, although now the established church idea is not as rigid and strict and much more flexible? Or is it because the UK courts want to stay out of the business of religious communities? Ironically, personal religious rights have taken off in the courts much more significantly than church-state relations.

All the cases we covered in this chapter are not of any great significance. They all deal with relatively mundane issues and none of any great controversy or import. In *Gallagher v. Church of Jesus Christ of Latter-Day Saints*, the case involved a Mormon church that wanted to be exempt from taxes. However, the Mormon Church only allowed worship in the building to those who subscribed to the Mormon doctrine. For this reason, the court ruled the church could not qualify

---

36 [1992] 2 All ER 249, 1 W.L.R. 1036.

37 [1994] ELR 495.

for a tax exemption. In *Aston Cantlow et al. v. Wallbank*, the case involved a dispute over a chancel repair, which under English law is the responsibility of the lay rectors or impropriators of the rectorial land; ownership of the land requires the duty to repair the land. While the rectors tried to claim rights under the Human Rights Act, the court rejected their claim, instead deferring to church authorities.

And in an interesting twist, in two cases involving Roman Catholic schools, the courts defer to school officials. In the *Lancashire County Council* case, efficient education was key; in *Crizzle*, religion is key. As in Germany, the UK refuses to recognize Scientology as a religion. This is in contrast to the USA, which in the past did not recognize Scientology as a religion, but presently does. It will be interesting to see with the increasing emergence of the UK as a more concrete constitutional order whether the church-state relations issue will become a forefront issue. That is a question to be addressed in the future.

Chapter 7
Church-State Relations in Germany

The German approach to church-state relations is one of cooperation between the two institutions. For example, the government provides the administrative apparatus to collect and disperse tax money to financially support churches. Government support of religion allows the government some control over religion. Religious education can be taught in public schools. And religious symbols can sometimes be displayed in public settings.

Religion and Ethics in School

I want to focus on the teaching of religious education and ethics in the public schools. I also want to cover prayer and religious symbols in schools, Sunday opening laws and minority religions. The deep tradition of church sponsorship of learning is a major reason why the traditional form of school in Germany was a confessional (religious) school, which was designed to teach religion as an influence alongside core secular topics.[1] The movement away from confessional schools began with the liberal movement of the nineteenth century, inspired by the French Revolution, which occurred mainly in southern areas, like the southwestern state of Baden. The nineteenth-century liberalization of parts of Germany led to a process of secularization throughout society, including the school system. In place of confessional schools, education was redesigned to take the form of "open" community schools, which sought to minimize religious influence in the schools by opening students' minds to a range of influences, religious and otherwise, along more Enlightenment ways.[2] The open community school—interdenominational in that a range of religious/philosophical views are to be presented, but with a distinct Christian orientation—thereby became the main model for schools in Germany. The Weimar Constitution essentially confirmed this school arrangement, which the Basic Law ratified as well.

Further confirmation of a Christian interdenominational community school as a general model for German schools came to the fore in a series of important rulings by the Constitutional Court, all issued on the same day. While we might say a Christian interdenominational community school is the general type of school present in Germany, there is, of course, variation in the characteristics of schools in different regions of Germany, given that each *Land* determines educational

1 *Baden Christian Community School Case*, 41 BVerfGE 29, 57 (1975).

2 Ibid.

policy. In the *Länder* of Berlin, Brandenburg and Bremen, the curriculum is generally non-religious and involves the teaching of ethics. And this variation is reflected by the three cases we now consider: *Baden Christian Community School Case*,[3] *Bavarian Christian Community School Case*[4] and *North-Rhein Westfalia Christian Community School Case*.[5] We will primarily consider the *Baden Christian Community School Case*, the main case. Then we will move on to the *Brandenburg* cases, which dealt with ethics and religion and were settled by arbitration.[6]

Baden Christian Community School Case

The Christian community school at the heart of the case emphasized the Christian roots of German and European society, but strictly limited teaching of religion as gospel to religion classes.[7] In religion class, the major religions—Catholicism, Lutheranism or other Protestantism—select teachers and materials to instruct in their faith. In this sense, the school is interdenominational. Recently, Islam has achieved a toehold to do the same.[8] The state of North-Rhein Westfalia has allowed the teaching of Islam in the schools. Religion class is a regular and required part of the school curriculum.[9] Parents (or students when they reach ages of 14 or 16) decide which religious instruction to receive. They can also decide to receive no religious instruction and be relieved from the requirement.[10] The school is also interdenominational in that there must be provision of a format for presentation of a range of religious/philosophical views. Outside of religion class, Christianity can only be mentioned as a historical or cultural force, but not as chosen tenets of faith. All classes, apart from religion, are shared commonly by students, the ideal of the nineteenth century liberal experiment.[11]

There can be other forms of school as well, as determined by the community. The alternatives to a Christian community school are a confessional, religious school (as formerly practiced widely in Germany) or a secular, non-religious school, which is quite rare outside of Bremen, Berlin or Brandenburg. Confessional schools are most popular in more religious areas of Germany. In the German states

3 41 BVerfGE 29 (1975).

4 41 BVerfGE 65 (1975).

5 41 BVerfGE 88 (1975).

6 *Brandenburg IV*, 106 BVerfGE 210 (2002).

7 GG. art. 7(3) codifies this arrangement of the Weimar era.

8 BVerwG, Nr. 9/2005 (23 February 2005) (teaching of Islam in North-Rhein Westfalia cannot be rejected out of hand because Islam is not organized as a legal corporation, as is the usual case. Further proceedings are necessary to determine whether Islam has the characteristics necessary to qualify as a legal religious order). www.bundesverwaltungsgericht.de (26 April 2005).

9 GG art. 7(3).

10 GG art. 7(2).

11 41 BVerfGE at 58.

of Bremen, Berlin and Brandenburg, the predominant school form is secular, not Christian.

Despite the long practice of Christian community schools, not all constitutional issues were resolved. The question in the *Baden Christian Community School Case* was a recent Baden-Würtemberg law that unified the school form in the state, but which had the effect of changing the form of community school in Baden to a distinctly more Christian orientation.[12] A father filed a constitutional complaint that the change in school to a more Christian orientation violated his Article 4 free exercise and Article 6 parental rights because it would be harder for him to raise his child in a non-religious environment, as he desired.[13] Of course, under Article 7 of the Basic Law, it was the province of the *Land* legislature to determine the appropriate form of school for the region, upon taking into consideration the full range of varied interests at stake.[14] Still, only the Constitutional Court could determine the permissible circumference of constitutionality within which the legislature could work, which it proceeded to do. The court found the complaint unfounded, which had the effect of confirming the constitutionality of a Christian community school.[15]

The constitutional issues are complicated, reflecting the principles of the German constitutional order. From the standpoint of the complaining parent, he could allege violations of his Article 4 free exercise rights (interference with his choice or religion/philosophy) and his Article 6 parental rights (interference with his right to raise his child according to desired religious/philosophical views).[16] However, his assertion of rights could only go so far. In the German constitutional order, rights holders are not isolated individuals or, as is sometimes the case in American law, lone rangers. Instead, German rights holders operate within a social community which instills values and responsibilities on social members. This had immediate consequences in the case. For at issue, according to the Constitutional Court, were not only the rights of the complaining parent, but the same set of religious and parental rights for other parents as well who might want a school to have a more distinctly Christian orientation or might be quite satisfied with the form of the school as it is.[17] It is fair to say no parent can demand a certain kind of school.[18] Further, the German conception of religious rights is different from the American, reflecting more an orientation of development and assertion of personality than mere exercise of claims and interests. There is an inner dimension to a person's religious rights that captures matters of faith and belief, as in the

12 41 BVerfGE at 36.

13 41 BVerfGE at 44. His wife did not join in the complaint.

14 Ibid. at 46–48.

15 Ibid. at 44.

16 41 BVerfGE at 36–37.

17 Ibid. at 50.

18 Ibid. at 46.

United States. But there is also an outer dimension to these rights that facilitates the ability of a person to practice outwardly chosen faith:

> Belief and freedom of faith encompasses not only the inner freedom to believe or not believe, but also the outer freedom to manifest belief in the world, to confess and to spread the word. Included also is the right of the individual to orient his whole life according to his inner conviction. In this sense Article 4 (1) and (2) comprise not only defensive rights, that prohibit the state from entering the highly personal area of individuality, but also endows a positive sense, which guarantees room for the active activity of conviction of faith and the realization of the autonomous personality in the religious/ideological arena.[19]

The outer dimension to German religious rights are far more pronounced than in American law, especially with the movement from *Sherbert v. Verner*[20] to *Employment Division, Department of Human Resources, Oregon v. Smith*.[21] The German movement toward holistic personhood has its roots in the architectonic principle of human dignity and accompanying free unfolding of personality that animates the German constitutional order. The transcendent dimension of human personality captured by religion/philosophy is part of the essence of being human.

The battle among competing parents is, as we might imagine, somewhat of a free-for-all, as any community of parents is likely to involve differing views as to the degree of religion desired in the community school. Only a compromise among contending views can achieve some equilibrium to this quandary; essentially that is what the Constitutional Court instructed. As the Constitutional Court stated: in today's pluralistic society, it is virtually impossible that any one parent can exercise religious rights without restriction; one parent's exercise of rights is likely to be limited by other parents' exercise of the same rights; thus, communities must search for a compromise addressing all views.[22] The struggle, moreover, was not just among contending parents; the state had supervisory duties over education as well.[23] The positive duties of the state flow from the positive nature of the German Basic Law, which bestows both rights and duties on official authority to manifest the core values of the constitution.

Following the devolution principle applicable to education, the Constitutional Court determined quite naturally that the *Land* legislature had the ultimate authority to fix the nature of religious education, upon taking into consideration the wide

19 Ibid. at 49.

20 374 U.S. 398 (1963).

21 494 U.S. 872 (1990) (free exercise claims judged not by strict scrutiny but by inquiry into whether law in effect is generally applicable and neutral). For discussion of this difference, see Edward J. Eberle, Free Exercise of Religion in Germany and the United States, 78 *Tulane L. Rev.* 1023 (2004).

22 41 BVerfGE at 50.

23 GG arts 6(2) and 7(1).

ranges of religious and educational matters at issue in such a crucial decision. The choice of school form appropriate for the community, however, is to be determined by the community, in accord with *Land* law. Deference to local authority over schools is, as in the United States, attributable to federalism principles. Because of federalism, there can be no unified school system in Germany.[24]

As instructed by the court, the legislature was obligated to consider relevant values of the Basic Law, including parental rights and, most importantly, children's welfare.[25] Under German law, the legislative judgment would involve Concordance (*Konkordanz*), by which an equilibrium is sought to balance the contending rights and interests.[26] Inevitably, this will be a compromise. Yet, the legislative judgment cannot be simply the product of majority vote. If it were, the majority would always get its way. Special regard must also be given to minority views.[27] A careful look at the constitutional principles set down by the court provides insight into the German solution of how to address religion in common schools.

In setting out guidelines governing the role religion can play in the Christian, community school, the Constitutional Court emphasized the need to minimize any coercion of conscience. Any religious instruction must be done with a minimum of forced persuasion; there can be no insistence on the truth of Christianity.[28] Second, there can be no religious instruction or proselytization in school except in religion class. Students who desire not to participate in religion class may be excused from doing so as a matter of free exercise of conscience. Third, outside of religion class, Christianity, as the dominant religion, can only be referred to as a historical or cultural force, not as religious doctrine. The more privileged position of Christianity reflects its dominance as a cultural force, not its truth as doctrine. Fourth, schools must be open and tolerant of other beliefs.[29] The role of the school is to offer a variety of religious/philosophical perspectives as forums for learning. There can be no discrimination against other religious/philosophical views.[30] These constraints on the role religion plays in common schools should afford, in the view of the court, parents adequate room to impart or inculcate religious/philosophical views to their children as they deem fit, without coercion of conscience.[31]

For those parents yet unhappy with this arrangement for their children, further options are available. First, a child may be excused from religious class. Second, a child can attend a secular school in communities where that option is available. Third, where no secular schools are available, a child can attend a private

24 Ibid. at 45.
25 41 BVerfGE at 47.
26 41 BVerfGE at 50–51.
27 Ibid. at 47–48.
28 Ibid. at 51.
29 Ibid. at 52.
30 Ibid.
31 Ibid. at 51–52.

school, secular or religious, according to choice.[32] We can thus see that a *Land* is obligated to provide parents/students with a wide range of religious/philosophical opportunities.

Notable about the German community school model is its transparently Christian orientation, reflective of the predominant Christian roots of the society. Yet, the role of religion is more constrained than the model would suggest. Religion instruction or indoctrination can only occur in religion class for those freely willing to participate, but not for the unwilling. Religion is a matter of choice, not obligation. Apart from religion class, Christianity can only be mentioned as a cultural force, not as a religious force.[33] In this regard, Christianity is to be treated like any other belief system under a school that is designed to be open to and tolerant of all views. In this aspect, the state acts somewhat neutrally, not taking sides on religious views and, instead, offering the school as a forum for the different communities of faith to teach their tenets.

Bavarian Christian Community School Case

The prohibition on teaching religious tenets in schools was put to the test in the *Bavarian Christian Community School Case*,[34] where what was at issue was an accord reached by Roman Catholic and Lutheran churches over the teaching of fundamental Christian gospel, such as the Ten Commandments, the Lord's Prayer and the Apostolic and Nicene creeds.[35] The churches had published their pedagogical inclinations in their official publications. Catholic and Lutheran sets of parents sued to enjoin the practice because they believed this would convert the Bavarian school from an interdenominational to a confessional one, but lost.[36]

The court attributed the choice of introducing this more distinctly Christian program to the churches themselves, and not the state.[37] Thus, the court had no constitutional objections.

The guidelines were published in church papers, not official ones.[38] The guidelines were only helpful aids; they were not binding on the schools or the state.[39] Moreover, any overt confrontation with Christianity can be dealt with by the fundamental constitutional norms announced in *Baden Christian Community*

32 Ibid. at 45. These options were part of the Weimar compromise that constitutionalized much of the German church-state relationship.

33 "The approval of Christianity is attributable to acknowledgment of its role as dominant cultural and educational forces, not as to the truth of its belief system …" Ibid. at 64.

34 41 BVerfGE 65 (1975).

35 Ibid. at 70.

36 Ibid. at 71, 77.

37 Ibid. at 85.

38 Ibid.

39 Ibid.

School Case: non-coercion; toleration and non-discrimination.[40] Concretely, this meant that the community school had to allow presentation of other religious/ philosophical views as well, unlike a confessional school. No person could be made to feel isolated.[41] The Bavarian choice illustrates the wide options of school form available under German federalism. The court noted that a community could decide to have even a confessional school, so long as room—likely by separate school—was made for dissenters. However, the court also decided, on the same day, that no parent can demand a confessional school.[42] Thus, the cases hold that no parent can demand a certain form of religious school, whether more religious (*North-Rhein Westfalia Christian Community School Case*) or more secular (*Baden Christian Community School Case*). Communities can reformat schools along distinctly more religious lines if there is a consensus to do so, as they can also do the same along more secular lines.

Viewed from afar, it would seem the complaining parents had a point. Orientation of education according to fundamental Christian teachings would seem to push, if not cross, the line from secular Christian orientation to religious indoctrination. It seemed that the schools did reformat along distinctly more Christian lines, quite likely crossing the neutrality border. What this reflects is the influence of religion in German culture. There can be no doubt that German public schools allow more overt religious doctrine, like the UK schools to an extent, and provide more influence of religion than American public schools.

Brandenburg

Eastern regions of Germany that were formerly under Soviet occupation and then became the German Democratic Republic are, not surprisingly, distinctly less religious, due to antireligious, Communist influence, than many areas of western Germany that formed the earlier Federal Republic of Germany before reunification. The eastern states tended to carry over the more distinctly antireligious orientation when they joined the reunited Federal Republic. This entailed essentially a severance of Christian morality. Today in Europe there is a movement toward secular morality. The USA is still quite religious, predominantly Christian in orientation, although there is a slight movement away from religion.

These issues came to the fore in the state of Brandenburg, where the *Land* legislature introduced an ethics and religion course as a substitute for normal religious instruction as the standard course in the school curriculum. The substance of an ethics and religion course is discussion over the meaning of ethics and religion in society, a distillation of secular morality and key religious principles. These ideas, of course, are rooted in the Basic Law, as it consists of three fundamental

40 Ibid. at 85–86.

41 Ibid. at 83.

42 *North-Rhein Westfalia Christian Community School Case*, 41 BVerfGE 88 (1975).

sources: natural law, rooted strongly in Kant; Christian natural law; and socialist morality. Brandenburg is rooted more in socialist morality.

For many in German society, teaching of ethics and religion is controversial. But this is mainly the concern of dedicated Christians. In contemporary Germany, belief in God is split; about 50 per cent believe in God and about 50 per cent do not believe in God or instead in some other transcendental idea.

The major difference was that the ethics and religion course would not be taught or organized by the religions, as is normally the case in the German schools. This met with stiff resistance from the churches, who felt threatened by and displeased with the antireligious orientation of the instruction, and asserted their authority as guardians of the faith in an attempt to preserve the domain of the believers. But in a novel solution, the parties were able to bury their hatchets and reach agreement, which the Constitutional Court supervised as an arbitration settlement, itself a highly novel use of judicial authority. The issue was contentious enough to go before the Constitutional Court four times. Each time the court confirmed the arbitration settlement, despite the challenges to introduction of the course.[43]

The terms of the agreement mirrored in reverse the constitutional solution reached in the trio of *Christian Community School Cases.* The ethics and religion class could be taught as a regular part of the school curriculum, but students who did not wish to take part had the right to be excused, a necessary condition of freedom from coercion of conscience. Students desiring to take religious instruction, as more common in other German *Länder*, could do so as well, provided there was a minimum of 12 students willing to do so.[44] The Brandenburg non-religious school curriculum is similar to those in place in the German *Länder* of Berlin and Bremen and could be instituted because of federalism principles that allow *Länder* to fix the content of their school curriculum.

Religious Symbols and Prayers

Classroom Crucifix II

Classroom Crucifix II concerned a Bavarian school ordinance that required the display of a crucifix in the classroom.[45] The case had come up four years earlier, but the Constitutional Court dismissed the appeal on the ground that the delineation of the facts and consequences of the crucifix fact scenario were not

43 *Brandenburg IV*, 106 BVerfGE 210 (2002); *Brandenburg III,* BVerfG, 1 BvQ 25/02 (July 28, 2002); *Brandenburg II*, 105 BVerfGE 235 (2002); *Brandenburg I*, 104 BVerfGE 305, 308 (2001).

44 *Brandenburg I*, 104 BVerfGE 305, 308 (2001) (Brandenburg school law, section 11, 2–4).

45 *Classroom Crucifix II*, 93 BVerfGE 1 (1995).

sufficient for the petition to be granted.[46] Parents of children attending the schools objected to the display of the crucifix in the classroom. They claimed that the display of the crucifix offended their children's religious beliefs. Many of these parents were members of a cult known as anthroposophy, based on the naturalistic quasi-religious teachings of Rudolf Steiner. School officials sought to quell the controversy by removing the large crucifix, which displayed Christ's body, and replace it with a smaller cross without the figure of Christ. This compromise did not work, leading to the lawsuit.[47]

The Constitutional Court is faced with a number of constitutional rights which need to be balanced against one another. These include Article 4 religious freedoms, Article 6 parental rights concerning their children and Article 7 state control of education. The court first starts by outlining the core elements of Article 4 religious freedoms. Article 4 protects belief, and it is up to each person to determine their conviction or non-conviction, not the state. The state is not allowed to prescribe or forbid a particular religion. Freedom of belief includes not only the freedom to follow a particular faith, but also to live and act according to one's own personal convictions. These could even include non-religious or cultist convictions. And a person can refrain from participating in religious activities. The religious freedoms also apply to symbols that incorporate a belief or religion.[48] As a matter of personal freedom, "each individual or group of people can determine themself which religious symbol they wish to acknowledge or venerate or which they wish to reject."[49] In a diverse society with many religious participants, a person does not easily have the ability to be spared from exposure to religious or non-religious actions or symbols.

However, a much different and more difficult situation arises when the state exposes people to the influence of a given faith, without allowing the person to avoid such influence. This is what is at issue with children being exposed in a classroom to a religious symbol. "Article 4(1) protects precisely areas of life … that the state protects … (which include also Article 140 of the Basic Law and Article 136(4) of the Weimar Constitution) …These provisions disallow the state from forcing a person to participate in a particular religious exercise."[50]

Under the norms of Article 4(1):

> the state is not limited to just being disallowed to interfere with a person's faith beliefs and commitments and those of a religious community. The state is also obliged to secure for each person a realm of freedom where they can realize their personalities within a philosophical or religious area. The state is designed to protect people from attacks or obstructions from believers of different religions

46 *Classroom Crucifix I*, 85 BVerfGE 94 (1991).
47 *Classroom Crucifix II*, 93 BVerfGE at 2–3.
48 Ibid. at 15–16.
49 Ibid. at 16.
50 Ibid.

> or competing religious groups. Under Article 4(1) an individual or religious group cannot have a right to have their faith commitments be supported by the state. Rather, the state is to remain neutral in matters of faith and religion. A state with members of various and even conflicting religious and nonreligious groups can guarantee a peaceful coexistence only if it remains neutral in matters of religious belief. … The state cannot endanger religious peace. … The state is obligated to treat each religious or nonreligious group the same. … Also, when the state supports or works together with a particular religious group, it may not identify with that particular religion.[51]

Parents have the right to raise their children as they like, and this includes the choice of a religious or non-religious upbringing. Parents can raise their children in a religious direction or choose to shield their children from religious or non-religious views.[52]

The problem with the Bavarian law that mandated the display of a cross in the classroom was that it forced students to study in the classroom under the influence of the cross. The students had no possibility of exercising their choice of whether wanting to leave or stay in the classroom or see or not see the cross. This contrasts with scenarios where a person might walk in public open spaces or other aspects of their daily lives. The length of time and intensity of the cross in a classroom is a greater violation of personal freedom than its presence in a courtroom. A major difference is that children are more impressionable than adults.[53] On the other hand, crosses can be displayed in private schools, especially those with a religious character.[54]

But the presence of a cross in a courtroom can also violate religious freedoms, as the Constitutional Court ruled in the *Cross in Courthouse* case, a case involving a Jewish person present in the courtroom.[55] Since 1949, the cross had a history of being in courtrooms. The object of the cross was to have people be serious and tell the truth. However, the presence of a cross in a courtroom impinges on the religious neutrality of the state and violates the religious freedom and dignity of participants in court proceedings. The majority cannot impose its religious view on minorities.[56]

The court next turns to an evaluation of the meaning of a cross:

> The cross is the symbol of a particular religious belief and not merely an expression of western culture. To be sure, many Christian traditions have found their way into the general culture of our society over the centuries, and these

51 Ibid. at 16–17.

52 Ibid. at 17.

53 Ibid. at 17–18.

54 93 BVerfGE at 18.

55 35 BVerfGE 366 (1973).

56 Ibid. at 367, 374–76.

> traditions cannot be denied, even by critics. However, there must be a distinction between these traditions and the particular Christian confessions, including ritual and symbolic manifestations. Any state support of particular religious tenets would undermine freedom of religion.[57]

The state can recognize Christianity as a part of Western culture, but not as a religious matter. For the court, the cross represents a religious matter, not a historical part of Western culture. "The cross represents a symbol of belief. It symbolizes man's redemption from original sin by way of Christ's sacrifice through death, as it also represents Christ's victory over Satan and death and his control over the world. The cross represents both suffering and triumph."[58] For Christians, the cross is a core symbol of their belief. But for non-Christians or Christians who do not want the presence of a cross in a classroom, a cross is a symbol of missionary zeal. "To view the cross as just an artifact of the western world … would constitute a profanation contrary to the understanding of Christians."[59] The Bavarian ordinance makes clear that the cross has religious significance.

While one can say the cross in a classroom does not always force children to adhere to or embrace the cross, still the cross exerts influence. Key is education. Education is not just the teaching of culture and the development of cognitive abilities. It also is important for schools to develop their emotional and affective abilities. "The mission of a school is to develop and promote a pupil's personality and influence the pupil's social behavior."[60] In this respect, the cross can take on great significance. The presence of a cross in a classroom can appeal significantly to religious influence and thus disrupt or interfere with students' participation in class; in particular, this will affect young and impressionable people who are still learning to develop their thinking abilities and social skills.

Religion, of course, is important and can have an influence on education. Christianity has had an important influence in the development of cultural and historical values and, according to the court, is not to be taken lightly. But with a pluralistic society, account must be taken of the diversity of views. No one can claim an absolute right over religious or educational matters. This results in an inevitable tension between the different aspects of religious freedom, negative and positive. It is up to the state to reach a reasonable compromise among the contending faiths. Concordance must be reached between Article 4 protection of religious freedoms and Article 7, which sets out the religious and ideological influences in education.[61]

The Constitutional Court has already recognized that Christianity can have an influence in school as part of culture and education, but not particular articles of

57 93 BVerfGE. at 19.

58 Ibid.

59 Ibid. at 20.

60 Ibid.

61 Ibid. at 21–22.

faith. Parents have the right to opt their children out of a religious class teaching religious tenets, as previously discussed in the *Baden Christian Denomination School Case*. The role of the state is to be neutral and accommodating of all faiths. The school is not to force or coerce students toward a particular religion; coercion must be reduced to a minimum. Students are not to be preached to over religious matters. Instead, they are to be taught to think and act autonomously so that they can develop their personalities as they emerge toward adulthood in society.[62]

The placement of the cross in the classroom exceeds the permissible bounds of religious freedoms, as it tends to coerce students. A cross is not just a symbol of Western culture. It is instead an essential manifestation of Christianity. The cross thus cannot be tied to Article 4, as the school is a non-confessional school. Parental rights also control; parents can choose how their children are or are not to be influenced by religion. Parents and pupils who adhere to the Christian faith cannot justify the display of the cross under their positive Article 4 religious freedoms. This conflict cannot be solved by the majoritarian process as the constitution is designed to protect the rights of minorities. Unlike the dissemination of religion in a classroom, where students can opt out, here there is no opportunity to be removed from the presence of a cross in the classroom. Instead, students are coerced to learn secular topics under the influence of the cross. This simply cannot be harmonized under the principle of Concordance. Non-believers will feel oppressed by the rights of believers.[63]

A number of judges dissented from the majority ruling, reasoning that Article 7(1) of the Basic Law confers exclusive power to the states to set the curriculum and that the Bavarian law did not violate the religious rights of parents. The dissenters believed that the states enjoy a wide degree of latitude in determining the curriculum and the style of a classroom. They also thought that the display of a cross had just a minimal effect on children who were not pleased with the cross being present in a classroom.[64] However, the role of the court in interpreting the Basic Law is to protect rights. It is not for the majoritarian process to control religious or other core rights. Protection of rights is central to society, as the role of courts is to protect minority members of society, as the majority determines most policy issues.

What *Classroom Crucifix II* illustrates is that the classroom setting for non-denominational schools is designed to be open and neutral and help advance a student toward being a productive member of society as they reach adulthood. Cooperation between church and state does not mean an intense mix between the two. Rather, the case seems to show that the state is to be neutral. Religion is not to have an immediate and deep impact on child education and development. Rather, students are to be sheltered from religious influences as they go on their path to adult life. So we might say this case seems more in line with a separationist

62 Ibid. at 23.

63 Ibid. at 23–24.

64 Ibid. at 25–26, 33.

approach, reflecting the diversity within German society and the need, in particular, to protect minorities from the influence of majoritarian groups.

School Prayer Case

The *School Prayer Case* dealt with the issue of whether religious prayer was permissible outside the offering of religious instruction.[65] For the school, the class day began with a Christian prayer. Parents objected to the allowance of religious prayer in the school setting, leading to the lawsuit. The case entailed the rights of parents and the rights of the state to set the curriculum, including even allowing prayer. Neither parents nor the school has the right to control one over the other. The problem that had to be considered was whether it was appropriate to have religion—here the prayer—outside of religious class, matters that were extensively discussed in the *Baden Christian Community School Case* and the *Bavarian Christian Community School Case*, among others.[66]

The Constitutional Court ruled that the rendering of a prayer during the school day was constitutional, even when a minority of parents may object to prayer in the school. The court assessed the prayer and determined that Christianity is significant in its role in influencing Western culture. The school cannot be a missionary school and cannot demand adherence to Christian beliefs. Instead, the school is to be tolerant of all religions. No one is to be compelled to be Christian or participate in the prayer. Instead, students can forego the prayer or leave the classroom when the prayer is being conducted and then return to the classroom after the prayer has been given.[67]

To be constitutional, the prayer cannot be part of the curriculum or a binding lesson plan. The prayer must be voluntary. Teachers cannot compel students to participate in the prayer nor direct the prayer. The rendering of the prayer is to be determined by the principal, teacher or student, at any time of the school day—before, during or after school. The state can sponsor the prayer, but it must be voluntary. The court does not see prayer as duty, but as a voluntary exercise. Putting voluntary participation of prayer in school falls within the authority of the states, under Article 7. Thus, the states establish a school system that allows students to acknowledge their beliefs. However, states cannot compel that prayer be rendered in schools.[68]

However, for students of a young age, not participating in the prayer or leaving the classroom can put the students in a difficult situation. Do the students feel discriminated against? Do they feel uncomfortable? Does it affect their ability to develop their critical reasoning skills? Does it affect the development of their psyche and emotional development? These are all difficult predicaments for the

65 52 BVerfGE 223 (1979).
66 Ibid. at 224–25, 236.
67 Ibid. at 223, 236–37.
68 Ibid. at 238–41.

students. It may cause them psychological harm. It is up to the teachers to instruct students how to proceed or not proceed with the rendering of prayer. But still, this puts students in a difficult position.[69] But for the court, because religion is part of the German school system, there is a stronger ground for allowing prayer in school. The German cases contrast with those of the USA, where prayer is banned in schools, as in, for example, *Engel v. Vitale*.[70]

Prayer in school came up again in 2003, dealing with kindergartners praying during kindergarten class.[71] This was a chamber decision by the Constitutional Court, with the court rejecting the appeal of the parent, who opposed prayer in school. The court was aware of the diversity of the kindergarten student body and wanted schools to be open to all young students. So, if the school was missionary and religiously oriented, then the rendering of a prayer would be constitutional. The court assessed the fact situation and observed that schools needed to be sensitive to all of the students, and not allow the implementation of core religious exercises. The context and setting of the class day was significant, and this had to be assessed and supervised. Balance and harmonization had to be achieved for all the parents and their children. The court left the current prayer in school exercise in place and observed that the prayer exercise could be assessed again; parents and visitors could visit the classroom and gather insight about the rendering of the prayer.

It will be interesting to see how prayer in school will come out. Is it better to allow prayer in public schools because it is a religious part of the curriculum? Or is it better not to have the rendering of prayer in school? Can a religion have an effect on the minds of young children who are looking for intellectual and emotional development? These are hard questions that merit serious consideration. With the increasing diversity in Germany society, perhaps matters of prayer in school will come up again for consideration in the courts.

Berlin Sunday Opening Law

The city of Berlin, which is actually a state, as are Bremen and Hamburg, passed a law allowing stores to be open on Sundays. Under the law, during Advent Sundays, stores are allowed to be open. The law is more precise concerning other goods. For example, on Sundays and holidays, the needs of tourists are addressed through the offering of maps, film and other travel accessories and tobacco, in addition to flowers, plants and food, pharmacy products and gas, among other things. A complaint was brought by religious organizations who were concerned about the infringement of religious liberties, which the Constitutional Court granted, with the court ruling that the law violated religious freedom under Articles 4 and

---

69 Ibid. at 248–50, 252.

70 370 U.S. 421 (1961).

71 *Prayer in Kindergarten*, BvR 1522/03 (2 October 2003).

140 and the incorporated Article 139 of the Weimar Constitution.[72] Article 139 of the Weimar Constitution is clear: "Sunday and public holidays recognized by the state shall remain legally protected as days of rest from work and of spiritual edification." Of course given the concern over people's welfare, exceptions are made for specific services and goods, such as police and fire services, medical and pharmaceutical services, transportation, energy, gasoline and other goods and services when necessity demands it.

In assessing the Berlin Sunday Opening Law against the Basic Law, the Constitutional Court observes that Article 139 of the Weimar Constitution in conjunction with Article 4 of the Basic Law guarantees respite from work and spiritual edification and that the Berlin law is not compatible with these norms of the Basic Law. Citing the Bible and the Christian tradition, the court observes that the seventh day should be a day of rest. If shops are open on Sunday, it places religious organizations in a position of disadvantage or prejudice and infringes on their religious freedom. Accordingly, the legislature is obligated to protect Sundays and holidays under the Basic Law.[73]

Again in a contrast to the constitutional orders of the UK and the USA, negative or fundamental freedoms are not only protected, but also the positive right and obligation of the state to carry out the core norms of the constitution, facilitating protection of religious people and organizations. Specifically, the state is obligated to provide room and security for the actions of religious convictions and the realization of autonomous personality and worldly and religious views. This applies also to religious organizations. It is up to the legislature to put these measures in place to guarantee religious freedom and autonomy. Generally, the court will defer to the legislature. However, if the law in place is inconsistent with the constitution or incompatible with its objectives, the court will strike it down.[74]

Under the religious guarantees of Article 4 and 140, and the incorporation of Article 139 of the Weimar Constitution, the states, through their legislatures, are obligated to put in place a day of rest during Sundays and holidays. The Sunday day of rest is rooted in the Jewish tradition of the Sabbath, which is a Saturday in the weekly calendar. Under the Christian tradition, the Saturday day of rest carried over to Sunday. Article 139 of the Weimar Constitution is rooted in the Christian tradition, but applies in a socially equal and neutral way to all people, regardless of their religious or non-religious affiliation. The state must be neutral in its treatment of all people, regardless of religious affiliation or non-affiliation. These religious guarantees provide for the protection of a day of rest and spiritual renewal of people. The concept of a day of rest is to free people from the pressures of daily life so they can partake in a rhythm of work and rest. It allows people to undertake physical and psychological regeneration. People are thus free to undertake religious practices or renewal or non-religious activities, like relaxation,

72 BVerfG, 1 BvR2857/07 (1 December 2009).

73 Ibid. at 18–20.

74 Ibid. at 20–21.

recreational activities and group undertakings. A day of rest is important to renew a person's spirit and personal freedom and is available for all people. It also allows religious organizations to realize their religious freedom, as Article 4 protects not only individuals, but also religious organizations.[75] For the court, the Berlin law was a clear violation of the express textual guarantee of Article 139 of the Weimar Constitution.

Interestingly, the German Sunday closing law is a clear contrast with American culture. In the twentieth century and up to the 1960s it was common for the USA also to have a day of rest, as the court ruled in *Braunfeld v. Brown*, which dealt with the free exercise rights of an Orthodox Jew who adhered to the Saturday Sabbath,[76] and in *McGowan v. Maryland*, where the court kept intact a Sunday closing law for large commercial enterprises.[77] However, since the late twentieth century, there are generally no longer Sunday closing laws. Most stores and businesses are now open on Sundays, with some exceptions in some states for certain goods, like alcohol.

The contrast between Germany and the USA over the Sunday closing law is the constitution. The German Basic Law sets out clearly, in the incorporation of Article 139 of the Weimar Constitution into Article 140 of the Basic Law, that Sunday and public holidays are days for rest and spiritual edification. By contrast, there is no clear mention of Sundays as days of rest in the US Constitution, as the Constitution is sparse. Sunday closing laws are set out only in state laws, as, for example, in the *McGowan v. Maryland* case. But now there are no state Sunday closing laws, as most business now goes on as normal.

Jewish Organization

The case of the *Jewish Organization* entailed an agreement between the state of Brandenburg and a Jewish organization that had recently been founded in 1999, a successor to the organization founded in 1922.[78] The agreement between the religious organization and the state of Brandenburg entailed celebration of Jewish holidays, aiding people in need, in locations such as homes and hospitals, schools and education for children, money contributions by the state of around 200,000 euros, Jewish cemeteries and memorials, among other matters.[79] However, the Jewish organization was not recognized as a public corporation because it did not belong to the state association run by the Jewish council. The Jewish organization at issue was not aligned religiously in the same manner as the Jewish organizations who were members of the state association.[80] Among other things, the Jewish organization at issue had members who were not Jewish and did not have a central

75 Ibid. at 21–22.

76 366 U.S. 599 (1961).

77 366 U.S. 420 (1961).

78 BVerfG, 2 Bv R 890/06 (5 May 2009).

79 Ibid. at 4–8.

80 Ibid. at 3.

organization, but instead consisted of a number of independent organizations. These characteristics of the Jewish organization did not align with the norms of Jewish communities. In considering the agreement between Brandenburg and the Jewish organization, the Constitutional Court determined that the agreement was invalid, violating the constitution, as it did not conform to the principle of neutrality that is central to religious freedom.

Claims were made by the organization under Article 3 equality and Article 4 religious freedoms, together with Article 19(3), dealing with basic rights, and Article 140, incorporating Weimar religious constitutional provisions. The court rejected these claims, noting that the organization had not demonstrated sufficient proof of violation of its basic rights. The second complainant, a member of the Jewish organization at issue, was totally rejected by the court, as the rules apply only to organizations, not members.[81]

The court observes that it is the duty of the state to treat all religious groups the same, rooted in the German constitutional tradition. Government cannot favor one religion over another, including religious groups of the same faith. Equality for all must be the case. Religious organizations are to operate on their own, with their own autonomy, determining their own rules and organization. Freedom of religion for religious organizations must be guaranteed. The state must operate neutrally, not favoring or disfavoring any particular religion, and it must apply the *Rechtsstaatsprinzip*, meaning adherence to the rule of law, applicable to all people and organizations, whether religious or not. However, if religious organizations do not comply with their obligations, the state will not support them. Further, if religious synods do not treat religious organizations in the same manner, it violates the fundamental principle of religious neutrality.[82] The court then ordered the Brandenburg parliament to keep the current law in effect until it passed a new law, which is a common practice in German constitutional law.

Minority Religions

Jehovah's Witness

Two years before *Ritual Slaughter*, the Constitutional Court rendered another important decision concerning the scope of religious freedoms that apply to minority sects. *Jehovah's Witness*[83] concerned the committed evangelical Christian group of Jehovah's Witnesses. Jehovah's Witnesses have long been considered exotic and different in the United States. A series of important Supreme Court cases helped to transform the public image of the sect so that today they have gained

81 Ibid. at 14–17.

82 Ibid. at 18–20.

83 102 BVerfGE 370 (2000).

more acceptance.[84] But Jehovah's Witnesses are still outside the mainstream in the United States. Their status in Germany is no different. They have long been considered a fringe group and were subject to severe persecution under the Nazis and the authorities of the German Democratic Republic.

The point of controversy of the case was the Jehovah's Witnesses' seeking of recognition as a public corporation under German law. Attainment of public corporate status is very important in Germany. As a public corporation, a religious group can achieve legal capacity, raise taxes from among its membership using the machinery of the state, run and administer extensively its affairs and workforce, determine membership, and set its own rules and internal structure, among other matters.[85] Public religious corporations are a main way by which the church-state cooperative model in Germany is implemented. Historically, mainstream religions have predominantly attained public corporate status, most notably the Roman Catholic church, Protestant denominations and Jewish congregations. However, some minority religions and other organizations have achieved this status as well. The Seventh-Day Adventist Church, Church of Jesus Christ of Latter-Day Saints, New Apostolic Church, Mennonites and the Salvation Army are among the groups that have achieved public corporate status.[86] Other minority religions have had some difficulty achieving official recognition.

Jehovah's Witnesses have historically been denied official privileges because the sect does not allow its members to vote or participate in the democratic process. Authorities thus viewed the group as animated by values antithetical to the social order and, accordingly, a danger to society. Germany is especially keen to inner threats to domestic security and democracy given its history under the Weimar Republic.[87] Because Jehovah's Witnesses did not vote or participate in the democratic process, German authorities and the administrative courts viewed the group as disloyal to the democratic order and therefore not deserving of public corporate status. This became the question of the case for the Constitutional Court to resolve: what constitutional conditions were required to obtain public corporate status.

The Constitutional Court treatment of the issue was more sensitive than that of the administrative courts. The Jehovah's Witnesses history of persecution and lack

84 See, e.g., *West Virginia State Board of Educ. v. Barnette*, 319 U.S. 624 (1943) (Court holds unconstitutional state statute requiring mandatory salute and pledge of allegiance to the flag of the United States, and thereby excuses Jehovah's Witnesses from being coerced to do acts against their conscience); *Cantwell v. Connecticut*, 310 U.S. 296 (1940) (Jehovah's Witness within his first amendment free speech rights to walk public streets attacking organized religion, especially Catholicism, and to proselytize).

85 GG art. 140 (incorporating WRV art. 137). *Jehovah's Witness*, 102 BVerfGE at 71.

86 Edward J. Eberle, Free Exercise of Religion in Germany and the United States,78 *Tulane Law Review* (2004) (citations omitted).

87 To help guard against threats to the democratic social order, the Basic Law embodies the idea of a "militant democracy," which obligates the state and citizens to resist threats to the democratic social order. *See* GG art. 20(4).

of official recognition might explain their skittishness about political authority and general reluctance to participate in the political process. But there were deeper religious reasons motivating their behavior as well. Jehovah's Witnesses believe with conviction in the world beyond. They view their time on earth as temporary, as just a passing phase until they can achieve fulfillment in heaven. Based on these tenets, Jehovah's Witnesses view all political authority as temporary and impermanent and, at root, the devil's work.[88] Therefore, the group did not believe in any need to vote or otherwise participate in the political process. Viewed in this manner, their lack of participation in politics was religiously motivated, based on a desire to remain apolitical and neutral in the affairs of the world, and not on account of any hostility to democracy or Germany.[89] Moreover, there is no legal obligation to vote.[90] Thus, it was manifestly unfair to demand of Jehovah's Witnesses what was beyond the law.

Because the Constitutional Court viewed the actions of Jehovah's Witnesses as primarily religiously motivated, denial of public corporate status was an affront to their religious belief, under Article 4, and could not be countenanced unless there were good reasons for such action. No good explanation was forthcoming.

Viewing the case from this perspective, the Constitutional Court found no basis for denying Jehovah's Witnesses public corporate status based on their non-voting.[91] The principle of official neutrality forbids government from valuing a religion.[92] Religious tenets and their exercise are matters for the religion, not for the state.[93] It is within the autonomy of a religion to define its relationship with the state and political authorities.[94] A determination not to vote fits within the province of religion.

In the view of the Constitutional Court, Jehovah's Witnesses' failure to vote did not evidence disloyalty to the social order. Placement of this condition on a group is not required by the Basic Law. Requiring more of one group than another is a violation of the equality of treatment obligatory on the state.[95] The proper focus of authorities should be on whether a group is loyal to the legal order (*Rechtstreue*).[96] The core of this duty is adherence to the norms anchored in the famous Article 79(3) of the Basic Law. These norms form the essence of Germany: commitment to human dignity and its unfolding in the ensuing catalogue of rights; the *Rechtsstaat*; and democracy.[97]

88 102 BVerfGE at 397.
89 Ibid. at 380–81.
90 Ibid. at 380.
91 Ibid. at 394.
92 Ibid.
93 Ibid. at 394–95.
94 Ibid. at 396.
95 Ibid. at 380–81.
96 Ibid. at 379.
97 Ibid. at 392.

Assessing the Jehovah's Witness against this standard, the Constitutional Court did not find their behavior evidenced any lack of commitment to democracy. Their actions were a better measure of this than their religious beliefs.[98] Thus, the group was not a danger to democracy and denial of public corporate status could not be made on this basis. Nevertheless, whether Jehovah's Witnesses could obtain corporate status depended on resolution of certain other questions, including investigation of whether the group mistreated children through their educational method and coerced departing adult members to remain in the fold.[99] These actions would implicate other German core values, such as human dignity.

Baha'i

In *Baha'i* the Constitutional Court ruled that Article 4 self-autonomy allows Baha'i religion to rule itself as it likes, even when supreme religious authorities outside Germany order affairs and vote differently than communities within Germany.[100] The lower courts had invalided the self-autonomy of the Baha'i religion on the ground that foreign influence on the formation of the Baha'i faith in Germany was not consistent with the rules in forming and governing a religious organization.[101] The Constitutional Court ruled that the lower courts had misinterpreted Articles 4 and 137 of the Basic Law.

The Constitutional Court examined the affairs of the Baha'i and the German Civil Code rules in place and determined that the institutional organization and process of the Baha'i is consistent with the German Civil code and not contrary to the Basic Law. While the Baha'i is not a public organization, and does not desire to be, it qualifies as a religious organization because it is a living reality, a cultural tradition and has a general philosophy of what religion is. It only has about 5,000 members.[102] Articles 4 and 137 recognize not only freedom to believe and practice but also freedom to organize itself as a religious entity; these freedoms include organizational freedoms. Thus, the Baha'i can determine the form of organization it wants to be, including the types of common religious purposes. The content of organizational freedom includes the guarantee of freedom of belief and right to organize and run religious affairs in the manner it likes. Ideas form a group of like believers to realize faith. Building a religious organization helps open the way to realize the common religious purpose and legal personality. The organizational form must not be hierarchal, as is common in the Roman Catholic Church.[103]

98 Ibid. at 397–98.
99 Ibid. at 399.
100 83 BVerfGE 341 (1991).
101 Ibid. at 346–48.
102 Ibid. at 357.
103 Ibid. at 355–57.

Under the concept of organizational freedom, the religious entity is allowed to determine the religious ideas and principles that form an inviolable guarantee of belief and conscience. With this idea, religious organizations have not only a degree of formative freedom, but also some discretion in interpretation. It is important that religious organizations determine their own fate and govern their own affairs as matters of autonomy and self-determination in the form and operation that they want.[104] What the case demonstrates is the high degree of deference the Constitutional Court is willing to go to allow outside, minority religious groups to participate in society.

OSHO

Germany is an increasingly diverse society. So it is not unusual that the Constitutional Court would consider new religious or philosophical groups, such as at issue here, an eastern-oriented meditation society known as OSHO (previously the Bhagwan) movement. *OSHO* raises the critically important issue of the appropriate role of government in respect of the growth of new religious or philosophical groups inspired by the new wave of religious or philosophical orientation arising from the cultural revolution of the 1960s and its aftermath.[105] These new world groups have mainly been viewed as being on the fringe and with suspicion by the public. Not surprisingly, groups like these are often referred to as "sects" or "psycho sects" or "young religions," as was the case here. The groups have been subject to much criticism and accused of alienating members from their family and friends and manipulating them psychologically and financially.[106]

As a response, officials in government made a number of statements about these groups, trying to keep the public abreast of these developments and inform and warn the public about them. The government was especially concerned about the susceptibility of the young to the enticements of these groups and, accordingly, sought to inform the young and their parents about these groups.[107] The justification for performance of this information function came from the duty of the government to lead the state and offer guidance to social members, crystallized around the concept of *Staatsleitung*, duties flowing from the positive role of the state under the German constitutional system, according to the Constitutional Court's creative interpretation.

For our purposes, it is interesting to observe, first, that the OSHO group achieved Article 4 religious/philosophical protections on account of its organization pursuant

104 Ibid. at 356.

105 105 BVerfGE 279. The First Senate also evaluated aspects of OSHO in a chamber decision, BVerfGE, 1 BvR 1044/93 (12 August 2002).

106 Ibid. Marion Albers, Rethinking the Doctrinal System of Fundamental Rights: New Decisions of Federal Constitutional Court, 3 *German L. J.* No. 12 (1 November 2002).

107 Ibid.

to and consistent with German constitutional principles. In this regard, we can observe, again, application of Article 4 norms on an equal, level basis. If a group fulfills the requirements for recognition as a religious/philosophical organization, it obtains the benefits due such organizations under German law. In this regard, *OSHO* is of a similar tenor to *Jehovah's Witnesses*: both groups reside at the fringe of society but, having made their case as to their religious/philosophical nature, merited Article 4 protection. Interesting for us, in contrast to *Jehovah's Witnesses*, OSHO was a philosophical (*weltanschaulich*), not religious organization. Of course, Article 4 protects both forms of groups—religious or philosophical—an innovative and notable characteristic of German constitutionalism.

Vitally important to Article 4 protections is the obligation of officials to remain neutral in religious/philosophical matters. At issue was a series of governmental statements made about religious groups, in response to parliamentary questions and a speech by the Federal Minister for Youth, Family Affairs and Health.[108] These official statements did not refer specifically to the OSHO movement, but grouped them in reports under characterizations of "sect," "youth sect," a "young religion," and a "psycho sect." Likewise, but more negatively, other official statements characterized OSHO as "destructive," "pseudo-religious," and "manipulative." The OSHO movement complained about these characterizations as violating its rights, and wanted the government to retract these statements.[109]

Determination of the propriety of these statements called for resolution of the bounds of official neutrality in religious/philosophical issues. According to the court, the state is justified, on account of the doctrine of *Staatsleitung*, in confronting relevant issues of the day, including, if necessary, disseminating information and, where appropriate, warning the public. Members of society may not be able to obtain complete information or perspectives on issues, and the role of government is to assist them in being more fully informed.[110] Still, official rendering of information is subject to the need to maintain neutrality. Forced to work out this concept, the court ruled that the state is not prevented from disseminating information about religious/philosophical groups to the public, and can even render critical information or facts on them, their goals or activities; state officials can critically engage in public discourse over organizations and events in society. However, the state may not describe or depict these groups in a defamatory, discriminatory, distorted or inaccurate manner.[111] In an increasingly pluralistic society, it is useful to clarify important concepts, such as neutrality. All groups, majority and minority, benefit from clarity and equal application of legal norms. Society benefits as well, as neutrality helps assure peaceful coexistence between government and religion and among different religious groups.

108 Ibid.
109 Ibid.
110 Ibid. at 6.
111 Ibid. at 3.

Applying these principles, the Constitutional Court determined that official characterization of groups, such as OSHO, as "sects," "psycho sects," or "youth religions" was within the zone of official neutrality and, therefore, permissible. However, characterizations of "destructive," "pseudo-religious," or "manipulative" were beyond the pale and exceeded the bounds of neutrality and, therefore, constituted a violation of Article 4.[112]

Underlying these holdings lay the court's re-conception, in part of the concept of fundamental rights and, more particularly, how such rights might be violated. Ordinarily, rights are violated by government when government undertakes some action that directly impairs a right holder's zone of protection. This could not be the case here, as government had done nothing directly against the OSHO group. Rather, what was at issue was whether statements made to others—here the Parliament and the public—could nevertheless impair the rights of OSHO. Certainly such third party statements might impact negatively on a group. For example, the statements at issue in *OSHO*, especially those that were demeaning, might influence members to quit, prospective members not to join, or people not to commit financial or personal resources to the group.[113] Recognizing this, the court was forced to confront the doctrine of what constituted a violation of fundamental rights. Impairment of rights could occur not just in the usual case of direct official incursion against a right holder, but also in situations where facts or information directed at someone else can negatively affect a rights holder, as here.[114] We might refer to this as an indirect or mediated incursion of rights. The concept of mediated impairment of rights is a somewhat novel and innovative doctrine with important consequences for German law. It will be interesting to see how this doctrine unfolds. For now, we can recognize it as evidence of the disposition of the Constitutional Court to be flexible in applying the Basic Law to contemporary needs. We observed another illustration of this in the *Muslim Teacher's Head Scarf*, as the court adjusted state neutrality requirements away from a strict concept and toward a nurturing, supportive one. These adjustments bespeak a certain sensitivity and willingness to adjust to the needs of a changing society, moving toward pluralism.

OSHO is a complicated case with important consequences for German religious freedoms. *OSHO*, like *Muslim Teacher's Head Scarf*, displays a certain sensitivity by the court to the needs of emerging, minority dissenting groups. In *OSHO*, this entailed recognition of mediated impairment of Article 4 religious rights, which allowed the OSHO group to be successful in parts of its religious claims.

Second, the court established an important component of Article 4 freedoms that protect right holders from defamatory, discriminatory or false or distorting statements. This development fortifies the court's commitment to equal application of norms, which benefits especially minority groups. Plausible, but arguable, was

112 Ibid.

113 105 BVerfGE 279.

114 Ibid.

the court's validation of official statements like "psycho sect" or "youth religion" as neutral. It might be argued, on the other hand, that such characterizations are themselves denigrating, in comparison to conventional views of religion, as a psycho sect or youth religion would seem to have the connotation as outside the mainstream and, therefore, suspicious. In fact, official warnings directed at or implicating a group are hard to understand as other than a violation of the group's claim to equal treatment.[115] More important, then, is whether such incursion of rights is justified. Furthermore, it seems questionable whether government should take sides at all, rendering information or warnings, in religious/philosophical matters. It seems preferable to let people themselves decide these issues. The court would have been better served in *OSHO* by more clearly describing the appropriate relationship between neutrality and *Staatsleitung* so that its reasoning in asserting these doctrines would have been more apparent.

Third, it seems fair to say that *OSHO* represents a cautious approach to alternative, emerging religious, philosophical groups. No doubt, what to do with such groups is a difficult matter for government and society, not unlike the question of Scientology or *Jehovah's Witness.*[116] Certain of these groups are thought to engage in threatening conduct such as exploitation, manipulation or denial of gender rights and, thus, present serious constitutional issues. Careful deliberation is necessary to resolve how to treat constitutionally such alternative groups.

OSHO would seem to suggest a model of reduced protection for groups viewed as threatening in some way. Rendering of official warning impairs the rights of a group like OSHO. True, warnings could also be issued against other, majoritarian groups, like Roman Catholics or Protestants. But it is more likely the case that government, responding to majoritarian pressure, will warn groups perceived to be on the fringe.

Other Cases

In a Scientology case, a famous Austrian artist who lived in Germany was successful in his claim that his dignity and personality rights had been violated by an article published that defamed him, calling him an absolute scandal given his adherence to Scientology and the claim that he was brainwashing people.[117] The artist was a leading figure in the Scientology movement, an auditor, having gained experience of the movement while living in the USA. Human dignity and personality rights are central in German constitutional law; and, thus, defamatory statements lead to a violation of personality rights.

---

115 Dietrich Murswiek, *Das Bundesverffungsgericht und did Dogmatik mittelbar Grundrechts eingriffe: Zu der Glykol und der Osho Entscheidung von 26.6.2002*, Neue Zeitschrift fuer Verwaltungsrecht 1, 6 (2003).

116 102 BVerfGE 370.

117 99 BVerfGE 185 (1998).

In the *Kalifstaat* case, the Constitutional Court rejected the application of the Islamic religious group for legal status as a religious organization because the court determined that the group posed a threat to democracy, wanting to act in a militant and violent way and thus did not comply with the norms of the Basic Law, including human dignity, democracy, the rule of law, justice and democratic ideals.[118] The Islamic group especially showed disdain for Jews and Turkish politicians. The Islamic group was interested in advocating violence to accomplish its goals. Posing these kinds of threat to society is not a legitimate purpose of religion.

Observations

Like *Ritual Slaughter* and *Islamic Teacher's Head Scarf*, *Jehovah's Witnesses* evidences the Constitutional Court's application of religious freedoms in ways that fit the needs and perspectives of outsider groups. These cases called for sensitivity and understanding in assessing religious claims from the perspective of the believers, even when such practices were contrary to convention. With respect to religious freedoms, of course, that seems totally appropriate, since religions freedoms, like all basic freedoms, are to be available to all. Naturally, a sound way to judge religious freedom is from the perspective of the believer. The faith of the believer has more to do with religion than the estimation of any supervising authority, such as a court. A court needs to determine only whether the belief is sincerely held and meaningful to the believer.

Each case called for an adjustment in thought. In *Ritual Slaughter*, conventional views on how to treat animals were upturned in order to accommodate the faith of the believers. In *Islamic Teacher's Head Scarf*, acknowledgment of Islam called for re-conception of state neutrality norms in religion and civil service obligations. In *Jehovah's Witnesses*, the adjustment in thought was perhaps even greater. For at stake was one of the cardinals of the German constitutional order: guarantee of the stability of the democracy. But this seemed of less moment once the issue was properly understood. Religious conviction lies at the root of the Jehovah's Witnesses' actions. There was no real threat to the democracy.

Once the underlying claims had been identified and understood as religious, the cases fell within the normal pattern of German law. When claims of free exercise of religion are placed against the requirements of the general law, the general law must accommodate religious claims unless there is a very strong argument to the contrary. In *Islamic Teacher's Head Scarf*, accommodation was made, tentatively, against the general norms of civil service rules. Notable in these cases is that this general rule manifestly applies to all, majority and minority sects. In this respect, the Constitutional Court has signaled that fundamental rights apply equally to

118 BverfG, 1 BvR 536/03 (2 October 2003).

all. Equality in treatment speaks to a certain strength and confidence of religious freedom in Germany today.

Equality of treatment in religious affairs is notable. Apart from the claims of Islam, Jehovah's Witnesses and the Baha'i described here, we might also observe that Jews[119] and evangelical Christians[120] have received accommodation under German religious freedom. It is true that other aspects of religious freedom in Germany have been the subject of severe criticism. Most notable has been the ongoing controversy with respect to Scientology. Germany still views Scientology with suspicion, treating it as a cult and a commercial enterprise, not a religion. The German position is similar to that formerly held by the Internal Revenue Service, which revoked Scientology's tax exemption for a period of more than 30 years because "even if religious in nature [it was operated] for the enrichment of specific private individuals."[121] Recently, the German office of finance exempted Scientology from taxes on the basis of a treaty on double taxation with the United States. German authorities were careful to observe that the tax ruling did not imply recognition of Scientology as a religion. However, Scientology officials viewed the ruling as a first step in setting Scientology on the same plane as other religions in Germany.[122] Thus, some change in thinking is apparent concerning Scientology. And the OSHO movement has received limited religious protection out of concern that the group might pose a threat, especially to young people.

What we see then as we turn to the United States for an evaluation of state support of religion in American schools is that the German model is very decentralized, with each *Land* determining the school curriculum. The idea of local control over education resonates in both countries. The Christian community school is the norm, but we have also observed how three German states are distinctly non-religious, including the major population center, Berlin. Both schools containing religion or ethics as a normal part of the curriculum must accommodate dissenters—those students choosing not to participate—by excusing them from required attendance in those classes and, upon request, reasonably creating options for them more suitable to their religious/philosophical beliefs. Further, in Christian community schools, teaching of religion must be restricted to religion class, and Christianity

119 *Cross in Courtroom*, 35 BVerfGE 366 (1973) (ruling that cross displayed in courtroom must be removed in view of objection from Jewish lawyer).

120 *Blood Transfusion Case*, 32 BVerfGE 98 (1971) (evangelical Christian husband relieved from criminal penalties for allowing wife to die due to loss of blood and abstinence from blood transfusion because actions were religiously motivated).

121 Michael Browne, Note, Should Germany Stop Worrying and Love the Octopus? Freedom of Religion and the Church of Scientology in Germany and the United States, 9 *Ind. Int'l & Comp. L. Rev.* 155, 191 (1998) (citation omitted). See also Arthur C. Helton and Jochen Müenker, Religion and Persecution: Should the United States Provide Refuge to German Scientologists?, 11 *Int'l J. Refugee L.* 310, 311 (1999).

122 Frankfurter Allgemeine Zeitung, "Steuerbefreiung für Scientology," No. 29, page 2 (4 February 2003); Spiegel Online, "Scientology ab sofort steuerfrei," at http://www.spiegel.de/wirtschaft;0,1518,233557,00.html (3 February 2003).

may be referred to, outside of religion class, only as a cultural or historical, but not religious force. Finally, there can be no discrimination against other religious/ philosophical views. In these respects, we can see that German doctrine is following its own version of state neutrality, non-discrimination and non-coercion. How these German doctrines compare with American doctrines is our next topic.

Chapter 8
Church-State Relations in the United States

Public Support of Religion in American Schools

Public Schools

It is strange, in a sense, to speak of public support of religion in American schools in the twenty-first century. With the dawn of modern Establishment Clause jurisprudence, in the 1947 *Everson v. Board of Education*, the idea of separation of church and state was launched, with mixed effect in Supreme Court jurisprudence, but with deep effect in the American psyche.[1] The *Everson* Court unanimously articulated a distinctly separationist approach to the Establishment Clause, although the justices split 5-4 over application of separationist philosophy to the issue under review. The court upheld provision of state-supported busing of Catholic students on the ground that the provision of busing was a neutral service, analogous to police and fire protection. The dissent disagreed, finding this to be a violation of separation of church and state under a more absolutist application of this principle.[2] As Justice Rutledge observed: "The great condition of religious liberty is that it be maintained free from sustenance, as also from other interferences, by the state. For when it comes to rest upon that secular foundation, it vanishes with the resting."[3] For the dissent, the purpose of the Establishment Clause was to "create a complete and permanent separation" of church and state.[4] Through the course of the Warren Court and into the early Burger Court, the court understood the Establishment Clause to hold for separation of church and state, although application of the principle yielded mixed results, sometimes prohibiting state aid of religion, sometimes supporting state aid of religion.

For some time in the modern age marked by *Everson*, and even today, the court and Americans believed in a model of separation of church and state. The clear principles of the separationist philosophy, originating in *Everson*, are that government may not set up a church, aid one religion over another or influence a person over religious beliefs.[5] A further clear principle of separationist philosophy

---

1 330 U.S. 1, 16 (1947) ("In the words of Jefferson, the clause was intended to erect a 'wall of separation between Church and State.'") (quoting *Reynolds v. United States*, 94 U.S. 145, 164 (1879)).

2 *Everson v. Board of Educ.*, 330 U.S. 1.

3 Ibid. at 53 (J. Rutledge, dissenting, citing James Madison's *Remonstrance*).

4 Ibid. at 31–32 (J. Rutledge, dissenting).

5 Ibid. at 15.

is that there can be no public support of religious instruction in schools. Until 1983, the court had never sustained any public support for religious instruction, being careful to approve state support for religion only over secular matters such as, for example, the lending of secular textbooks.[6] Since the public school is the forum for inculcation of democratic and constitutional values, adherence to separationism made sense as a plausible interpretation of constitutional text as influenced by Enlightenment tradition.

Most American students attend public schools, where religious instruction does not occur as part of the public school curriculum, as is the norm in German schools and UK schools, although many English schools avoid religious instructions. A case like *Epperson v. Arkansas*[7] would appear to place an insurmountable roadblock to public support for religious instruction in public schools. In *Epperson*, the court held unconstitutional an Arkansas statute that prohibited "the teaching in its public schools and universities of the theory that man evolved from other species" [evolution] because it was "tailored to the principles or prohibitions of [any] religious sect or dogma."[8] Creation science, the court concluded, is a religiously based theory and therefore incompatible with Establishment Clause principles.

The closest the court has come to allowing religious instruction in public schools during the school day are time-release programs for religious instruction, which must occur off public school premises. For example, in *Zorach v. Clauson* the court held that students can constitutionally be dismissed from school premises to attend religious education conducted in off-school premises. Non-participants in religion are required to stay on school premises.[9] The movement toward allowing religious instruction in the schools has progressed in the recent *Good News Club v. Milford Central School*, where the court held that prayer and Bible lessons could be held after school hours, on public school premises, for students who attended the public schools.[10] *Good News* is distinguishable from *Zorach* on the ground that the religious instruction occurs outside the regular school curriculum and day, but certainly is a dramatic movement in the direction of public support for religious instruction. By contrast, in *McCollum v. Board of Education*, the court found it unconstitutional to release public school students from regular classes to attend religious instruction on public school premises during the school day.[11] What these

6 *Bd. of Educa. v Allen*, 392 U.S. 236 (1968) (permissible to lend textbooks on secular topics). The path-breaking case was *Mueller v. Allen*, 463 U.S. 388 (1983) (court sustained Minnesota state tax deduction for tuition, textbook and transportation expenses; 96 per cent of the benefits of which went to religious schools).

7 393 U.S. 97 (1968).

8 Ibid. at 98, 106. Accord, *Edwards v. Aguillard*, 482 U.S. 578 (1987) (Louisiana statute requiring teaching of "creation science" alongside evolution unconstitutional because such curricular choice advanced a religious viewpoint).

9 *Zorach v. Clauson*, 343 U.S. 306 (1952).

10 *Good News Club v. Milford Central School*, 533 U.S. 98 (2001).

11 *McCollum v. Board of Education*, 333 U.S. 203 (1948).

cases show is that religious instruction can occur during regular school days off school premises and on school premises after the school day has finished, but religious instruction cannot occur on school premises during the regular school day.

So, with respect to religious instruction in public schools, it seems fair to conclude that the United Kingdom and Germany diverge from the approach of the United States. The standard United Kingdom and German model allows religion to be taught as a regular part of the school curriculum, in contrast to the United States. There are, of course, exceptions. The German *Länder* of Berlin, Bremen and Brandenburg do not include religion as a regular part of the school curriculum, although the option is available. It is also possible for communities in other *Länder* to have secular, non-religious schools. And many of the UK schools do not respect the law requiring religious instruction in the school. In the United States, off-public school premises time release programs[12] allow religion to be taught and religious instruction may also occur after school hours at public schools.[13] However, religious instruction cannot occur during the regular school day, a contrast with British and German law.[14] Thus, neither country is absolutist in its teaching or non-teaching of religion in public schools.

Private Religious Schools

The forum for public support of religion in the United States shifted dramatically since *Mueller v. Allen*,[15] in 1983, from public schools to private, religious schools under the leadership of Justice William Rehnquist. Public accommodation of religion through its treatment as an equal claimant on the public fisc ranks with other notable accomplishments of the Rehnquist Court, such as diminished free exercise rights,[16] stronger federalism[17] and enhanced police powers with respect to criminal due process rights.[18] At war with the stricter separationist direction of Establishment Clause jurisprudence shepherded by prior courts (most notably the Warren Court), the Rehnquist Court reworked Establishment Clause doctrine away from a separationist orientation (represented most prominently by *Lemon v. Kurtzman*)[19] toward an approach of formal neutrality, which holds that government

12 *Zorach v. Clauson*, 343 U.S. 306 (1952).

13 *Good News Club v. Milford Central School*, 533 U.S. 98 (2001).

14 *McCollum v. Board of Education*, 333 U.S. 203 (1948).

15 463 U.S. 388 (1983).

16 *Employment Division, Dept. of Human Services v. Smith*, 494 U.S. 872 (1990).

17 *Lopez v. United States*, 514 U.S. 549 (1995).

18 See, e.g., *Illinois v. Caballes*, 125 S. Ct. 834 (2005) (police can allow trained dog to sniff stopped car for drugs without any need for suspicion of a narcotics violation).

19 403 U.S. 602 (1971). Under *Lemon*, the court synthesized various strands of Establishment Clause jurisprudence employed by the Warren Court to ask whether, first, the measure had a secular purpose, second, its main effect neither advanced nor inhibited religion and, third, did it foster an excessive government entanglement with religion. Many

must treat religion on terms equal to other, non-religious institutions with respect to the distribution of public benefits. Stated a different way, government may not favor one religion over another or over non-religion, nor disfavor any particular religion/non-religion, but government may support religion generally on the same terms as it supports secular institutions.[20] Under the *Lemon* test, the Burger Court synthesized various strands of Establishment Clause jurisprudence employed by the Warren Court to ask whether, first, the measure had a secular purpose, second, its main effect neither advanced nor inhibited religion and, third, did it foster an excessive government entanglement with religion?

It is this concept of formal neutrality we want to compare to German law. Some caveats are in order. First, there is little constitutional authorization of public support for religion in American public schools, where most American students attend. Secondly, formal neutrality to date has mainly been applied to non-public, primarily religious schools. Approximately 11 per cent of American students attend private schools, and approximately 87 per cent of private school students attend religious schools, with Catholicism constituting about 55 per cent of these religious schools.[21] Thus, the degree of national public support for religion in school is, relatively speaking, small. Third, our focus is one of following constitutional doctrine and jurisprudence. Our concentration is on a comparative look at British, German and American doctrine on church-state relations in the schools. Let us now turn to an examination of American doctrine.

The court's translation of formal neutrality into a rule of law consists of two main inquiries. Government may aid religion when the government program is "[1] neutral with respect to religion, and provides assistance directly to a broad class of citizens who, in turn, direct government aid to religious schools [2] wholly as a result of their own genuine and … independent private choice."[22] Neutrality and individual, private choice are the two ingredients of the test.

Unpacking these ideas, we can see, first, that the inquiry into neutrality is designed to place religious claimants on par with other claimants in society

---

current justices on the court decry the test, none more notably than Justice Scalia, *Lamb's Chapel v. Center Moriches Union Free School District*, 508 U.S. 384, 398 (1993) (Scalia, J., concurring), but the court has not yet formally repudiated *Lemon.* Justice Scalia criticized the *Lemon* test by analogizing it to a ghost:

> a ghoul in a late-night horror movie that repeatedly sits up in its grave and shuffles abroad, after being repeatedly killed and buried. [I]t is there to scare us [when] we wish it to do so, but we can command it to return to the tomb at will. When we wish to strike down a practice it forbids, we invoke it, when we wish to uphold a practice it forbids, we ignore it entirely. [Such] a docile and useful monster is worth keeping around, at least in a somnolent state; one never knows when one might need them.

20 This description reworks the description of non-preferentialism in Stone, Seidman et al. *Constitutional Law* 1495 (5th ed. 2005).

21 National Center for Education Statistics, at www.nces.ed.gov (visited June 2005); Council for American Private Education, at www.capenet.org/facts.html.

22 *Zelman v. Simmons-Harris*, 536 U.S. 639, 652 (2002).

for governmental aid, as seems consistent with a doctrine of formal neutrality. The driving force of the idea is to discourage government hostility to religion as seemed the case, to some, by an approach of separationism. Moreover, publicly supporting religion increases its ability to advocate its values in the marketplace of ideas. For many believers, public articulation and acknowledgment of religion is an indispensably sacred part of their lives. Historically, formal neutrality is rooted in Puritan philosophy as it influenced the more accommodationist civic republican views of framing generation people such as George Washington and John Adams, who advocated for the importance of religion as a source of morals in society and the two, together, as a prop for the promotion of civility in society.[23]

Fine and good. There is certainly an equality component to religious protection,[24] as with other rights, such as free speech[25] or privacy rights.[26] In fact, an equality component may underlie most, if not all, human rights. Every person has an equal claim to basic rights. But the source for church-state relations in the United States Constitution is the Establishment Clause, which provides government "shall make no law respecting an establishment of religion," not the Equal Protection Clause, which more reasonably bestows textual authority for a norm of neutrality. The Establishment Clause itself does not self-evidently bestow an equality claim, although equality and neutrality are certainly core components of "the essential rights and liberties" of religion.[27] If questions concerning equal treatment of religion were raised under the Equal Protection Clause, it would make sense to inquire into neutrality, a driving force of equal protection under the rubric that similarly situated people or institutions must be treated similarly or, if dissimilar treatment is to be allowed, it must be justified by a persuasive reason. Equal protection would seem to handle well claims for equal treatment.

---

23 Arlin M. Adams and Charles J. Emmerich, A Heritage of Religious Liberty, 137 *U. Pa. L. Rev.* 1579 (1989); John Witte, Jr., The Essential Rights and Liberties of Religion in the American Constitutional Experiment, 71 *Notre Dame L. Rev.* 386–87 (1996). Chief Justice Rehnquist developed his historical case for non-preferentialism in his important dissent in *Wallace v. Jaffree*, 472 U.S. 38, 91–114 (1985) (Rehnquist, J., dissenting).

24 *Memorial and Remonstrance*, cited in *Everson*, 330 U.S. at 66.

25 *Police Dep't of Chicago v. Mosley*, 408 U.S. 92, 96 (1972) ("There is an 'equality of status in the field of ideas,' and government must afford all points of view an equal opportunity to be heard.").

26 *Lawrence v. Texas*, 539 U.S. 558, 575 (2003) ("Equality of treatment and the due process right to demand respect for conduct protected by the substantive guarantee of liberty are linked in important respects, and a decision on the latter point advances both interests.").

27 Witte, *supra* note 23, at 388. The court itself has acknowledged that inquiry into neutrality is an Equal Protection norm. See, e.g., *Church of the Lukumi Babalu Aye v. City of Hialeath*, 505 U.S. 520, 540 (1993) ("In determining if the object of a law is a neutral one under the Free Exercise Clause, we can … find guidance in our equal protection cases."); *Walz v. Tax Comm'n of New York*, 397 U.S. 664, 696 (1970) (Harlan, J., concurring) ("Neutrality in its application requires an equal protection mode of analysis.").

It may certainly be helpful to borrow equal protection components to buttress Establishment Clause arguments, as is done, for example, in free speech claims.[28] By comparison, however, a free speech claim fundamentally relies on tests more derivable from textual authority.[29] The point, simply stated, is that free speech, as other constitutional provisions, has a main test to gauge its infringement derived from textual authority and relies on equality interests as important, but supplemental, support. By contrast, formal neutrality does not center around the textual enumeration of the Establishment Clause but instead drafts an equality component as a main part of the test. In this respect, the neutrality inquiry is a curious choice for the court, at least based on a textual methodology.

The choice is also curious as a matter of text in that it does not directly address the Establishment Clause textual prohibition on governmental establishment of religion. The language choice of the Establishment Clause, after all, delimits governmental authority over religion. Government "shall make no law respecting an establishment of religion," not an establishment of politics, economics or postmodernism. The focus, therefore, should more appropriately center around governmental choices in respect of religion. For example, does government establish, promote, aid, favor, disfavor, inhibit or impede religion, to name a few possibilities. In this respect, the three-part *Lemon* test has a stronger textual tether in that the three questions posed concern themselves with the degree of governmental support for religion. Under *Lemon*, the court asks "First, the statute must have a secular legislative [not religious] purpose; second, its principal or primary effect must be one that neither advances nor inhibits religion; finally, the statute must not foster 'an excessive government entanglement with religion.'"[30]

Moving beyond text to substance, it is also notable that the court's questioning of neutrality is simply a formal, facial one. The court only looks to see if measures are designed to make benefits generally available to claimants, religious or non-religious. As the court states in *Zelman,* "a government aid program is neutral with respect to religion, and provides assistance directly to a broad class of citizens … ."[31]

28 *Mosley*, 408 U.S. at 96.

29 For example, the prohibition on governmental abridgement of ideas has as its center a presumption against censorship or other official tampering with ideas, which seems consistent with a textual mandate that specifies government is to make no law abridging speech. See, e.g., *R.A.V. v. St. Paul*, 505 U.S. 377, 382 (1992) ("The First Amendment generally prevents government from proscribing speech [because] of disapproval of the ideas expressed.").

30 403 U.S. 602, 612–13 (1971).

31 See, e.g., *Zelman*, 536 U.S. at 652. To follow Professor Laycock's dichotomy, the Rehnquist Court's formal neutrality doctrine would constitute formal neutrality, not substantive neutrality. Douglas Laycock, Formal, Substantive, and Disaggregated Neutrality Toward Religion, 39 *Depaul L. Rev.* 993, 999–1003 (1990). Formal neutrality has great appeal in its "simplicity and apparent even-handedness." Ibid. at 999. But it also has drawbacks.

The court does not engage in a more intense scrutiny of the substance of neutrality, as is more characteristic of free speech[32] or equal protection[33] questions.

A review of several of the measures upheld under formal neutrality illustrates the point. Focusing first on formal neutrality, the court in *Mueller v. Allen* upheld a Minnesota statute that permitted taxpayers to deduct as expenses from gross income "amounts not exceeding $500 [for students in grades kindergarten to sixth grade] and $700 [for students in grades seven to twelve] for tuition, textbooks and transportation expenses.[34] In *Zelman*, the court upheld an Ohio pilot program designed to aid the Cleveland schools by providing tuition aid for students in K-3 to attend public or private schools and tutorial aid for students who remain in public schools.[35] On their face, both measures apply evenhandedly to public and private school students. So far, so good.

As a matter of substance, however, there is a significant disparity between allocation of public monies to religion as compared to non-religious claimants. In the Minnesota program at issue in *Mueller*, the vast bulk of tax benefits were claimed by religious students, likely as high as 96 per cent.[36] In *Zelman*, 96 per cent of the students participating in the pilot program were enrolled in religious schools and 82 per cent of the private schools participating in the program were religious schools.[37] Certainly statistics may be misleading.[38] But any fair assessment of the evidence reasonably discloses that the substance of the measures approved in *Mueller* and *Zelman* impacts disproportionately favorably on religion. At a minimum, these measures constitute indirect official subsidies of religion.[39] Since most legislators are likely aware of the composition of their constituencies—including their general religious makeup and number of parochial schools—the subsidies may even be more overt. But the court does not examine the underlying motivations of legislators.

Nor does the court examine the empirical data resulting from the programs.[40] As stated baldly by Chief Justice Rehnquist, "We would be loath to adopt a rule grounding the constitutionality of a facially neutral law on annual reports

---

32 See, e.g., *Gooding v. Wilson*, 405 U.S. 518 (1972) (fighting words statute unconstitutional because applied overly broad by Georgia).

33 See, e.g., *Yick Wo v. Hopkins*, 118 U.S. 351 (1886) (facially neutral ordinance unconstitutional because selectively applied negatively against Chinese).

34 463 U.S. 388, 391 n. 1 (1983).

35 536 U.S. 639, 645 (2002).

36 *Zelman*, 536 U.S. at 658; *Mueller*, 463 U.S. at 401.

37 536 U.S. at 647.

38 Chief Justice Rehnquist observed that school programs in other states, such as Maine or Utah, would likely result in a lesser percentage (perhaps less than 45 per cent) of the aid going to religious schools. Ibid. at 657–58.

39 *Mueller*, 463 U.S. at 404 (Marshall, J., dissenting).

40 The failure to employ effects analysis is in contrast to other constitutional domains, such as dormant commerce clause, where effects analysis is a primary inquiry into the constitutionality of measures. See, e.g., *Hunt v. Washington State Apple Advertising*

reciting the extent to which various classes or private citizens claimed benefits under the law."[41] The point is simple: the inquiry into neutrality is facial only and has the effect of favoring religion, which, in fact, may be the point. Public schools, of course, are directly funded by tax monies and, accordingly, do not need to participate in these aid programs. In fairness, parents of parochial students already pay taxes to support the public schools. Receiving the benefits of some tax dollars for religious educational costs could certainly be viewed as only fair. Still, regardless of the equities, our focus must be on the constitutional question.

The second element of formal neutrality involves breaking the direct link between government and church by making monies available to people, who then exercise "genuine and … independent private choice" to spend the monies as they like, including for religious education if they so desire.[42] In this way, the choice to support religion is made by the individual, and not the government.[43]

There is something to be said for this. Channeling money to people, not government, facilitates individual choice, which might plausibly break the link between government and religion. This is a point well worth considering. Private decision-making is different from government decision-making. No doubt, reasonable people will differ over this. Moreover, this doctrine has the added benefit of encouraging voluntary group-based religious value-formation, which can help animate a democracy and add a significant and worthy voice to public debate.

Yet, the Establishment Clause delimits governmental power; it does not speak to individual behavior. Personal choices are quite irrelevant to the Establishment Clause.[44] Thus, the relevant question would seem to be whether the governmental action constitutes an establishment of religion. Whether the governmental choice is accomplished by direct or indirect means should have some bearing on this question, but not be dispositive. The real question is whether a governmental choice to support religion, directly or indirectly, is an establishment of religion. There can be, no doubt, a difference of opinion on this.

To determine whether government is, indeed, supporting religion heavily enough to constitute an "establishment" should entail a probing examination of the purpose, background and effects of the measure. Certainly the seriousness of the question merits a careful review of such a measure, one more probing than the facial review employed under formal neutrality. The significant amount of aid and its transparently primary effect in benefitting religion under formal neutrality would suggest tilting more on the side of finding an establishment of religion. It is certainly an open question as to what constitutes an "establishment."

Comm'n, 432 U.S. 333 (1977) (North Carolina facially neutral statute unconstitutional because practical effect of measure is to burden Washington state apples).

41 *Mueller*, 463 U.S. at 401.

42 *Zelman*, 536 U.S. at 652.

43 *Witters*, 474 U.S. 481, 488 (1986).

44 *Zelman*, 536 U.S. at 685–86 (Stevens, J., dissenting).

Is an establishment to be judged by text, originalism, accommodationism, separationism or some combination of all or some of them? We would first need to set forth a plausible theory of the Establishment Clause—establishing a principled standard of law—in order to make this judgment. That endeavor will call for significant effort.

At bottom, we can see that the court applies a facial review of these formally neutral governmental programs that has the effect of supporting indirectly religion. We can also see that formal neutrality is a far cry from the separationist approach of the Warren Court and of the philosophy of Thomas Jefferson and James Madison. Instead, formal neutrality is more in accord with the aspects of the Puritan tradition that encouraged and advanced official support of religion and influenced the religious orientation of notable civil republicans, like George Washington and John Adams. There is also some evidence that evangelicals, like Isaac Backus, would willingly accept official support of religion, insofar as it did not interfere with the core concern of liberty of conscience.[45] In this respect, formal neutrality has more in common with the Massachusetts experience than the 1784–86 Virginia one.[46]

In sum, as a matter of constitutional methodology, formal neutrality does not seem clearly rooted in the text of the First Amendment, but is firmly rooted in the Puritan tradition that carried over to influence important accommodationist civic republicans, like George Washington and John Adams. For sure formal neutrality—with its appeal to equality and neutrality—can draw upon one of the main "essential rights and liberties" of religion.[47] And formal neutrality, consistent with accomodationist civic republicans, can draw upon a long history of official United States accommodation of religious practice. As a matter of constitutional methodology, formal neutrality is on weakest ground as a matter of text; it is on strongest ground as a matter of tradition; and is on solid ground as a matter of the Puritan-influenced strand of historical practice. Thus, we can see that the debate between separationism and accommodationism is itself a titan struggle over constitutional methodology: text; framers' intent; and historical practice.

For our purposes, we are concerned with two primary objectives. First, assessing the degree of public support for religion in schools in the United States. Second, how does American church-state law on this question compare to British

45 Mark Howe, *The Garden and the Wilderness: Religion and Government in American Constitutional History* 11–12 (1985) ("The evangelical principle of separation endorsed a host of favoring tributes to faith [so] substantial that they have produced in the aggregate what may fairly be described as a de facto establishment of religion [in which] the religious institution as a whole is maintained and activated by forces not kindled directly by government"). See also Adams and Emmerich, *supra* note 23, at 1593 ("Backus expressed no opposition to Sabbath laws, teaching Calvinistic doctrine in the public schools, proscribing blasphemy, and conducting official days of fasting and prayer.").

46 Witte, *supra* note 23, at 379–80, 385–87.

47 Witte, *supra* note 23, at 388.

and German law. A third objective, to be pursued later, is what we can learn from this comparative experience.

The court's change in doctrine from separationism to formal neutrality has resulted in a decisive shift to state support of religion. The shift is brought out dramatically by observing the state of affairs prior to formal neutrality. Under a separationist approach, it was unconstitutional to aid non-public (mainly religious) schools by reimbursing parents for portions of tuition costs;[48] engaging public school teachers in remedially educating parochial students;[49] lending instructional materials and equipment;[50] or paying the costs of field trips for purposes related to secular courses.[51] Today, these forms of state support of religion are constitutional under formal neutrality.

Interestingly, however, we must observe that there has never been absolute or, perhaps, even strict separationism in the United States. Even under a separationist approach, government could support religious schools in certain respects. For example, as noted by the court in *Lemon*: "Our prior holdings do not call for total separation; total separation is not possible in an absolute sense. Some relationship between government and religious organizations is inevitable."[52] The court in *Lemon* goes on to say, "the line of separation, far from being a 'wall,' is a blurred, indistinct and variable barrier depending on all the circumstances of a particular relationship."[53] Still, what is quite important is that some line between church and state is necessary so that there will not be political divisiveness.

So, we might say that even in the pre-Rehnquist Court era, the court vacillated somewhat uneasily between separationism and accommodationism. However, a major difference was that under this earlier approach of separationism, the court distinguished between state support of religious schools over secular matters[54] and sectarian matters. It was absolutely off limits for government to aid religion in core religious matters,[55] and it was irrelevant whether the nature of official

48 *Sloan v. Lemon*, 413 U.S. 825 (1973); *School Dist. of Grand Rapids v. Ball*, 473 U.S. 373 (1985).

49 *Aguilar v. Felton*, 473 U.S. 402 (1985) *o.r.*, *Agostini v. Felton*, 521 U.S. 203 (1997).

50 *Meek v. Pilterger*, 421 U.S. 349 (1975) and *Wolman v. Walter*, 433 U.S. 229 (1977), *o.r. Mitchell v. Helms*, 530 U.S. 793 (2000).

51 *Meek.*

52 *Lemon*, 403 U.S. at 614. Under separationism, government could support religious schools by busing parochial students, *Everson*; lending textbooks on secular topics, *Bd. of Educa. v. Allen*, 392 U.S. 236 (1968); or reimbursing them for costs of state-mandated and state-composed testing requirements. *Comm. for Public Educa. v. Regan*, 444 U.S. 646 (1980).

53 403 U.S. at 614.

54 E.g. *Everson*, 330 U.S. 1 (state support of busing of parochial students is neutral social welfare aid, analogous to police and fire protection).

55 E.g., *Lemon v. Kurtzman*, 403 U.S. 602, 617 (1971) (in invalidating state subsidy of religious teachers, court observes: "We cannot ignore the danger that a teacher under

support was accomplished directly or indirectly.[56] Moreover, the court in the pre-Rehnquist Court era tended to agree on doctrine. Most of the justices of this era were committed to separation of church and state as stating the proper relationship. Their disagreements were over how strict to apply separationism to particular factual settings.[57]

By contrast, under formal neutrality significant amounts of public aid have been directed to religion. Although the aid was formally neutrally available to all claimants, the vast majority receiving the aid were religious schools.[58] The most dramatic sums of public aid directed to religion include subsidization of parental costs of parochial school tuition;[59] supply of computer, media, laboratory, library and teaching aids;[60] and provision of public school remedial education.[61] Let us examine some of these cases more carefully.

In *Mitchell v. Helms*, the court sanctioned federal provision of educational materials to religious schools. The material included library and media materials, computer hardware and software, and instructional materials such as books, movie projectors and overhead projectors.[62] *Mitchell* breaks ground in one notable respect. The plurality simply brushed aside the clear diversion of the public aid from secular to sectarian purposes.[63] Perhaps the court was reluctant to scrutinize recipients' use of monies. But we might more plausibly understand this as simply a consequence of formal neutrality. The real point of formal neutrality is equal treatment for religious groups as compared to non-religious groups. Such equality

---

religious control and discipline poses to the separation of the religious from the purely secular aspects of precollege education").

56 *School Dist. of Grand Rapids v. Ball*, 473 U.S. 373, 393–94 (1985).

57 So observes Justice Souter in his recounting of the history of the Establishment Clause. E.g., *Mitchell v. Helms*, 530 U.S. at 876 (dissenting).

58 Of the participating schools in the year in question evaluated in *Mitchell v. Helms*, 530 U.S. 793 (2000), 41 of 47 were religious (87 per cent), a percentage close to other cases, like *Zelman* (96 per cent) and *Mueller* (96 per cent).

59 *Zelman*, 536 U.S. 639 (2002) (public money supports 90 per cent of parochial school tuition costs in instances of severely poor students), Ibid. at 707 (Souter, J., dissenting) ("sheer quantity of aid unprecedented"); *Mueller v. Allen*, 463 U.S. 388 (1983) (state tax deduction for parochial school tuition costs up to $500 or $700, depending on case).

60 *Mitchell v. Helms*, 530 U.S. 793 (2000).

61 *Agostini v. Felton*, 521 U.S. 203 (1997).

62 530 U.S. 793, 803 (2000).

63 *Mitchell*, 530 U.S. at 833–34 ("[W]e agree with the dissent that there is evidence of actual diversion and that, were the safeguards anything other than anemic, there would almost certainly be more such evidence. … In any event … evidence of actual diversion and the weakness of the safeguards against actual diversion are not relevant to the constitutional inquiry, whatever relevance they may have under the statute and regulations."); *contra*, ibid. at 840 (O'Connor, J., concurring) ("I also disagree with the plurality's conclusion that actual diversion of government indoctrination is consistent with the Establishment Clause.").

of treatment leads, of course, to official support of religion, as it could to official support of non-religion if the social reality of statistical configurations was different.

In *Agostini*, the court approved provision of federally funded remedial education, provided by public school teachers, to parochial students on the school premises of the religious schools, in direct contradiction of the court's earlier finding that such was unconstitutional.[64] The symbolic presence of public school employees rendering services to parochial schools was no longer relevant in determining whether such constituted an official endorsement of religion.[65] Likewise, it was no longer relevant whether an excessive entanglement of state in religion occurred by reason of the significant monitoring by government of religion as to the uses of the aid for secular purposes required by the statute. The court abandoned the presumption that any mixing of church and state meant religious indoctrination.[66] The contrast in approach between *Agostini* and *Aguilar* simply illustrates the difference in approach between formal neutrality and separationism, as would a comparison of almost any case decided before or after the advent of formal neutrality. And the court went on to acknowledge the change in Establishment Clause doctrine rendered by decisions like *Zobrest v. Catalina Foothills School District*,[67] *Witters v. Wash. Dept. of Services for the Blind*,[68] and *Rosenberger v. Rectors and Visitors of the Univ. of Virginia*.[69] These decisions undermined *Aguilar*, and *Ball*;[70] accordingly, the court overruled them.

For our purposes what is relevant to observe is the quite substantial channeling of governmental aid to religious schools accomplished through the indirect route of formal neutrality. As the court frankly acknowledges, a governmental program that is neutral and operates by way of the private choice of people permits governmental aid to reach religious institutions.[71] So blessed, therefore, is official provision of tuition relief;[72] library and teaching aids;[73] remedial educational services[74] and learning;[75] and vocational aids.[76]

The direct/indirect role of government in funding religion is the doctrinal line the court is drawing at present. The endpoint of formal neutrality, for now, is

64 521 U.S. 203 (1997), *o.r., Aguilar v. Felton*, 473 U.S. 402 (1985).

65 Ibid. at 234–35.

66 Ibid. at 233–34. The court observed that the financial costs associated with compliance with *Aguilar* were significant and burdensome. 521 U.S. at 213.

67 509 U.S. 1 (1993).

68 474 U.S. 481 (1986).

69 515 U.S. 819 (1995).

70 473 U.S. 373.

71 *Zelman*, 536 U.S. at 652.

72 *Zelman*; *Mueller*.

73 *Mitchell*.

74 *Agostini*.

75 *Witters*.

76 *Zobrest*.

reached by *Locke v. Washington*, where the court upheld Washington's prohibition of direct funding of pastoral education.[77] Such open, overt official funding of the religious mission went too far, at least for some.[78] And so we are left again with a distinction between direct governmental funding of religion (unconstitutional) and indirect funding (constitutional).

Public subsidy of religious education is at odds with much of the early American theoretical writing on liberty of conscience and its protection from mixing of church and state that informed the framing of the First Amendment religious protections. It would appear to violate the fundamental norm of freedom from coercion of conscience insofar as it forces any dissenting taxpayers to fund religious education against their will. Most formally neutral programs do not provide opportunity for opt-out provisions for dissenters, in contrast to early American practice and current British and German practice.[79] The conception of liberty of conscience forms the core of Establishment Clause protections, both historically[80] and today.[81]

As formulated by Roger Williams, for example, the integrity of freedom of conscience included a freedom from coercion of conscience as the essence of the religious experience and the basis for religious freedom.[82] As stated by Thomas Jefferson, coercion of conscience is inconsistent with true belief because: "no man shall be compelled to frequent or support any religious worship, place or ministry whatsoever … "; official support of religion leads to its corruption; and that opinion, including religious opinion, is not within the jurisdiction of government.[83] As reworked by James Madison, religion is a fundamental, natural right we owe to our Creator, and it "can be directed only by reason and conviction, not force or violence." Religion is to be left "to the conviction and conscience of every man;

77 540 U.S. 712 (2004). Even though decided on Free Exercise grounds, *Locke* represents the same type of programs considered under formal neutrality, as does *Rosenberger v. Rectors and Visitors of Univ. of Virginia*, 515 U.S. 819 (1995), decided under free speech grounds.

78 Chief Justice Rehnquist wrote then majority opinion sustaining Washington's constitutional prohibition on funding religious education. Perhaps he was motivated by federalism concerns; Washington could determine to prohibit what Ohio, for example, in *Zelman* allowed. Justices Thomas and Scalia would have found the funding constitutional, relying in part on *Witters*. *Locke*, 540 U.S. at 729–30.

79 Noah Feldman, The Intellectual Origins of the Establishment Clause, 77 *N.Y.U. L. Rev.* 351 (2002).

80 Ibid. at 346, 398.

81 *Lee v. Weisman*, 505 U.S. 577 (1992).

82 Roger Williams, *The Bloody Tenet, of Persecution, for Cause of Conscience* (1644).

83 Thomas Jefferson, *A Bill for Establishing Religious Freedom* (12 June 1779) (reprinted in 5 *The Founders' Constitution* 77 (Philip B. Kurland and Ralph Lerner eds, 1987).

and it is the right of every man to exercise it as these may dictate."[84] For Madison, forced payment of tax monies in support of religious education constituted an establishment of religion.[85] Any "authority which can force a citizen to contribute three pence … of his property for the support of any one establishment, may force him to conform to any other establishment in all cases whatsoever."[86]

Viewed from the lights of Thomas Jefferson, James Madison and other Enlightenment authority, the variety of formal neutrality advanced by the Rehnquist Court, most notably in cases like *Zelman* and *Mueller*, would appear to be at odds with these core American religious principles. First, not all taxpayers would agree to apply their monies in support of religious education. In this respect, the court would appear to miss the Establishment Clause question. "The Establishment Clause question is whether Ohio is coercing parents into sending their child to religious schools … ."[87] The court tries to save the point by observing that this question must be considered within the overall context of school choice available to parents, public or private.[88] But the real Establishment Clause question is not a focus on the parents sending children to religious schools. Of course, faced with a failing public school system, most parents will choose a better school system, religious or not. The real Establishment Clause question is whether taxpayers who don't approve of public funding of religious schools are being coerced against their conscience to support them, as would appear in *Zelman*.[89] For these uncooperative, dissenting taxpayers, application of their tax monies in support of religious education would seem to constitute coercion of conscience. So forcing conscience is likely to induce resentment and hostility in those coerced. Nobody likes being forced against their will. The resentment is likely to lead to divisiveness in the body politic, already abundant. Some form of opt-out provision for dissenting

84 James Madison, *Memorial and Remonstrance Against Religious Assessments*, cited in *Everson v. Bd. of Educ.*, 330 U.S. 1, app at 64.

85 Ibid. at 65–66.

86 Ibid. at 65–66. In *Rosenberger v. Rectors and Visitors of the University of Virginia*, 515 U.S. 819 (1995), Justices Thomas and Souter debated the meaning of Madison's *Memorial and Remonstrance*. According to Justice Thomas, Madison simply saw the Establishment Clause "as a prohibition on governmental preferences for some religious faiths over others. … [T]here is no indication that at the time of the framing he took the [extreme] view that the government must discriminate against religious adherents by excluding them from more generally available financial subsidies." Ibid. at 855–57. Thomas then pointed to historical examples of state funding of religion, such as elected chaplains to Congress, tax exemptions for religious bodies and sale of land reserved by Congress to support religion. Ibid. at 858–59. Justice Souter, by contrast, read Madison to oppose aid to religion and to advocate strict separation of church and state. Ibid. at 868–72.

87 *Zelman*, 536 U.S. at 655–56.

88 Ibid. at 656.

89 Accord, *Everson,* 330 U.S. at 22–25 (Jackson, J., dissenting) (unconstitutional to tax those unwilling to expend their monies for religious purposes); ibid. at 36–37 (Rutledge, J., dissenting).

taxpayers is necessary to ameliorate the concern of coercing conscience, as done in early America and in contemporary UK and Germany.

Second, the mixing of church and state occasioned by indirect public subsidy of religion may lead to corruption of religion, as warned by separationist doctrine. These first steps are evident in *Zelman*. A condition of participating in the pilot program is that religious schools may not "discriminate on the basis of … religion."[90] Being obligated to follow a non-discriminatory policy is likely to dilute the purity of religion and involve government in supervision of religion.[91] In these respects, religion may become beholden to government, a root concern of separationism.[92]

As we conclude our assessment of formal neutrality, we can discern the design of constitutional guideposts for the public funding of a parallel, religious school education. Whether this becomes a reality or not will depend on the democratic processes at work in federal and state legislatures. In this respect, we can see that formal neutrality approximates—operating indirectly—but does not mirror, the more direct UK and German system of public support for religious education.

Prayer and Bible Reading in School

With the landmark case of *Engel v. Vitale*,[93] prayer in public schools was rendered unconstitutional as a violation of the Establishment Clause. One year after *Engel v. Vitale*, the court also determined that the reading of Bible verses in public schools was unconstitutional in *Abington School District v. Schempp*.[94] At this time of the Warren Court, in the early 1960s, the cases provoked great outrage in the public. With the changes in the court's makeup—from the Warren Court, to the Burger Court and then to the Rehnquist Court—there was concern that prayer in public schools might be considered constitutional. The matter came up in *Lee v. Weisman*,[95] and the court ruled again that the rendering of prayer at a middle school graduation was unconstitutional, keeping intact *Engel v. Vitale*. The Rehnquist Court also considered a number of cases rendered by the Warren and Burger Courts, but also kept all of these intact. These cases included *Planned*

90 Ibid. at 639, 712 (Souter, J., dissenting).

91 As Justice Souter observed, compliance with governmental requirements of non-discrimination means that religious schools will not be able to give preference to members of the chosen faith; may not be able to choose members of their own clergy as instructors; and might be prohibited from teaching certain articles of faith dealing with faith, sinfulness or ignorance of others due to the official mandate of not teaching hate." Ibid. at 712–13.

92 Ibid. at 712.

93 370 U.S. 421 (1962).

94 374 U.S. 203 (1963).

95 505 U.S. 577 (1992).

Parenthood v. Casey,[96] which kept intact the core of *Roe v Wade*[97] and *Saenz v. Roe*,[98] which kept intact *Shapiro v. Thompson*;[99] the Roberts Court in *Berghuis v. Thompkins*[100] kept the essence of *Miranda v. Arizona*[101] intact, but stated that the right to remain silent must be unambiguous. Let us now evaluate prayer and Bible readings in public schools.

Engel v. Vitale

The controversy in *Engel v. Vitale* starts with the New Hyde Park Board of Education directing the school district to cause a prayer to be read aloud by each class in the presence of a teacher at the beginning of each school day. Under the state prayer program, the prayer is neutral and non-denominational and students are free to remain silent or leave the room. The court simply does not buy this argument. The court is quite clear: the Establishment Clause absolutely prevents government from composing and then rendering prayers in public schools. It is simply not part of government to compose official prayers as a religious exercise or any religious activity.[102] As the court states:

> The First Amendment was added to the Constitution to stand as a guarantee that neither the power nor the prestige of the Federal Government would be used to control, support or influence the kinds of prayer the American people can say—that the people's religions must not be subjected to the pressures of government for change each time a new political administration is elected to office.[103]

Religious exercises are, at their core, a matter of personal belief and conviction and it is simply not part of government to have a role in initiating or rendering religious exercises. Use of the power or prestige of government to back a particular religious belief will result in placing coercive pressure on minority religious groups. Any union of government and religion will result in degrading religious practices. Religion, after all, is a personal, sacred affair, and must be left to people, not government and governmental influences.[104]

Historically, many of the colonists from England and other European countries left those countries out of fear of religious persecution. But interestingly, many of these colonists, who then became American citizens, wanted essentially to

96 505 U.S. 833 (1992).
97 410 U.S. 113 (1973).
98 526 U.S. 489 (1999).
99 394 U.S. 618 (1969).
100 78 U.S. L.W. 4479 (2010).
101 384 U.S. 436 (1966).
102 370 U.S. at 425.
103 Ibid. at 429–30.
104 Ibid. at 430–33.

continue their religious exercises, including prayer. *Engel v. Vitale* demonstrates the bedrock value of the religious freedoms in the First Amendment to guarantee people their core religious beliefs. It is the role of government to be neutral and separate its affairs from religion.

Abington School District v. Schempp

The controversy in *Abington School District v. Schempp* involved the reading of 10 verses from the Holy Bible to open the public school day.[105] As in *Engel v. Vitale*, the court rules that this religious practice is also unconstitutional under the Establishment Clause. Religion has been closely aligned with American government, including such acts as oaths of office for the Presidency, the opening of legislative and United States Supreme Court sessions in a prayer or religious oath and Thanksgiving proclamations.[106] "In God We Trust" is stamped on American coins, starting in 1864, with paper currency stamped on beginning in 1957. But it is clear again that the Establishment Clause forbids the rendering of religious exercises in public schools. The Establishment Clause is designed to keep the affairs of church and state separate from one another in order to preserve the freedom of religion for people. If the two are mixed, state or church could well destroy or degrade the other. Governmental neutrality is essential to free people to follow their own religious beliefs. Government is not to advance or inhibit religion. To be compliant with the Establishment Clause, there must be a secular purpose and a primary effect that neither advances nor inhibits religion.[107] As the court states, "The breach of neutrality that is today a trickling stream may all too soon become a raging torrent … ."[108] It simply is not the power of government to invade "the inviolable citadel of the individual heart and mind."[109] People must be free to practice their own religious beliefs free from any official compulsion. State intrusion into religion can have a coercive effect on the rights of dissenters and non-comformists. But *Schempp* made clear that the study of religion and of the Bible in literature and history classes is an essential part of public education.[110] What the court means is that religion is a crucial part of education. It just cannot be done in a religious manner.

Engel and *Schempp* are foundational cases for the establishment of a separationist jurisprudence, designed to separate as much as possible church from state, leaving an inner citadel of religious freedom for people. After all, religion is a private affair, a matter of great moment. Any intrusion by government into

---

105 374 U.S. 203 (1963).

106 Ibid. at 212–13.

107 Ibid. at 222.

108 Ibid. at 225.

109 Ibid. at 226.

110 Paul G. Kauper, The Warren Court: Religious Liberty and Church-State Relations, 67 *U. Mich. L. Rev.* 269, 283, 287 (1968).

religion is damaging. For the Warren Court, its focus is on protecting minorities and dissenters, as the role of fundamental rights is to protect freedoms from the majoritarian process, which determines the laws that govern society.

Lee v. Weisman

In *Lee v. Weisman*[111] the controversial matter of school prayer came up again. This time the prayer was rendered at the end of graduation at the Nathan Bishop public middle school in Providence, Rhode Island. Rhode Island, interestingly, has been the subject of a number of important Supreme Court cases, including *Lemon v. Kurtzman*[112] and *Lynch v. Donnelly*.[113] Rhode Island, in fact, is an incubator for religious freedom. Roger Williams founded the state and it was the origin of the idea of freedom of religion for all people, no established church and separation of church and state. At the school, they rendered an invocation for the graduation of middle school students. Trying to accommodate the Weismans, who were Jewish, the principal wrote a pamphlet setting prayer guidelines for a Jewish rabbi, who was to render the prayer. The invocation mentioned God a number of times. The school board thought that provision of a graduation prayer was of profound significance for students, providing for divine guidance and deep spiritual aspiration. In setting the guidelines, the school tried to have a non-sectarian prayer in order to not have a flashpoint for religious animosity. The Weismans were adamantly against the rendering of prayer and filed the lawsuit.[114]

The court evaluated the school's rendering of prayer during the graduation and found, easily, that it violated the Establishment Clause. Any governmental involvement in prayer violates the central tenets of religious freedom. The court observed while government can accommodate the free exercise of religion, limitations are imposed by the Establishment Clause. For one thing, government may not coerce a person to support or participate in a religious exercise. It is important that government stay out of religious affairs and instead leave that exercise to people.[115]

The presence of a religious figure, in this case a rabbi, leads to divisiveness. While there can always be an issue with divisiveness, it is especially going to be the case with young people, here middle school students. Tension over religious matters can lead to subtle coercive pressure. This puts the student in the position of having to conform to the religious exercise, something they would prefer not to do.[116] While the guidelines provided by the school called for a non-sectarian, civic invocation, it is still clear that invoking the name of God has a negative effect on

111 505 U.S. 577 (1992).
112 403 U.S. 602 (1971).
113 465 U.S. 668 (1984).
114 505 U.S. at 582–84.
115 Ibid. at 586–87.
116 Ibid. at 588.

students and is not compatible with the Establishment Clause. As the court notes in *Engel v. Vitale*, "it is no part of the business of government to compose official prayers for any group of the American people to recite as a part of a religious program carried out by government."[117] While common ground can sometimes be found with a shared conviction and a sense of ethics and morality, which may result in a sense of community, still, it is not the role of government to undertake the composition and rendering of prayer.[118]

The religious clauses of the First Amendment are designed to safeguard the religious beliefs and expression of people; it is not the business of government to proscribe or prescribe religion. As the court observes:

> The design of the Constitution is that preservation and transmission of religious beliefs and worship is a responsibility and a choice committed to the private sphere, which itself is promised freedom to pursue that mission. It must not be forgotten then, that while concern must be given to define the protection granted to an objector or a dissenting nonbeliever, these same Clause exist to protect religion from government interference.[119]

Under the First Amendment, all creeds are to be tolerated and none favored. The idea that government might try to further an official or civic religion as a way to not have an establishment of religion strikes the court as a contradiction that cannot be accepted. Here it is clear to the court that the graduation prayers have the imprint of the state and put school children in a difficult spot.[120]

A major purpose of exposure to ideas, whether false or offensive, is to provide students with the learning ability to participate in a pluralistic society. The idea of society is to provide an open discourse toward the development of a tolerant citizenry. Tolerance is designed to provide a mutuality of obligation. The constitutional vision of American free society bestows confidence in the ability of people to accept or reject ideas. Exposure to a wide range of ideas is important to the development of the young and participation in society in an open and mutual way. Still, there is a difference between expression of views on any subject and expression of religion that is sponsored by the state.[121]

As the court states, there is a difference between free speech and religious rights.

> The First Amendment protects speech and religion by quite different mechanisms. Speech is protected by ensuring its full expression even when government participates, for the very object of some of our most important speech is to

117 370 U.S. at 425.
118 505 U.S. at 589.
119 Ibid. at 589–90.
120 Ibid. at 590.
121 Ibid. at 591.

> persuade the government to adopt an idea on its own.... The method for protecting freedom of worship and freedom of conscience in religious matters is quite the reverse. In religious or expression the government is not a prime participant, for the Framers deemed religious establishment antithetical to the freedom of all. The Free Exercise Clause embraces a freedom of conscience and worship that has close parallels in the speech provisions of the First Amendment, but the Establishment is a specific prohibition on forms of state intervention in religious matters with no precise counterpart in the speech provisions.... The explanation lies in the lesson of history that was and is the inspiration for the Establishment Clause, the lesson that in the hands of government what might begin as a tolerant expression of religious views may end in a policy to indoctrinate and coerce. A state-created orthodoxy puts at grave risk that freedom of belief and conscience which are the sole assurance that religion is real, not imposed.
>
> The lessons of the First Amendment are as urgent in the modern world as in the 18th century when it was written. One timeless lesson is that if citizens are subjected to state-sponsored religious exercises, the State disavows its own duty to guard and respect that sphere of inviolable conscience and belief which is the mark of a free people. To compromise that principle today would be to deny our own tradition and forfeit our standing to urge others to secure the protections of that tradition for themselves.[122]

The problem with prayer exercises in school is that it places students in a position of indirect coercion. While many might think provision of religious exercises is a good thing, and non-believers should respect the religious exercises of students, for a non-believer or dissenter it might involve the machinery of the state in enforcing a religious orthodoxy. This ends up in placing pressure on students, whether subtle or indirect, to show respect for believers. But such coercion places dissenting students in an untenable position. Students are often susceptible to pressure from their peers toward conformity. This poses a real conflict of conscience for the young.[123]

The school is arguing that students are free not to participate in the prayer. But for the court, this:

> turns conventional First Amendment analysis on its head. It is a tenet of the First Amendment that the State cannot require one of its own citizens to forfeit his or her rights and benefits as the price of resisting conformance to state-sponsored religious practice. To say that a student must remain apart from the ceremony at the opening invocation and closing benediction is to risk compelling conformity in an environment analogous to the classroom setting, where we have said the risk of compulsion is especially high.[124]

---

122 Ibid. at 591–92.
123 Ibid. at 593.
124 Ibid. at 596.

For the court, Establishment Clause jurisprudence is a sensitive matter that calls for line-drawing. While prayer at public schools cannot be allowed, legislatures can open their session with a prayer.[125] But this is the difference between young people and adults. Young people are simply more vulnerable to induced religious exercises.

Lee v. Weisman is an important case for the Supreme Court, reaffirming the significance of the Establishment Clause in keeping the barrier between church and state intact. There is always a danger that religiously inspired acts can have a negative effect on people. While some people are very supportive of public religious acts—which may be common in countries that support religion—it should not be the case in countries where church and state are to be separated. Religion, after all, is a private affair, and it is not the business of government to play a role in religion.

Justice Scalia, in his dissent, observes that psychological coercion is strange. Why can students, in grade school, middle school and high school be psychologically coerced, but not adults? Justice Scalia wonders whether jurisprudence will be distinguished from mature and immature adults. He refers to the psychological effect as "psycho-journey" and "psycho-coercion test;" and he believes that *Lee v. Weisman* "suffers the double disability of having no roots whatever in our people's historic practice and being as infinitely expandable as the reasons for psychotherapy itself."[126] He goes on to say that "To deprive our society of that important unifying mechanism, in order to spare the nonbeliever what seems to be the minimal inconvenience of standing or even sitting in respectful nonparticipation, is as senseless in policy as it is unsupported in law."[127] He then goes on to cite the tradition of religious exercises that have occurred in the history of the nation, such as invocations in legislatures, inaugural addresses and Thanksgiving Proclamations.[128] Should that tradition stay in place? Or is it better not to have religious rituals? What is the purpose of the Constitution: protect people's freedom under the religious rights listed in the First Amendment or allow religion to have a role in American society? Much will depend on the complexion of the Supreme Court.

What we see in the *Lee v. Weisman* case, as with other cases, is a debate on the meaning of the Establishment Clause. Should the Establishment Clause be applied in a separationist approach, as the First Amendment clearly states that there should be no establishment of religion? Or should religion be allowed to play a role in government? What we can observe is contention over the meaning of the Establishment Clause.

125 *Marsh v. Chambers*, 463 U.S. 783 (1983).

126 Ibid. at 643–44.

127 Ibid. at 648.

128 505 U.S. at 633–35, 637–38.

Santa Fe School District v. Jane Doe

Following *Lee v. Weisman*, *Santa Fe v. Jane Doe* also involved the rendering of prayer, here over a public address system before a football game.[129] The process was different than that of *Lee v. Weisman*. Here students held elections authorizing prayers, which the students determined, with the student spokesperson acting, essentially, as a student chaplain. The school was trying to stay out of the religious affairs, leaving it to the private choice of the students. When the case went to the District Court, the court modified the policy, calling for a non-sectarian prayer, which the Circuit Court found unconstitutional.[130]

Following the principles of *Lee v. Weisman*, the court observed that the principle that government may accommodate the free exercise of religion does not supersede the restraints imposed by the Establishment Clause. The school district is arguing that this matter of student prayer involves private, not public, speech. But the court is unwilling to buy into the argument that private speech is constitutionally permissible. For the court, the invocations are authorized by a government policy that take place on government property—here the school setting—and is a government-sponsored school event. This element of government sponsorship is, according to the court, a publicly sponsored prayer which is a clear violation of the Establishment Clause.[131]

As in *Lee v. Weisman*, majority student determinations result in the isolation and lack of protection for minorities. A major role of fundamental freedoms is to protect minority groups, as much of general legislation is determined by majoritarian power. The degree of school involvement "makes it clear that the pregame prayers bear 'the imprint of the State and thus put school age children who objected in an untenable position.'"[132] School sponsorship of prayer or a religious message is wrong. It sends a message to members of the audience that are non-adherents "that they are outsiders, not full members of the political community, and an accompanying message to adherents that they are insiders."[133] It is clear that young people are especially susceptible to pressure from their peers. There is a sense that adolescents must conform to the influence of the strongest members of the community. The school cannot force students to forfeit their rights at the price of conformance. The delivery of a pregame prayer has the effect of coercing students, a clear violation of the Establishment Clause.[134]

For the court, the school's involvement in the school prayer is a clear endorsement of religion. The students' involvement in the prayer is delivered to

---

129 530 U.S. 290 (2000).

130 Ibid. at 294–95.

131 Ibid. at 302.

132 Ibid. at 305 (citing *Lee v. Weisman*, 505 U.S. at 590).

133 Ibid. at 309–10 (citing *Lynch v. Donnelly*, 465 U.S. at 688) (O'Conner, J., concurring).

134 Ibid. at 312.

a large audience at a school-sponsored event. The prayer is delivered over the school public address system. The pregame ceremony is clothed in the traditional manner of a school sporting event, which includes the team, cheerleaders and band members, all dressed in the school uniforms. The school's name is likely written on large banners and flags. And the crowd will likely wear clothes that display the school's logo. For the court, the text and history of this policy is that the prayer policy is encouraged by the school.[135]

An essential element of the Establishment Clause is to keep government out of the affairs of people's religious freedoms. Government debate over religion is to be excluded from the private sphere. Religious matters are designed to be a choice of people, not government. Nothing in the Constitution prohibits students from voluntarily praying at any time, before, during or after school. But the school cannot sponsor prayer. The purpose of the religious clauses is to secure religious freedom for people. The current policy, as in *Lee v. Weisman*, results in divisiveness in society, something at odds with the Establishment Clause. For the court, the policy is invalid on its face "because it establishes an improper majoritarian election on religion."[136] The majority should never control religion. Religion is a private affair to be determined by each person.

Observations

With the advent of Establishment Clause jurisprudence, in the 1947 *Everson v. Board of Education* case, the court has mainly followed an approach of separation of church and state, although in *Everson*, the court ruled that provision of bus services to Roman Catholic students was constitutional as it was a governmental service, like police and fire protection, or the rendering of textbooks to religious schools over secular topics. Under the idea of separationism, government is not to set up or support churches, synagogues, mosques or other religious buildings nor is the role of government to aid one religion over another or a person's religious belief. And there can be no public support of religious instruction in public schools.

The line of jurisprudence has changed with the 1983 *Mueller v. Allen* case, which allowed state tax exemptions for tuition costs for private schools, most of which were religious. With *Mueller* in effect, public accommodation of religion, through state subsidy, has been allowed for textbooks, computers, and other laboratory and teaching aids, remedial education over reading, writing and math and, with *Zelman v. Simmons-Harris*, the court has allowed greater public aid for tuition for private schools, most of which are religious.

At present, we have two approaches to Establishment Clause jurisprudence: separationist, which originated in the first sets of Establishment Clause cases, and now formal neutrality. Separationist is rooted in James Madison and Baptists;

135 Ibid. at 307–08.

136 Ibid. at 310–11, 313, 317.

formal neutrality is rooted in accomodationist civic republicanism. Both these approaches now apply to school systems: separationism applies to public schools, where religion is not allowed, and private schools, primarily religious, that incur some public subsidy to support their educational mission are rooted in a form of accomodationism. How these two philosophies will work is something to be considered in future jurisprudence.

School prayer is still not allowed in public schools, as also not allowed is the reading of Bible verses. Exercise of religious practices in public schools can hinder, at times, students' emotional and intellectual development.

Chapter 9
Comparative Observations

Personal Religious Freedom

Our review of personal religious freedoms in the United Kingdom, Germany and the United States has led us to clarify the values underlying free exercise of religion and the purposes it serves in constitutional democracy. Comparative law has a useful role to play in clarifying constitutional values and tenets of public philosophy. Fundamentally, religious freedom empowers a person to act freely on affairs of the soul within the constraints of society. Personal religious freedom recognizes a dilemma of human existence within constitutionally organized society: what to do when faced with competing claims of conscience and law. Should a person follow affairs of the soul—"soul liberty"[1]—or the demands of society?

Our review of the three countries discloses different ways of unraveling this dilemma. German law is very empowering. Viewing the conflict between conscience and legal obligation as one requiring an individual to pay an unacceptably high price, German law unravels the dilemma by strongly favoring claims of conscience over claims of law. On the whole, German law is willing to grant wide accommodation to the realm of faith-based activities—including suspending legal claims that ordinarily would apply (even when generally applicable)—so that a person may be free, legally and spiritually, to act on conscience. The goal of German law is to empower a person to live according to chosen tenets relatively unimpeded. German law strives to so accommodate conscience in ways that complement social order. The German solution thereby demonstrates how balance between religious liberty and social order may be achieved.

American law solves the dilemma exactly opposite of German law. For the most part, conflicts between conscience and law are resolved by demanding obedience to the law over conscience. Great danger is seen in "each conscience [becoming] … a law unto itself."[2] Yet, there is danger to religious liberty in overemphasizing order as well. Under the rule of *Smith*, Free Exercise rights consist only of the right to believe, act on such belief pursuant to ritual or worship, and claims to fair treatment under a principle of non-discrimination

1 Edward J. Eberle, Roger Williams' Gift: Religious Liberty in America, 4 *Roger Williams Univ. L. Rev.* 425, 442 (1999) (describing Roger Williams' thought).

2 *Smith*, 494 U.S. at 890.

whereby the social order may not disfavor religion in relation to other activities.[3] This rule of *Smith* largely follows the position of John Locke, of the seventeenth century, and eclipses the earlier position of the court expressed in *Sherbert.* On this review of the law, American law is unwilling as a matter of right to grant accommodation to religiously motivated actors except by majoritarian grace, discrimination or as otherwise noted, things like religious ritual and worship. We might therefore characterize American law as rather restrictive of Free Exercise rights. American law makes only minimal effort to achieve equilibrium between religious liberty and social order, instead reflexively deferring to authorities' demands for order.

UK law has made significant progress in protecting religious freedoms. The UK evaluates carefully the conflict between the demands of conscience and the law, and then reaches a judgment as to which should prevail. Under the rules of UK law, the courts will protect entirely freedom of belief and will also protect religiously based conduct if the court determines that the value of religion outweighs conformity with the general law. Allowing such religious practice will call for a very persuasive ground based on religion. But in that respect, UK law is, in ways, more tolerant of religious practice than the current American law under *Smith.* But UK law is certainly not as protective of religious freedoms as German law.

A further notable contrast between the three laws is the breadth of accommodation present in German law. German law presumptively favors conscience-based actors faced with constraints imposed by the social order. Accommodation is the rule, not the exception. Pursuant to this methodology, the German Constitutional Court has suspended general legal requirements concerning rules of the marketplace,[4] criminal negligence,[5] the rendering of oaths,[6] and requirements of the slaughter of animals.[7] This pattern of law—predictably favoring accommodation—reveals a rich mosaic of people's chosen acts of conscience forced to the brink by social requirements.

The broad accommodation of religion manifest in German law contrasts again with American law. Under *Smith*, obviously, accommodation no longer exists as a matter of constitutional right. The forum for accommodation is the democratic process. However, even under the prior rule of judicial accommodation in *Sherbert*, exemption was an extremely rare occurrence. Recall again that accommodation occurred in only three instances: unemployment compensation,[8] mandatory high

3 See *Church of the Lukumi Babalu Aye v. City of Hialeah*, 508 U.S. 520 (1993).

4 *Rumpelkammer*, 24 BVerfGE 236 (1968).

5 *Blood Transfusion*, 32 BVerfGE 98 (1971).

6 *Bavarian Official Oath*, 79 BVerfGE 69 (1988); *Denial of Witness Oath*, 33 BVerfGE 23 (1972).

7 *Ritual Slaughter*, 104 BVerfGE 337 (2002).

8 See, e.g., *Frazee v. Illinois Dept. of Employment Security*, 489 U.S. 829 (1989); *Sherbert.*

school attendance,[9] and barring ministers from holding a public office.[10] It was more common the case that accommodation was denied than granted.[11]

The UK fits somewhere in the middle on determining where a religious practitioner fits between conscience-driven conduct and the constraints of the general laws. Certainly the UK is not as liberal in protecting religious rights as Germany; instead, it leans more toward the American model, under *Smith*: looking mainly toward discrimination or non-discrimination. In this respect, UK and US law seem more in accord: looking to equality as the governing norm. However, this reflects a major difference in the constitutional orders. The USA sets out clear textual protection for free exercise of religion in the Constitution. In contrast, in the UK there is no written constitution and no clear law setting out religious protections. Instead, the UK must rely on equality norms set out in the Race Relations Act and the Equality Act. Of course, this reflects the tradition of the UK of a continuous constitutional order where norms are not always clearly spelled out in a constitutional document.

An additional contrast between the three countries is who, among members of society, has been granted accommodation. A country's commitment to religious liberty is especially revealed in how it treats minority sects. Religious liberty is always popular from the viewpoint of majorities. Whether equal rights are accorded minorities is an acid test of religious liberty.

Here too we can observe that German law evidences certain solicitude toward minorities. First, accommodation of traditional Christians and fundamentalist Christians is noteworthy: in *Blood Transfusion*, where the court allowed the husband to allow his wife to die for her refusal, on religious grounds, to have a blood transfusion; and in *Denial of Witness Oath* and *Bavarian Official Oath*, where the court allowed Christians not to take an oath. Evangelical Christians are considered as outside the mainstream in Germany, viewed with suspicion, notwithstanding the predominantly Christian orientation of the country. Granting of public corporation status to Jehovah's Witnesses[12] is further evidence of this toleration. Second, apart from these cases involving Christians, notable further is accommodation of minority sects, as concerning Muslims in *Ritual Slaughter*, *Islamic Teacher's Head Scarf* and *Turkish Sales Clerk's Head Scarf*, and Jews, such as removal of a Christian cross from a courtroom,[13] and recognition of

9 *Wisconsin v. Yoder*, 406 U.S. 205 (1972).

10 *McDaniel v. Paty*, 435 U.S. 618 (1978).

11 See, e.g., *Lyng v. Northwest Indian Cemetery Protective Association*, 485 U.S. 439 (1988); *O'Lone v. Estate of Shabazz*, 482 U.S. 342 (1987); *Bowen v. Roy*, 476 U.S. 693 (1986); *Goldman v. Weinberger*, 475 U.S. 503 (1986); *United States v. Lee*, 455 U.S. 252 (1982); *Braunfeld v. Brown*, 366 U.S. 599 (1961) (applying methodology that evolves into rule of *Sherbert*).

12 *Jehovah's Witness*, 102 BVerfGE 370 (2000).

13 *Cross in Courtroom*, 35 BVerfGE 366 (1973) (ruling that cross displayed in courtroom must be removed in view of objection from Jewish lawyer).

religious autonomy rights for the Baha'i.[14] Thus, German law evidences certain accommodation of minority sects, consistent with a principle of religious equality. It is also fair to observe that most of the German cases involve accommodation of the dominant Christian group.

By contrast, American Supreme Court case law has not exhibited much solicitude toward minorities. First, we must observe again that American law has been quite restrictive generally of Free Exercise rights, granting accommodations only in three instances—unemployment compensation, not allowing ministers to take a public office position, and mandatory high school attendance. Part of accommodation of religious rights depends on the status of citizens: are they good citizens and law-abiding members of society? In *Sherbert*, the court observed that the claimant was a good citizen. "This is not a case in which an employee's religious convictions serve to make him a nonproductive member of society."[15] In *Wisconsin v. Yoder*, the court made a point of emphasizing that the Old World Amish were law-abiding citizens.[16] These accommodations were granted to Christians only. Perhaps Americans overemphasize order in society over religious matters.

Minority sects have never been granted an accommodation in Supreme Court case law. The Supreme Court has rejected accommodations for Jews,[17] Muslims,[18] and Native Americans.[19] The treatment accorded practitioners of the Santeria religion in *Church of the Lukumi Babalu Aye v. City of Hialeah*, 508 U.S. 520 (1993), was not an accommodation, of course, but rather discrimination under the rule of *Smith*.[20] On the other hand, in view of the pattern of presumptive rejection of accommodation of religious actors, it is fair to say that predominant Christian beliefs have fared only marginally better than minority sects.

The UK seems to fit, again, somewhere in the middle. Accommodation has been granted to Jews[21] and Muslims,[22] although these accommodations are fairly uncommon. In the *JFS* case, a leading decision of the recently instituted Supreme Court, the court upheld the Court of Appeals decision that the school had committed direct discrimination against the applicant student under the 1976

14 *Baha'i*, 83 BVerfGE 341 (1991).

15 *Sherbert*, 374 U.S. at 410.

16 *Yoder*, 406 U.S. at 222 ("the Amish community has been a highly successful social unit within our society, even if apart from the 'mainstream.' Its members are highly productive and very law-abiding members of society; they reject public welfare in its usual modern forms.").

17 See *Goldman v. Weinberger*, 475 U.S. 503 (1986); *Braunfeld v. Brown*, 366 U.S. 599 (1961).

18 See *O'Lone v. Estate of Shabazz*, 482 U.S. 342 (1987).

19 See *Smith; Lyng v. Northwest Indian Cemetery Protective Association*, 485 U.S. 439 (1988).

20 *Lyng v. Northwest Indian Cemetery Protective Association*, 485 U.S. 439 (1988).

21 *JFS* [2009] UKSC 15.

22 *R. v. Aberdare Girls' High School*, [2008] EWHC 1865 (Admin); 3 FCR 203.

Race Relations Act. The court determined that the boy did qualify as Jewish and therefore could be admitted to the school.

Under current UK law, Muslims are also granted significant accommodation. Much depends on the religious grounds of the wearing of certain attire. A key case is *Mandla*, which, as we have observed, sets out the key definition as to what constitutes a religion that qualifies under the Race Relations Act, which is critical to the UK definition as to what constitutes religion.[23] In *Mandla*, the court determined that Sikhs do qualify as a racial group under the Race Relations Act and that the wearing of a turban is an indispensable part of being a Sikh. Accordingly, the court ruled that denial of the Sikh's admission to school, for not complying with the dress code, was discrimination and, therefore, unconstitutional. Likewise, in *R. v. Aberdare Girls' High School*, the Queen's Bench Division Court determined that the school's decision not to grant a waiver for the Muslim girl's wearing of a plain steel bangle, known as a kara, was discrimination.[24] The wearing of a small piece of jewelry poses no health or security threat.

On the other hand, the UK courts have often deferred to school authorities over Muslim women's wearing of religious attire. This occurred in *R. v. Denbigh High*, where the House of Lords deferred to school authorities over the Islamic girl's wearing of a jilbab, a full-length dress, which was not compatible with the school's dress code, although other schools allowed the wearing of a jilbab.[25] Likewise, in *R. v. Head Teachers and Governors of Y School*, the court deferred to school authorities over the wearing of a niqab, a veil that protected the whole face except the eyes.[26] And in *Azmi v. Kirklees Metropolitan Borough Council*, a teacher of Muslim faith wanted to wear a head veil.[27] The school allowed her to wear the head veil in open areas and while walking around the school, but not in the classroom. The Employment Appeal Tribunal upheld the school policy. Where Muslim workers wear religious attire that poses health hazards in work settings, the courts defer to companies. Health is more important than practice of religion.

The significance of the *Williamson* case is the House of Lords setting the benchmark for the definition of religion. In the case, the House of Lords upheld the UK law that banned corporal punishment in all schools, public or private.[28] Corporal punishment can be allowed under present law only by parents in their homes, and only if they do not severely beat their children.

What we see in the three countries is the significance of the courts defining rules of law. After all, the job of the court is to set forth workable definitions of legal standards. Concerning defining religion, we see a contrast between Germany, the UK and the USA. The German Constitutional Court sets out a clear definition

23 [1983] 2 AC 548.

24 [2008] EWHC 1865 (Admin); 3 FCR 203.

25 [2006] UKHL 15.

26 [2007] EWHC 298 (Admin); 1 All ER 249, ELR 278.

27 UKEAT/0009/07/MAA, (transcript).

28 [2005] UKHL 15, All ER 1.

of religion, in the *Rumpelkammer* case. Defining religion is critical to valuing religion. After all, the job of courts is to define constitutional norms. Likewise, the House of Lords sets out a fairly clear definition of religion in the *Williamson* case. By contrast, for the US Supreme Court, it believes it is not the role of judges to determine the centrality of religious beliefs. However, in past cases, like *Yoder* and *Seeger*, the court did define religion. In almost all other areas of constitutional law, the Supreme Court sets out workable definitions of a rule of law. So, if the court sets out clear rules of law for other parts of the Constitution, why would it not do the same for religion?

These developments point to the conclusion that individual religious freedoms are accorded much broader scope in Germany than in the United States and the United Kingdom. Viewed from an American sense, this observation is somewhat startling. A person would not ordinarily expect personal religious freedoms to be more vibrant in Germany than in the United States, at least as viewed from the standpoint of accommodation within society of religiously motivated actors. Upon further consideration, it is perhaps less startling that Germany has strong religious liberty. Under the Basic Law, the Federal Republic is constituted as a social democratic state committed to human dignity and human rights. Capturing the transcendent nature of the human condition, religious rights are an integral part of this central focus on the human person. Personal religious rights, like other rights, are tangible radiations of human dignity that facilitate realization of human capacity. Human rights stand at the fore of a dignitarian vision searching to gird society to higher principles of justice and human fulfillment. Given such a constitutional order, it is quite natural that religious rights will be highly preferred.

It is more surprising that American personal religious liberty pales in comparison to German. America was founded on principles of religious liberty more than 350 years ago, with Rhode Island being the first settlement founded on religious liberty in the Western world. In view of such history, it is surprising that the impulse of American law is to constrain religious liberty rather than empower it.

Viewed this way, there is much American law could learn from the dignitarian focus of German law. For one thing, focusing on individual dignity would not likely lead to excessive deference to majoritarian rule as a means to constrain religion. Instead, a dignitarian focus would accord greater regard to human needs. Human needs require acknowledgment of the importance of the spiritual and transcendent dimension to life that Free Exercise rights capture. Being more attuned to the needs of the believer, as the German Constitutional Court shows, and less attuned to the exigencies of law and order would help.

Second, the Constitutional Court demonstrates how an independent court can judge the boundaries of religious freedoms without impugning religion or courting anarchy. The point is partly one of methodology. Weighted balancing favoring religion (as in Germany and under the United States approach in *Sherbert*) is more likely to give religion its due than a black-line rule protecting belief but not action (*Smith*). And the point is partly one of judgment. The Constitutional Court shows how to cut to the heart of a personal religious claim, explicate the relevant considerations—assessing the demands of religion as they relate to the social claim—and then formulate a clear, workable rule of law that respects religion without undermining society.

In this respect, the Constitutional Court serves as an alternative standard by which to measure the work of the US Supreme Court and the UK Supreme Court. A key factor for American law is to determine whether the rule of *Smith* is appropriate to protect free exercise of religious freedoms. Should the USA go back to the rule of *Sherbert*, the standard rule of strict scrutiny that applies to fundamental rights? After all, is not religious freedom one of the core values of basic rights? Or should the USA keep the *Smith* rule intact, which has resulted in diminished free exercise rights protections? Likewise, which way should the UK go: should they look to Germany or the USA or determine their own rules to govern freedom of personal religion? Should native countries look outside their borders for inspiration and advice as to how to interpret constitutional norms? As currently measured, which of the three countries has the most vibrant protection of free exercise rights? Is it Germany, the USA or the UK? Most people would likely think Germany at present.

Church-State Relations

As we assemble the observations we have gathered from our comparative examination of British, German and American law concerning church-state relations, we are left with this observation: German law is in distinct ways committed to religious values of neutrality, toleration and non-discrimination, values we commonly associate with American law, but should not exclusively, as they resonate today as core religious values in Western culture. In this respect, German law is moving somewhat in a separationist direction. Conversely, American non-preferentialism is a distinct move in the direction of the church-state cooperative model in place in Germany. The UK system is still an establishment model, but the establishment approach is not as concrete as in the past. Instead the UK is moving to a much more accommodating approach. We might say the UK is also moving somewhat to a cooperationist model. Let us look at this more carefully.

The German community public school model presupposes a Christian orientation and, in this respect, is well out of line with American law. Yet, a closer look at what role religion actually plays in German schools may suggest the relationship is less disconnected. First, pure instruction in religious tenets is restricted to religion class. Religion class itself is the domain of the religious community, which picks teachers and determines religious instruction. Thus, we might think of the public school as neutrally providing the forum for religious instruction, but otherwise staying out of the affairs of religion. Government is in all respects to be neutral concerning religious/philosophical beliefs. Further, each student/parent can choose the religious instruction of choice, or none at all. We can thus see that ample consideration is given to liberty of conscience.

Under UK law, religious education is also part of the school curriculum. Under the law state-funded schools are required to provide a daily act of collective worship. As in Germany, parents may request that their children be excused from religious teachings. Despite the law being in effect, only about one-quarter of secondary schools comply with the law.

Aspects of American law approximate, but do not mirror, this element of German law. American students may be released from public school premises for religious instruction during the school day[29] and religious instruction can occur on public school premises after school hours.[30]

Outside of religion class in Germany, there can be no dissemination of religious tenets or proselytization. Teaching of religion is confined to religion class. There is room for experimentation in the laboratory of the *Länder*; some *Länder* are more overtly Christian than others, as most graphically indicated in the *Bavarian Community School Case*; some *Länder* are more secular, as in Bremen, Berlin and Brandenburg. Outside of religion class, Christianity is to be referred to only as a cultural and historical force, not a religious one.

These elements resonate partly with American law as well, although not in the same way as in Germany. For example, a Christmas crèche can be displayed as a symbol of culture as a Christmas holiday, as can a Jewish menorah displayed next to a Christmas tree.[31] There can be study of religions and of the Bible from a literary and historic point of view as part of secular education.[32]

Another contrast between Germany and the USA on religion is the presence or display of religious symbols in the classroom and the practice of religious rites, like prayer. Under the American system, display of religious symbols is not permissible in public schools. However, a private school that is religiously affiliated is allowed to display religious symbols, as the Constitution does not apply to private actors.

An interesting trend in German law is that it has moved somewhat in the direction of US law. The most notable case is *Classroom Crucifix II*, where the court held that display of a crucifix offended children's religious beliefs. The problem for the court was that a display of a cross in the classroom forced students to study under the influence of a cross. This was especially discomforting to

29 *Zorach v. Clauson*, 343 U.S. 306 (1952).

30 *Good News Club v. Milford Central School*, 533 U.S. 98 (2001).

31 *Allegheny v. ACLU*, 492 U.S. 573 (1989); *Lynch v. Donnelly*, 465 U.S. 668 (1984) (Christmas crèche symbol of culture as Christmas holiday, not religious message).

32 *Epperson v. Arkansas*, 393 U.S. 97, 106 (1968) ("study of religions and of the Bible from a literary and historic viewpoint, presented objectively as part of a secular program of education, need not collide with the First Amendment's prohibition … "); *School Dist. of Abington Township v. Schempp*, 374 U.S. 203 (1963) (Bible can be read in public schools as work of literature or culture).

students of a young age. The purpose of the classroom setting is to be open and neutral to students.

A further contrast between German and US law involves the rendering of prayer in school. Because Germany is a cooperationist model, prayer can be rendered in the classroom. The prayer must be voluntary, not compulsory. Because the USA is a separationist model, prayer or rendering of Bible verses is not permissible in public schools. The Bible can only be treated as a literary or historical work, not a religious work.

Another contrast between Germany and the USA is over minority religions. The German constitutional order is very solicitous of minority religions, including Christian fundamentalist religions, such as Jehovah's Witnesses and other minority religions, like Islam and the Ba'hai. These minority religions have been granted the right to freely exercise their religions. These religions are granted accommodating status as public corporations, such as Jehovah's Witnesses and the Ba'hai. In the *OSHO* case, the court allowed certain religious rights to the OSHO movement, but less strong rights, as there was some concern that the OSHO movement was somewhat on the fringe, and could at times be viewed as a threat.

By contrast, in the USA, the court has generally not been as favorable to allowing minority religions, such as Islam, Native Americans and Jews, to freely practice their religions. However, the court has generally treated minority religions the same as majority religions. Both majority and minority religions are entitled to tax exemption status, deferring to religious authorities to control their own affairs.

Beyond these elements of overt religious exercise, government is to be neutral, tolerant and non-discriminatory concerning all religious/philosophical beliefs, particularly those not in a dominant position. The community school is obligated to facilitate a dialogue of pluralistic religious/philosophical views to expose and develop students' intellectual and spiritual capacities. In recognition of the increasingly pluralistic composition of German society, the Constitutional Court is recalibrating religious freedoms toward a distinctly more neutral position and one that identifies less with any dominant sect so that each religious community can more freely compete on a level playing field. For example, "A regulation that prohibits teachers from displaying overtly their membership in a particular religious community or adherence to beliefs … is clearly in tension with especially pronounced growing diversity of religion in society."[33] The court also recognized that acceptance of growing religious diversity in society might call for readjustment of legal concepts, such as stricter neutrality in the obligations of members of the civil service. The state role is to be "not a distant, absent role … but rather a respectful, nourishing neutrality" that accords "equality to the beliefs of all believers, understanding the attitudes advanced [by people] on equal terms."[34] Commitment to these values of neutrality, tolerance and non-discrimination are also substantially in accord with American and, indeed, international norms of

33 See, e.g., *Muslim Teacher's Head Scarf*, 108 BVerfGE 282, 310 (2003).

34 Ibid. at 298–99.

religious freedom.[35] There is a certain resonance of core values that comprise a human right to religious freedom.

German law evinces further similarity with American law in that the Basic Law sets down in some detail principles of institutional separation of church and state. For example, recall that Article 137 of the Weimar Constitution incorporated into the charter prohibits a state church; religious bodies are authorized to regulate their own affairs within the limits of the law, including the ability to run their affairs according to their tenets. For example, a Catholic hospital can fire a doctor who took a public position on abortion contrary to Catholic doctrine.[36] Under Article 136, government is prohibited from inquiring into memberships of religious bodies, except for statistical purposes. These principles of institutional separation of church and state are broadly in line with American law, including the Puritan tradition. In these respects, German law is similar to American law.

Neutrality, non-discrimination and tolerance are hallmarks of American law as well. Under formal neutrality, neutrality and non-discrimination are central elements of Establishment Clause doctrine. The American idea of neutrality here is a formal, facial one which involves no substantive evaluation of the effects of government programs. But perhaps this more flexible, more malleable concept of neutrality has similarities to German doctrine as well. For, we can recall under German doctrine, the state acts somewhat as a neutral public forum in allowing the major religions—Roman Catholicism and Protestantism—to teach their tenets in the public schools. Opportunities are in the process of being expanded, as Islam too may soon achieve the same benefit. There is, thus, some surprising overlap in core values of both countries' jurisprudence.

There is also similarity in the nature of state support of religious education. Germany, the UK and the United States overtly fund religious education. German law straightforwardly funds religious education through making it a regular part of the public school curriculum, as does the UK. It is noteworthy here that the religious bodies mainly pay the administrative costs of the state taxes collected on behalf of religions that then go toward paying for the costs of religious education. The German government acts somewhat as a neutral conduit through which the monies go to religion. And the religions can only tax members of their sect. Non-

35 See Michael Perry, A Right to Religious Freedom? The Universality of Human Rights, The Relativity of Culture, 10 *R.W.U. L. Rev.* 385 (2005) (discussing Universal Declaration of Rights, the International Covenant on Civil and Political Rights and the International Covenant of Economic, Social and Cultural Rights); John Witte, Jr., The Essential Rights and Liberties of Religion in the American Constitutional Experiment, 71 *Notre Dame L. Rev.* 433–43 (1996).

36 Cf. *Catholic Hospital Case*, 70 BVerfGE 138 (1985) (Catholic hospital can fire doctor who took public position on abortion contrary to Catholic doctrine) with *Corp. of the Presiding Bishop of the Church of Jesus Christ of Latter Day Saints v. Amos*, 483 U.S. 327, 345–46 (1987) (exempting the church from federal antidiscrimination laws so that it may run autonomously its affairs).

adherents of particular religions are exempted from the religious tax. There is, thus, a minimum of coercion of conscience, as dissenters may opt out of funding religious education they disagree with.

By contrast, the American approach involves indirect funding of religious education through subsidization of private, parochial school education under formal neutrality. In this respect, the American approach accomplishes indirectly what the Germans accomplish directly. But perhaps this difference is more formal than substantive. Under the American approach, private, individual choice is said to break the link between state and church. But individuals simply endorse the financial benefits over to religious schools of their choosing. Public monies thus go to religious schools through the conduit of individual exercise, even those monies of taxpayers who may dissent from funding religious education; American programs do not normally have opt-out provisions to guard against coercion of conscience. In essence, the American program uses government as a conduit through which tax monies pass to religion, as the German program allows religions to use the apparatus of the state to raise and administer the monies to support religious education. A major difference in the German program is that monies are collected only from members of particular sects for the benefit of that sect; non-members are not taxed. Thus, perhaps the two programs are more alike than different, although using different schemes. In fact, it would appear that the German scheme is more solicitous of the core value of liberty of conscience. On the other hand, there is a big difference in the scale of aid disbursed. Public funding of religious instruction is the norm in Germany. It is clearly a small part of American education. Only about 11 per cent of American students attend private schools; of these, approximately 87 per cent of private school students attend religious schools.[37]

Assessing the programs of both countries more carefully, it seems fair to acknowledge that they constitute, in essence, de facto establishments of religion. The significant expenditure of public monies to support religious education would seem to suggest this. Whether the American program is a formal, unconstitutional establishment of religion is, of course, a difficult and disputed inquiry highly contested in the court[38] and in the scholarly literature.[39] Under German law, of course, no problem is presented even if the program is a formal establishment of religion given explicit German constitutional textual and historical authorization

---

37 National Center for Education Statistics, at www.nces.ed.gov (visited June 2005); Council for American Private Education, at www.capenet.org/facts.html.

38 Compare, for example, the positions of the majority, 536 U.S. at 634, and dissent, Ibid. at 684, in *Zelman*.

39 Compare, e.g., Noah Feldman, The Intellectual Origins of the Establishment Clause, 77 *N.Y.U. L. Rev.* 418 (2002) (governmental funding of religion unconstitutional) with Michael McConnell, Accommodation of Religion: An Update and a Response to the Critics, 60 *Geo. Wash. L. Rev.* 685, 693 (1992) (historical record indicates non-preferentialism constitutional).

of such a church-state cooperative model. But under American law, such is a problematic outcome given the lack of textual authority and the contested history between separationism and accommodationism. In contrast to German law, American formal neutrality cannot point to definitive constitutional authority.

A further striking similarity between the two countries is that both programs effectively empower majoritarian political constituencies to fund their majoritarian religious counterparts. Majoritarian configurations of political and religious power work to support each other. Only the dominant religions of Roman Catholicism and Protestantism are taught in German public schools, but now with a movement also to allowing Islam to be taught. And, again, this is not problematic given the German church-state cooperative model. American formal neutrality mainly funds Christian religious schools—the dominant religious groups—especially Catholicism, as Catholic schools are the main competitors to the public schools, given the long history and effective infrastructure and administration of the Catholic Church.[40] In fact, the Rehnquist Court has largely succeeded in converting important components of First Amendment religious protections into vessels of community, democratic control.[41]

Another interesting contrast between the three countries is over the Sunday closing laws. In Germany, Article 139 of the Weimar Constitution, which is incorporated into the Basic Law, states clearly that Sunday and public holidays are protected as days of rest or spiritual edification. Of course, exceptions are made for people's welfare over matters like police and fire services, medical supplies and other goods and services. Berlin passed a Sunday opening law, which allowed most businesses to operate. The Constitutional Court considered the Berlin law and declared it unconstitutional, as it was not compatible with the incorporated Article 139 of the Weimar Constitution.

In the UK, a 1950 Shop Act law, which severely restricted trading on Sundays, was in place until a 1994 law repealed many of the provisions of the 1950 Act. Under the new law, the Sunday trading restrictions are in force only to large shops. Large shops can only be open if they qualify for an exemption or are occupied by people who have observed the Jewish Sabbath, traditionally a Saturday, and now want to shop on Sunday. Small shops are now allowed to be open under the 1994 law.

By contrast, in the USA the situation is different. In the timeframe up until the modern age, roughly up to the 1960s, it was common for Sundays also to be a day of rest, a part of the Christian heritage. For example, in the 1961 case of *McGowan v. Maryland*, the court kept intact Sunday closing laws for major commercial

40 National Center for Education Statistics, at www.nces.ed.gov (visited June 2005); Council for American Private Education, at www.capenet.org/facts.html.

41 Compare *Zelman* with *Employment Division, Dep't of Human Services v. Smith*, 494 U.S. 872 (1990) (Free Exercise rights circumscribed according to norms of generally applicable neutral laws of democratic process).

enterprises.[42] At this time on Sundays, open for business were only enterprises for things like gasoline, milk and dairy supplies and other food products, many of which were located in gas stations and restaurants. Today, all states allow almost all commercial enterprises to be open.

In now assessing the three countries over Sunday closing laws, we can conclude that Germany is the most restrictive, keeping intact this core principle in its constitution. Sunday closing laws in the UK lie in the middle of Germany and the USA, as the USA is the most open, allowing essentially almost all businesses to be open on Sundays.

Concerning church-state relations in the UK, there is little case law. Most of the law on church-state relations entails statutes. The UK court cases are generally not of much import. They do not cover issues of great controversy and instead are of little import. They involve matters like tax exemptions, repairing church buildings or admission standards to religious schools. Nor do the UK courts delineate important rules of law to guide the issue of church-state relations. In this respect, the UK is not of a similar tenor to the German and US courts. With the UK's adoption of the 1998 Human Rights Act and the Constitutional Reform Act of 2005, there is some possibility that the UK constitutional order will be more aggressive in managing church-state relations.

In conclusion, in capturing this snapshot of German, UK and American religious protections, it seems reasonable to conclude that Germany's model of church-state cooperation is firmly rooted in constitutional authority and tradition. With that observation, however, Germany is trending toward a model of more open and welcoming accommodation of minorities in recognition of the increasing diversity of German society, including over religion. Commitment to values of neutrality, non-discrimination and tolerance are marks of this. There is, thus, a discernible movement to values long associated with the American model of church-state relations.

The UK still has in place an establishment model. However, the current establishment model is more lenient and less strict than the past model. There is now much more accommodation of other Christian and non-Christian religions.

By contrast, the United States yet evidences strong commitment to a model of separation of church and state in certain areas, most notably public school education. But in other areas, especially our topic of discussion—public funding of private religious education—the American approach is more in line with a church-state cooperative model, characteristic of Germany and most Western nations,[43]

42 366 U.S. 420 (1961).

43 See, e.g., *Stephen v. Monsma* and J. Christopher Soper, *The Challenge of Pluralism: Church and State in Five Democracies* 57, 67–69, 103–07, 136–44 (1977) (observing how the Netherlands, Australia and the United Kingdom all publicly fund religious education). Witte, *supra* note 35, at 440 (most international norms suggest church-state cooperation; separation of church and state is exceptional); *Religious Education and Globalised Economy*, at www.studyoverseas.com/re/jmh.htm (14 June 2005) (noting state-funded

than one of separation. Certainly formal neutrality is a paradigm of the church-state cooperative model. Other examples would be granting of tax exemptions to religious bodies[44] and funding of legislative chaplains,[45] ideas rooted in the American tradition.

Concluding Observations

Looking outside our borders has allowed us to gain insight into the purpose and utility of personal religious freedoms and church-state relations in constitutional democracy. Today, Germany can be thought of as a model for protection of constitutional values. The court is an incubator of many ideas, with many foreign courts looking to German constitutional law. The Constitutional Court serves as an alternative standard by which to measure the work of the Supreme Court. Perhaps that is something the Supreme Court should do.

Comparative law has a useful function to perform in holding native ways up to the light of another way, and seeing how native ways compare and also, when viewed in this more detached manner, how they compare with the design of other countries' laws and traditions. With this broader visage, we can gain perspective on whether we are true to our best intentions or whether we stray. In the case of personal religion, the comparison in approach of the German and American courts is so dramatic, notwithstanding similarities in text and constitutional design, that perhaps it ought to give us pause to ponder whether the rule of *Smith* is appropriate. Or should the USA go back to the conventional rule of strict scrutiny in protecting essential human rights of the American people, including especially freedom of religion?

Evaluating the UK, what should the UK do? What we have seen is that the UK is moving in a direction of protecting basic human rights. The UK constitutional order is increasingly looking to protect basic human rights. It is doing so by looking outside its borders and observing European models, resulting in adoption of UK laws modeled on European laws.

Viewed from the unique dimensions offered by comparative law—looking outside native borders to observe workings in other constitutional orders and then reflecting the insights learned on native law to see how we stand, for better or for worse—we seem left with this insight: A model of separation of church and state was uniquely instituted in the New World of America, in Providence colony, then Virginia, and then in the United States in essential respects. Operating under the model of separation, religion thrived in America in the past, and thrives today,

religious education in Canada, Greece, Italy, Spain and the United Kingdom. However, in the United Kingdom, purpose of religious education is to deepen and enlighten students' awareness of values associated with religion, not to indoctrinate or proselytize).

44 *Walz v. Tax Comm'n*, 397 U.S. 664, 677–80 (1970).

45 *Marsh v. Chambers*, 463 U.S. 783 (1983).

perhaps like in no other Western country. The question Americans must now face is: are Americans losing one of the unique traits that has characterized the American "livlie experiment"—separationism— and, if so, at what cost and at what benefit?[46] Is a European model of church-state cooperation better suited to American shores? And for the UK, should they keep in place the established church model, which they are likely to do? Or should they go toward a cooperationist model? For now, it seems clear that while the established church model is still in place, the UK is moving toward a much more flexible model, being tolerant of all religions, and not demanding adherence to the tenets of the Church of England.

46 *McCreary*, 545 U.S. 844, p. 20 (O'Connor, J., concurring) ("Those who would renegotiate the boundaries between church and state must therefore answer a difficult question: Why would we trade a system that has served us so well for one that has served others so poorly?").

Selected Bibliography

Adams, Arlin M. and Emmerich, Charles J., A Heritage of Religious Liberty, 137 *U. Pa. L. Rev.* 1559 (1989).

Currie, David P., *The Constitution of the Federal Republic of Germany* (1994).

Eberle, Edward J., Free Exercise of Religion in Germany and the United States, 78 *Tulane L. Rev.* 1023 (2004).

Eberle, Edward J., Religion in the Classroom in Germany and the United States, 81 *Tulane L. Rev.* 67 (2006).

Eberle, Edward J., Roger Williams' Gift: Religious Freedom in America, 4 *Roger Williams L. Rev.* 425 (1999).

Feldman, Noah, The Intellectual Origins of the Establishment Clause, 77 *N.Y.U.L. Rev.* 346 (2002).

Fischer, Judith D. and Wallace, Chloe J., God and Caesar in the Twenty-first Century: What Recent Cases Say About the Church-State Relations in England and the United States, 18 *Florida J. of Int'l L.* 485 (2006).

Hall, Timothy L., Roger Williams and the Foundations of Religious Liberty, 71 *B.U.L. Rev.* 455 (1991).

Hill, Mark, The Permissible Scope of Legal Limitations on the Freedom of Religion or Belief in the United Kingdom, 19 *Emory Int'l L. Rev.* 1129 (2005).

Kommers, Donald P., *The Constitutional Jurisprudence of the Federal Republic of Germany* (2nd ed.) (1997).

Krotosynski, Jr. and Ronald J., If Judges Were Angels: Religious Equality, Free Exercise, and the (Underappreciated) Merits of *Smith*, 102 *Nw. U. L. Rev.* 1189 (2008).

Krotosynski, Jr. and Ronald J., The Apostle, Mr. Justice Jackson, and the "Pathological Perspective" of the Free Exercise Clause, 65 *Wash. & Lee L. Rev.* 1071 (2008).

McConnell, Michael W., The Origins and Historical Understanding of Free Exercise of Religion, 103 *Harv. L. Rev.* 1409 (1990).

McConnell, Michael W., Establishment and Disestablishment at the Founding, Part I.: Establishment of Religion, 44 *Wm. & Mary L. Rev.* 2105 (2003).

Muehlhoff, Inke, Freedom of Religion in Public Schools in Germany and in the United States, 28 *Ga. Int'l & Comp. L.* 405 (2000).

Witte, Jr., John, The Essential Rights and Liberties of Religion in the American Constitutional Experiment, 71 *Notre Dame L. Rev.* 371 (1996).

Wuerth, Ingrid Brunk, Private Religious Choice in German and American Constitutional Law: Government Funding and Government Religious Speech, 31 *Vand. J. Transnat'l L.* 1127 (1998).

Index